ON LIFE & LETTERS
BY ANATOLE FRANCE

SECOND SERIES

TRANSLATED BY
A. W. EVANS

Edited by
FREDERIC CHAPMAN
and
JAMES LEWIS MAY

Essay Index Reprint Series

 BOOKS FOR LIBRARIES PRESS
FREEPORT, NEW YORK

First Published 1914
Reprinted 1971

INTERNATIONAL STANDARD BOOK NUMBER:
0-8369-2358-8

LIBRARY OF CONGRESS CATALOG CARD NUMBER:
77-156643

PRINTED IN THE UNITED STATES OF AMERICA

PREFACE

THIS volume contains the articles which I have published in the "Temps" for about two years past. The literary public has welcomed the first series of these chats with a kindness that honours and touches me. I know how little I deserve it. But I have been forgiven a great deal, doubtless because of my sincerity. There is a means of attracting which is within the reach of the most humble, and that is naturalness. One seems to be almost attractive as soon as one is absolutely true. It is because I have given myself completely that I have deserved some unknown friends. The only cleverness of which I am capable is not to attempt to hide my faults. It has succeeded with me just as it would have succeeded with any one else.

People have noticed, for instance, that I sometimes happened to contradict myself. A short time ago, a man of excellent parts, M. Georges Renard, pointed out some of these contradictions with an indulgence all the more exquisite in that it pretended to hide itself. " M. Leconte de Lisle," I once said, " has doubts about the existence of the universe, but he has no doubts about the goodness of a rhyme." And M. Georges Renard had no difficulty in showing that I myself fell into this

v

202981

contradiction every moment, and that, after having proclaimed philosophic doubt, I was in the greatest hurry to leave the sublime peace, the happy quietude of the sage, and to throw myself into the regions of joy and sorrow, of love and hatred. In the end, he forgave me, and I believe he did well. Poor human beings must be permitted to have their maxims not always in accord with their feelings. Each of us must even be allowed to possess two or three philosophies at the same time ; for, unless you have created a doctrine, there is no reason for believing that any single one is good ; that partiality is excusable only in an inventor. Just as a vast country has the most diverse climates, there is hardly an expanded mind that does not contain numerous contradictions. To tell the truth, souls that are exempt from everything illogical frighten me ; not being able to imagine that they are never mistaken, I am afraid that they may be always mistaken, whilst a mind that does not pride itself on its logic can rediscover the truth after it has lost it. Some one will doubtless reply to me on behalf of the logicians that there is a truth at the end of all reasoning just as there is an eye or a claw at the end of the tail which Fourier has promised men on the day when they shall be in harmony. But this advantage will remain to meandering and floating minds—they can amuse others by the errors which amuse themselves. *Happy is he who, like Ulysses, has made a prosperous journey !* When the road is strewn with flower, do not ask whither it leads. I give you this advice in contempt for vulgar and at the dictate of a superior wisdom. Ever the goal is hidden from man. I have asked my way of all those, priests, scholars, wizards, or philosophers, who claim

to know the geography of the Unknown. None of
them has been able exactly to point out the perfect way to me. That is why the road I prefer is
the one on which the greatest number of leafy elms
uprear themselves beneath the most smiling sky. The
feeling for the beautiful leads me on. Who is sure
of having found a better guide ?

Like my contradictions, my innocent mania for
telling stories at every turn as well as my memories
and my impressions, has been forgiven. I think
this indulgence has not been ill inspired. A superior
man ought to speak of himself only in connection
with the great affairs in which he has been engaged.
Otherwise he seems disproportionate and therefore
unpleasing ; at least unless he consents to show himself similar to us, which, to tell the truth, is not
always impossible, for great men have many things in
common with other men. But the sacrifice is too
costly for certain geniuses. How much more successful have ordinary men been in recording and depict-
ing themselves ! Their portrait is that of all ; each
of us recognises in the adventures of their minds
his own moral and philosophical adventures. Hence
the interest we take in their confidences. When
they speak of themselves, it is as if they spoke of
everybody. Sympathy is the pleasant privilege of
mediocrity. When we listen to their admissions
they seem to issue from ourselves. Their examination of conscience is as profitable to us as it is to
them. Their confessions form a manual of confession for the use of the entire community. And
manuals of this sort contribute to the amelioration
of the moral person, provided that in them the sin
be represented without hypocritical extenuation,
and above all without those horrible exaggerations

that produce despair. If I have spoken a little of
myself here and there in our chats, these considerations reassure me.

In this volume, as in its predecessor, there will
not be found any profound study of the younger
literature. The fault is doubtless mine, for I have
not been able to comprehend either the symbolist
poets or the decàdent prose writers.

It will perhaps also be conceded that the
younger school does not allow itself to be easily
comprehended. It is mystical, and one fatality of
mysticism is that it remains unintelligible to those
who do not lead the life of the sanctuary. The
symbolists write in a particular emotional condition ; and in order to enter into communion
with them it is necessary to find oneself in an
analogous disposition. I say it without jesting:
their books, like those of Swedenborg or those of
Allan Kardec, are the product of a sort of ecstasy.
They see what we do not see. A simpler explanation
has been attempted : it has been said that they
are hoaxers. But when we think of it, we never
find the true reasons for either a literary or a
religious movement, however small it be, in fraud
and imposture. No, they are not hoaxers. They
are ecstatics. Two or three of them have had a
seizure, and the whole coterie is raving, for nothing
is more contagious than certain nervous states. Far
from throwing any doubt upon the marvellous
effects of the new art, I hold them to be as certain
as the miracles which were wrought on the tomb
of Pâris, the deacon. I am sure that the young
author of the " Traité du Verbe " is speaking very
seriously when he says, assigning to the sound of each
vowel a corresponding colour : " A black, E white,

I red, U green, O blue." Before such an affirmation, there is some frivolity of mind in smiling and scoffing. Why not admit that, if the author of the treatise on words says that A is black and O is blue, it is because he feels it, because he sees it, because, indeed, sounds, like bodies, have really colours for him ? People will cease to doubt this when they know that the case is not unique, and that physiologists have demonstrated that in a fairly large number of subjects there exists a similar aptitude for *seeing* sounds. This sort of nervous affection is called " *coloured audition.*" I find its scientific description in an extract from " Progrès Médical," quoted by M. Maurice Spronck on p. 33 of his " Artistes Littéraires " :

" Coloured audition is a phenomenon which consists in two different senses being simultaneously put into activity by a stimulus produced by only one of these senses, or, to put it differently, in the sound of a voice or an instrument being translated by a characteristic and constant colour for the person possessing this chromatic peculiarity. Thus certain individuals can give a green, red, yellow, or other colour to every noise, to every sound which strikes their ears." (J. Baratoux, " Progrès Médical," December 10, 1887, and following numbers.)

Coloured audition brings about, in minds endowed with artistic and poetic gifts, a new æsthetic sense to which the poetics of the younger school responds.

The future belongs to symbolism if the nervous affection that has produced it becomes general. Unfortunately M. Ghil says that O is blue and M. Raimbault says that O is red. And these afflicted exquisites dispute with one another beneath the indulgent eyes of M. Stéphane Mallarmé.

A 2

I understand why the adepts of the new art should love their disease and even pride themselves on it; and even if they have some little contempt for those who are not refined by so rare a nervous affection, I shall not complain. It would be in bad taste to reproach them for being ill. I prefer, placing myself in the highest regions of natural philosophy, to say with M. Jules Soury: "Health and disease are vain entities." Let us learn, with the gracious Horatio of the poet, that there are more things in nature than in our philosophies, however comprehensive they be, and let us take care not to believe that contempt is the summit of wisdom.

There will not be found in this volume a general view of the contemporary literature of our country. It is not easy to form a general idea of the things in the midst of which one lives. We lack space and perspective. And if we succeed in distinguishing what is coming to an end, we discern badly what is beginning. It is doubtless on this account that the most indulgent minds have been ready to judge of their own time with severity. Men are inclined to believe that the world will end with them, and this thought, which they express, not without melancholy, consoles them inwardly for their fleeting days. I rejoice in my heart that I am exempt from so pitiable and vain an illusion. I do not believe that the forms of beauty will be exhausted, and I look for new ones. If I do not sing old Simeon's canticle every day, it is doubtless because the gift of prophecy is not in me.

I have always thought, perhaps very wrongly, that nobody creates masterpieces, that that is a task superior to individuals whoever they may be, but that the happiest among mortals sometimes produce works which may become masterpieces with the aid of Time, who is a man of honour, as Mazarin said. What reassures me, in spite of the Universal Exhibition and the dangerous nonsense which it has inspired in most of my compatriots, is that there are still in this country men equal, and, in a certain faculty for understanding, perhaps superior, to all the writers of past ages. I do not imagine, for example, that any one has ever been more intelligent than M. Paul Bourget or M. Jules Lemaître. I think there is a certain elegance in mentioning here only the younger writers.

As for the nature of these chats, I should be greatly embarrassed to define it. I have been told that it is not critical and æsthetic. I have had some doubts of this. As far as possible nothing ought to be done against the grain. The technical conditions under which novels and poems are elaborated have, I confess, but a very moderate interest for me. They interest, in short, only the vanity of authors. Each of them believes that, to the exclusion of others, he possesses all the secrets of the trade. But those who produce masterpieces do not know what they are doing ; they play the benefactor in all innocence. It is useless to tell me that critics should not be innocent. I shall still endeavour to keep as a celestial gift the impression of mystery that the sublimities of poetry and art leave on me. The better part is sometimes to be a dupe. Life teaches us that we are never happy except at the price of some ignorance. I am going to make an admission which will perhaps appear singular on the first page of a collection of chats upon literature. All books in general, and even the most admirable, seem to me infinitely less precious for what they contain than for what he who reads them puts into them. The best, in my opinion, are those that are most suggestive, and suggestive of the most diverse things.

The great advantage of the works of the masters is that they inspire wise conversations, grave and familiar topics, images that float like garlands unceasingly broken and unceasingly re-tied, long reveries, a vague and buoyant curiosity which attaches itself to everything without desiring to exhaust anything, the memory of what was dear, the forgetfulness of mean cares, the emotional return upon oneself. When we read them, these excellent books, these books of life, we make them pass into ourselves. The critic must imbue himself thoroughly with the idea that every book has as many different aspects as it has readers, and that a poem, like a landscape, is transformed in all the eyes that see it, in all the souls that conceive it. Some years ago, as I was spending the summer beneath the fir-trees of Hohwald, I was surprised, during my long walks, to find a bench at every point where the shade is pleasantest, the view most extended, nature most engaging. These rustic benches bore names which betrayed the sentiment of those who had placed them there. One was called "Friendship's meeting-place"; another "Sophie's rest," a third "Charlotte's dream."

These good Alsatians who thus provided "rests" and "meeting-places" for their friends and for passers-by, taught me the sort of good that can be done by those who have lived in the realm of culture and long been wayfarers there. I resolved, for my own part, to go about placing rustic benches in the sacred woods and near the fountains of the Muses. This

modest and pious woodman's occupation suits me
wonderfully. It demands neither system nor learning, and only requires a pleasant astonishment
before the beauty of things. Let the village
dominie, the land surveyor, measure the road and
set up the milestones! The kindly care of the
" rests," the " meeting-places," and the " dreams "
will be sufficient occupation for me. The critic's
task, as suited to my tastes and proportioned to my
strength, is lovingly to place benches in beautiful
places, and to say, following the example of Anytus
of Tegæa:

" Whoever thou art, come and seat thyself beneath
the shade of this fine laurel, so that here we may
celebrate the immortal gods ! "

A. F.

CONTENTS

CONTENTS

ON LIFE & LETTERS

ON LIFE & LETTERS

M. ALEXANDRE DUMAS
(THE YOUNGER)

THE famous novel * which a poet of talent, M. Dartois, has just dramatised, dates from more than twenty years back. When he published it, M. Alexandre Dumas, though already famous, was not, as he is to-day, a formidable moralist, one of the spiritual directors of his age. He had not yet proclaimed the gospel of punishment and revoked the Magdalen's pardon. He had not yet said: " Kill her ! " It is precisely in " L'Affaire Clémenceau " that he expounded for the first time that pitiless doctrine. It is true that he did not speak in his own person, and that the book, as its title indicates, is a presentation of the case for a prisoner. But one divined the philosopher beneath the novelist, one saw the thesis in the work of art. " L'Affaire Clémenceau " contained in germ " L'Homme-Femme " and " La Femme de Claude." Need I remind you that the novel deals with a natural child, the son of a poor, deserted girl who

* " Affaire Clémenceau, Mémoire de l'Accusé."

I

works for her living ?   Clémenceau has never known
his father.   He is still quite young when his companions at the boarding-school make him ashamed
of his birth.   He is handsome, he is strong, he is
intelligent and good.   His genius reveals itself from
his childhood : led by chance to a sculptor's studio,
he recognises his vocation.   He is destined to model
in clay ; he is dedicated to the delightful torment of
fixing in durable matter the forms of life.   Work
keeps him chaste.   But young, ignorant, and
vigorous, he is the chosen prey of love.   One night
he meets at a masked ball a child dressed as a page,
who accompanies an opulent and magnificent Marie
de Medici, her mother.   Iza, this child, is perfectly
beautiful.   But she is only a child.   Moreover, she
only appears as a presage.   She goes away with her
mother, Countess Dobronowska, a Polish adven-
turess, to seek a fortune in Russia.   The Countess,
not being able to marry her, tries to sell her.   Iza
escapes, and, either from love or from fancy, she
comes and asks shelter from the sculptor, Clémenceau, who in a few years has become celebrated.   He
was waiting for her.   He marries her, he loves her.
He loves her with a love at once ideal and æsthetic.
He loves her because she is the perfect form and
because she is the infinite of which we all dream,
in that dream of an hour which is life.   Iza, brought
up by an infamous mother, is naturally immodest,
ungrateful, and wanton.   Still, she loves Clémenceau,
who is handsome and robust.   But she deceives him,
for to deceive is her natural function.   She is false
to the man she loves, for the sake of jewels, or merely
for the pleasure of being false.   She gives herself to
the celebrities who frequent her house, and that for
the pleasure of indulging certain ideas when those

personages are gathered together in the evening at the table of which she gravely does the honours along with her husband. She is like those great artists who take pleasure only in difficulties: she increases, complicates, intermingles her falsehoods ; she dares everything, so that her husband is soon the only man in Paris ignorant of her conduct. By an accident he is undeceived. He discards her. But he still loves her. What is there to be surprised at in this ? That she is unworthy is no reason why he should love her less.

Love does not give itself as a prize for virtue. The unworthiness of a woman never kills the feeling that one has for her ; on the contrary, it sometimes reanimates it: the author of " La Visite de Noces " knows this well. The unhappy Clémenceau flees to Rome, where he takes refuge in his ideal of art. He begins a copy of Michael Angelo's " Moses " upon a block of marble with such a fury that one would think he wants to smash himself against the marble he is carving. He has wished to fly from her. But the wretched man is waiting for her.

He waits for her with open arms. She does not come : she remains at Paris, the mistress of a royal prince who is in luck's way. There, placid in her luxury, she is preparing a final masterpiece of perfidy: she seduces the only friend left to her husband. Clémenceau learns this; it is too much ; he hurries, he flings himself into her house, he sees her again, he finds her charming, amorous, for she still loves him. She is beautiful, she is irresistible. What does he do ? He possesses her once more and he kills her.

Such is the subject, the argument, as they used

to say in the old-fashioned rhetoric. You know that it is treated with a skill all the greater since it is hidden beneath an appearance of naturalness and ease. It is superfluous to-day to praise the skilful simplicity of this book, its sober and impassioned eloquence. I have said that in " L'Affaire Clémenceau " there is a work of art and a moral thesis. The work of art is admirable in all respects. As for the thesis, it inspires horror, and all the forces of my being rise in revolt against it.

If Clémenceau said: " I have killed this woman because I loved her," we should think: " That, after all, is a reason." Passion has every right, because it goes forth to meet every punishment. Whatever evil it may do, it is not immoral, for it carries in itself its own terrible retribution. Moreover, those who love say: " I will kill her ! " but they do not kill. But Clémenceau not only pleads his love, he invokes justice. That is what offends me. I do not like to see this violent husband, who becomes a lover, taking on the airs of a judge. I do not like to see him brandishing, as if it were the august instrument of public vengeance, the knife, " with its jasper handle, with its vermilion guard encrusted with garnets, with its blade of steel inlaid with gold."

He is a thinker. He is an ideologist. Sometimes he speaks as if, in truth, he had made an attempt on the life of an opportunist or a radical deputy. There is in him something of the Baffiers and of the Aubertins. He has general ideas, he has a system ; he gives I know not what humanitarian intentions to his crime. He is too pure. It is disagreeable to me that he should assassinate out of virtue. His defence is that of an ideologist murderer. If I were on the jury I would not acquit him. That is unless the doctors informed me that I had to deal with a man suffering from general paralysis, a thing, to tell the truth, that would hardly astonish me. He assures me that he was a man of worth and a good son. I do not want to dispute it. But he gives it to be understood that he was a great artist and that he made very beautiful figures; and there I have some difficulty in believing him. A great artist carries within him the generous instinct of life. He creates and does not destroy. To assassinate a woman is a stupid piece of work. Men capable of such a butchery must be intolerable. Admitting that they are not completely insane, they must have very little grace in their minds, very little flexibility in their intelligence. I imagine that they remain torpid and hard even in the midst of happiness, and that their souls have not those charming shades of distinction without which even love seems dull and monotonous.

The case for the accused says nothing about it, but Iza must have passed some terribly tedious hours with this man. He must have bored her before he assassinated her. He was worthy, doubtless; but an unpitying worth is a poor equipment in love. No, he had not a beautiful soul. In beautiful souls a divine indulgence is mingled with the most furious passion.

If it is true that one rarely finds love without hatred, it is true also that one rarely sees hatred without pity. This unhappy man had a narrow brain. He was a fanatic; that is to say a man of the worst sort. All fanaticisms, even that of virtue, create a horror in cheerful and indulgent souls. The evil comes solely from this Clémenceau who made the mistake of marrying a woman not

suited to that state. The Greeks knew well that
all women are not equally suited to make legitimate
consorts. He did not penetrate deep enough
into the mystery of the appetites and the instincts.
If he had had the faintest suspicion of the obscure
workings of animal life, he would have said to
himself, like good Doctor Fagon, that nature must be
forgiven for a great deal. He would have murmured
in the depths of his soul what Byron's amiable
Sardanapalus said from his funeral pyre to young
Myrrha :

> " If at this moment,—for we now are on
> The brink—thou feel'st an inward shrinking from
> This leap through flame into the future, say it :
> I shall not love thee less ; nay, perhaps more,
> For yielding to thy nature."

And he would have wept, and his heart would have
been softened, and he would not have killed poor
Iza, whom, moreover, he would not previously have
married.

Without doubt, she was bad. She had perverse
instincts. But are we entirely responsible for our
instincts ? Do not education and heredity weigh
upon all our acts ? We are born incorrigible, alas !
We are born so old ! If Clémenceau had reflected
how all the elements which composed the delightful
body of that poor child existed and had been tossed
hither and thither in the immoral universe of all
eternity, he would not have shattered that delicate
mechanism. He would have forgiven that unenlightened soul for the crime of her nerves and her
blood. Listen to what natural philosophy says in
verse. It says :

> " Les choses de l'amour ont de profonds secrets.
> L'instinct primordial de l'antique nature,

Qui mêlait les flancs nus dans le fond des forêts,
Trouble l'épouse encor sous sa riche ceinture ;
Et, savante en pudeur, attentive à nos lois,
Elle garde le sang de l'Eve des grands bois." *

I know, I know all that we owe to morality.
Heaven keep me from forgetting it! Society is
founded on the family, which itself rests upon
the faith of domestic contracts. The virtue of
women is a virtue of State. That dates from
the Romans. The heroic victim of Sextus, the
chaste Lucretia, practised modesty as if it were
a magistracy. She killed herself for an example :
Ne ulla deinde impudica Lucretiæ exemplo vivet
(Lest hereafter any immodest woman should live
having Lucretia as her exemplar). In her eyes
marriage was a sort of public function with which
she was invested. That is well. Those Romans
built up marriage as they did aqueducts and drains.
They joined flesh and stones with the same
cement. They built for eternity. There have
never been in the world masons and lawyers like
them. We still dwell in the house that they built.
It is august and holy. That is true ; but it is also
true that it is written : " Thou shalt not kill."
It is true that clemency is the most intelligent of the
virtues and that natural philosophy teaches forgive-
ness. Besides, when it is a question of love, can
we discern our own cause ? Which of us is pure
enough to throw the first stone ? We must go
back to the Gospel. In matters of morals religions
are always right, because they are inspired by

---

* " The things of love have profound secrets. The primordial
instinct of antique nature, which mingled naked limbs in the depth
of the forest, still troubles the wife beneath her rich girdle ; and,
skilled in modesty, attentive to our laws, she still keeps the blood of
the wood-land Eve."

feeling, and it is feeling that misleads us least. Religions would not unite men if they addressed themselves to the understanding, for the understanding is proud and takes pleasure in disputes. Creeds speak to the senses ; that is why they bring the faithful together: we all feel almost alike, and piety is made out of the common feeling.

It has happened to each of us to be present in some church, hung with black, at the funeral of some illustrious person. The chosen of society, honoured men, some of them famous, admired and respected women, have been ranged on both sides of the nave, in the midst of which the catafalque arose surrounded with tapers. Suddenly the *Dies irae* has burst forth on the air thick with incense, and those stanzas, composed in some unshaded garden by a gentle disciple of St. Francis, have rolled over our heads like threats mingled with hopes. I do not know if you have thus been touched even to tears, as I have been, by that poetry bearing the impress of the austere love which overflowed from the soul of the first Franciscans. But I can tell you that I have never heard the thirteenth strophe without feeling myself shaken by a religious tremor. That strophe says:

> " *Qui Mariam absolvisti*
> *Et latronem exaudisti*
> *Mihi quoque spem dedisti.*"

> " Thou the sinful woman savest ;
> Thou the dying thief forgavest ;
> And to me a hope vouchsafest."

The singer who launches forth these Latin words in the vessel of the Church is here the voice of the entire assembly. All present, those pure, great, exalted persons must inwardly repeat:

"Thou the sinful woman savest;
Thou the dying thief forgavest;
And to me a hope vouchsafest."

That is what the Church desires, the Church which has condemned theft and has made marriage into a sacrament. It humiliates, in its wisdom, the virtues of those happy people who are called the just, and it reminds the best among us that, far from being able to erect themselves into judges, they ought themselves to crave for pardon. This Christian morality seems to me infinitely sweet and infinitely wise. It will never completely prevail against the violences of the spirit and the pride of the flesh; but it will sometimes spread its divine peace over our tired hearts, and it will teach us to pardon, with all other offences, the treasons committed against us by those whom we have loved too well.

CHILDREN'S PLAYTHINGS

HAVE just had the pleasure of reading some children's tales, " La Comédie des jouets," * which M. Camille Lemonnier has given us. M. Camille Lemonnier has taken his place in the front rank of Belgian men of letters. He writes real romances in a language full of savour. He is a natural story-teller who pleases the Parisians as well as the people of Brussels. I knew from his books that he adored the various aspects of life, and that his artistic dreams have eagerly pursued the infinite forms of beings. I discover to-day that he sometimes amuses himself with children's playthings, and this taste inspires me with new sympathies for him. I am his well-wisher because of his poetic interpretations of playthings, and also because he possesses the mystic sense. Without the smallest effort he is able to give life and animation to his Jumping Jacks and his Punches. He reveals the spiritual nature of Father Christmas, who reappears every year covered with frost in the grocer's shop. At the breath of his thought a forest, which really consists of only six trees painted green, with chips for foliage, stretches forth every night out of its deal box, and becomes a haunt of shadow, mystery, and terror.

* " La Comédie des jouets." By Camille Lemonnier.

That is what pleases and touches me. For, like him, I practise the fetichism of lead soldiers, Noah's arks, and wooden sheepfolds. Think of it, this fetichism is the last that is left us. When humanity felt itself young, it gave souls to all things. That charming faith departed little by little, and to-day our modern thinkers no longer perceive souls in this disenchanted universe. At least M. Camille Lemonnier and I have a profound belief left us : we believe in the souls of toys.

For my own part, I do not hesitate to formulate my creed. I believe in the immortal soul of Punch. I believe in the majesty of marionettes and dolls.

Doubtless there is nothing human according to the flesh in those little personages of wood or cardboard, but there is in them something divine, however little it may be. They do not live as we do, but still they live. They live the life of the immortal gods.

If I were a scholar I should endeavour to build up their symbolism, as Guigniant, following Creutzer, attempted to establish the symbolism of the divinities of ancient Greece. Assuredly dolls and marionettes are very tiny gods ; but they are gods all the same.

For, look you : they are like the lesser idols of antiquity. They bear even a still closer resemblance to those ruder figures by which savages attempt to show the invisible. And what should they be like if not idols, since they are themselves idols ? Theirs is an absolutely religious function. They bring to little children the only vision of the divine which would be intelligible to them. They represent all the religion that is accessible to tender years. They are the cause of our earliest dreams. They inspire our first fears and our first hopes. Pierrot and Punch contain as much divine anthropomorphism as brains, as yet scarce fashioned though terribly active, can conceive. They are the Hermes and the Zeus of our babies. And every doll is to this day a Proserpine, a Cora, for our little girls. I would have these words taken in their most literal sense. Children are born religious. M. Hovelacque and his municipal council do not perceive a god anywhere. Children see them everywhere. Their interpretation of nature is mystic and religious. I will even say that they have more relations with gods than with men, and this proposition will not appear strange if we remember that since the divine is the unknown, the idea of the divine is the first which must engage the attention of growing thought.

Children are religious, but that does not mean that they are spiritual. Spirituality is the supreme elegance of intelligence on the down grade. Humanity began with fetichism, and children begin humanity anew. They are profound fetichists. What have I said ? Little children go back farther than humanity itself. They reproduce not only the ideas of the men of the Stone Age, but even the ideas of animals. And these, be sure of it, are also religious ideas. St. Francis of Assisi, in his beautiful mystic soul, recognised the piety of animals. You need not watch a dog for long to realize that his soul is full of sacred terrors. The faith of a dog, like that of a child, is a pronounced fetichism. It would be impossible to remove from a dog's mind the belief that the moon is divine.

Since children, then, are born religious, they worship their toys. They ask of their toys what men have always asked of the gods : joy and forgetfulness, the revelation of·mysterious harmonies, the secret of being. Toys, like the gods, inspire terror and love. Are not the dolls, whom the ancient Greeks called their Nymphs, the divine virgins of early childhood ? The devils who pop out of boxes, do they not, like the Greek Gorgon or the Christian Beelzebub, represent the sympathetic alliance between visible ugliness and moral evil ? It is true that children are familiar with their gods, but have men never blasphemed theirs ? Children sometimes break their dolls, but what symbols has not humanity broken ? The child, like the man, continually changes his ideal. His gods are always imperfect because they necessarily proceed from himself.

I will go further. I will show that this religious character, inherent in all toys, and above all in anthropomorphic toys, is implicitly recognised not only by all children, but even by those adults who still preserve the simplicity of childhood. Those who are good enough to read me know my respect for sacred things. I can say, without fear of being suspected of any irreverence, that even to-day entirely puerile images take their place in the ceremonies of the Church, and that innocent and pious souls ingenuously associate actual toys with the mysteries of worship. Are not the shops of the Rue Saint-Sulpice full of liturgical dolls ? And what are the Bethlehems that are put in the churches during Christmas time but pious toys ? Not a week ago, in a chapel opened by the English Catholics in the Étoile district, I saw the scene of the Nativity represented in the apse by modelled and painted figures. Gentle women came and knelt before them. With joy they recognised the grotto

of Bethlehem, the Holy Virgin, St. Joseph, and the
little Jesus opening His arms to the world from His
cradle.   Prostrate at the feet of the Child-God,
the three wise men presented gold, frankincense,
and myrrh.   Melchior could be recognised by his
white beard, Gaspar by his youthful air, and the
good Balthazar by the naïve expression on his
ebony countenance.   The latter was smiling under
his enormous turban.   O the candour of the good
negro !   Imperishable sweetness of Uncle Tom !
None of the figures were bigger than my hand.
Shepherds and shepherdesses as large as a finger
occupied the approaches to the grotto.   There were
also camels and camel-drivers, a bridge over a
stream, and a house with glass windows which
were lit up at night by tiny candles.   The scene
answered exactly to the æsthetic needs of a little
girl of six years old.   During the time that I
remained in the church, I heard the sounds of a
musical box which aided contemplation.

Thus the innocent ladies were deeply affected by
this pretty pastoral.   In order to be able to impart
such emotions, it is necessary that these half-comic,
half-sacred images must have a soul, a little doll's
soul.   It would be ungracious for me to sneer at
an ingenuousness which I myself shared : those
worthy souls who knelt and yearned before the
dolls seemed to me quite charming.   And if I
point out the elements of fetichism that entered
into the composition of their orthodoxy, it is not
with any intention of depreciating such an alloy.
I hold with that generous chief of positivism, M.
Pierre Laffite, that the creed of fetichism has good
in it, and, indeed, I do not believe that there is
any true religion which has not a little fetichism.

I go further: every deep human feeling leads back to that ancient religion of men. Look at gamblers or lovers: they must have fetiches.

I have just shown you the doll in the sanctuary. I shall not have much difficulty in showing it to you also on the threshold of the museum. It belongs at once to the invisible gods, and to the museums. Because the toy is religious, it is artistic. I beg you to regard that proposition as demonstrated. The creeds and the arts come from the same inspiration. From the infant laboriously arranging his lead soldiers on a table, to the venerable M. Ravaisson enthusiastically grouping the Venus Victrix and the Borghese Achilles in his studio at the Louvre, there is but a shade of difference. The principle of the two actions is precisely the same. Every little ragamuffin who grasps his toys is already an æsthete.

It is quite true to say that the doll is the rough draft of the statue. The learned M. Edmond Pottier hesitates before certain little figures from the Necropolis of Myrrhina, not knowing whether he has before him a doll or an idol. The dolls which the little girls pressed against their hearts in the days of beauty in holy Hellas have perished; they were made of wax, and have been melted by the sun. They have not survived the charming arms which, after having carried them, opened in love or closed in despair, and then froze in death. I regret those waxen dolls; I imagine the genius of Greece must have given beauty to their fragility. Those that remain to us are made of baked earth; they are poor little dolls found in the tombs of children. Their frail limbs are jointed like the arms and legs of marionettes. That is another special characteristic that ought to be considered.

B

If the doll precedes sculpture by its form, it owes several other precious properties to the suppleness of its joints. The child communicates gestures and attitudes to it, the child makes it act, and speaks for it. And there you have the theatre created !

Who was it that said, " Dolls and songs, almost all Shakespeare is in them " ?

GUSTAVE FLAUBERT *

T was an autumn Sunday in 1873. I was quite worked up as I went to see him. I could feel my heart beating when I rang at the little flat in the Rue Murillo where he then lived. He himself came to open the door. All my life long I had never seen anything like him. He was tall and broad-shouldered; he was huge, splendid, and sonorous. He wore easily a sort of chestnut-coloured cloak, a regular pirate's garment; ample trousers fell over his heels like a petticoat. Bald and hairy, with wrinkled brow, keen eyes, red cheeks, and colourless, hanging moustache, he was in real life all that we read of the old Scandinavian chiefs whose blood flowed, though not without some mixture, in his veins.

Sprung from a father who belonged to Champagne and a mother of an old South Norman family, Gustave Flaubert was indeed the woman's son, his mother's child. He seemed thoroughly Norman, not the Norman of the soil, the peaceful and degenerate descendant of Rolf's companions, citizen or serf, lawyer or labourer, of covetous and crafty temperament, not saying either "yes" or "indeed"; but a true Norman of the seas, a king of combat, an old

* On his " Correspondance."

17

Dane who came by the road the swans come, having never slept beneath a plank roof nor emptied his beer-horn beside a human hearth, loving the blood of the priests and gold pillaged from the churches, tethering his horse in the chapels of palaces, a swimmer and a poet, intoxicated, raging, magnanimous, full of the vague deities of the North, and even in pillage retaining his unalterable generosity.

And his appearance did not lie. He was this in his dreams.

He stretched out to me his fine hand, the hand of a leader and of an artist, said some kind words to me, and thenceforward I had the pleasure of loving the man whom I admired. Gustave Flaubert was very good-natured. He had a prodigious capacity for enthusiasm and sympathy. That is why he was always in a rage. He went to war on every possible occasion, having continually an insult to avenge. He was in the same case as Don Quixote, for whom he had so high a regard. If Don Quixote had cared less for justice and felt less love for beauty and less pity for weakness, he would not have broken the Biscayan mule-driver's head, nor run his lance through the innocent sheep. Both of them had brave hearts. And both dreamt the dream of life with an heroic pride which it is easier to laugh at than to imitate. I had scarcely been five minutes in Flaubert's company when the small drawing-room, hung with Oriental tapestry, was streaming with the blood of twenty thousand slaughtered Philistines. As he walked backwards and forwards, the good-natured giant crushed beneath his heels the brains of the municipal councillors of the city of Rouen.

He plunged both his hands into the entrails of

M. Saint-Marc Girardin. He nailed to the four
walls the palpitating limbs of M. Thiers, whose
crime, I believe, was that he had written of grenadiers
biting the dust on ground that had been muddied by
rain. Then, passing from rage to enthusiasm, he
began to recite in a loud, deep, and monotonous
voice the beginning of a play inspired by Æschylus,
" Les Érinnyes," which M. Leconte de Lisle had
just had produced at the Odéon Theatre. The
verses were, in truth, very fine, and Flaubert was
quite right to praise them. But his admiration
extended to the actors ; he spoke with violent and
terrible cordiality of Madame Marie Laurent, who
in that play had the part of Klytaimnestra. As he
spoke of her, he seemed to be caressing some monstrous animal. When it came to the turn of the
actor who played Agamemnon, Flaubert blazed
forth. That actor was usually cast for the part
of the confidant in tragedies, had grown old in his
modest employment, and was dispirited, disillusioned, and crippled by rheumatism ; his performance showed many signs of these physical and
moral misfortunes. There were days when the
poor man could hardly move on the stage. Late in
life he had married a work-woman belonging to the
theatre, and he reckoned soon on settling down with
her in the country, far from the boards and the rotten
eggs. His name, I believe, was Laute ; he was of a
peaceful disposition, and he was reasonably asking
for the peace promised to men of good will. But
our kindly Flaubert would have none of it. He
required the worthy Laute to enter upon a new and
royal career.

" He is immense ! " he cried. " He is a barbaric
chief, a dynast of Argos, he is archaic, pre-historic,

legendary, Homeric, rhapsodic, epic! He has the sacred immobility! He does not stir . . . It is great! It is divine! He is formed like a statue of Dædalus, dressed by virgins. You have seen in the Louvre a little bas-relief in the old Greek style, quite Asiatic, which was found in the island of Samothrace, and which represents Agamemnon, Tathybios, and Epeus with their names written alongside them! Agamemnon is to be seen there, sitting on an X-shaped throne, with goat's feet. He has a pointed beard and his hair is curled in the Assyrian manner. So is Tathybios. They are terrible chaps ; they have the appearance of fishes and seem to be very old. One would say that Laute had emerged from that group. Good Lord! he is superb! "

This was the way that Flaubert breathed forth his ardour. He saw all the poetry of Homer and Æschylus incarnate in the worthy Laute, exactly as the ingenious hidalgo recognised in the person of a simple sheep the ever intrepid Brandabarbaran de Boliche, the ruler of the three Arabias, whose breast-plate was a serpent's skin, and his crown a gate which was said to be one of those that Samson carried away from the city of Gaza. I agree that they were both mistaken ; but one must be out of the ordinary to make a mistake of that sort.

You will never see fools falling into such illusions. Flaubert seemed to me to regret sincerely that he had not lived in the time of Agamemnon and the Trojan war. After having said a great deal in praise of that heroic age, as well as generally of all barbarous epochs, he launched out into invectives against the present time. He found it common-place. It was in this that his philosophy seemed

to me to go wrong. For every epoch is common-
place for those who live in it ; whatever the time
in which one is born, one cannot avoid the impression
of the vulgarity of the things amid which one lingers.
Our manner of living has always been monotonous,
and men have at all times been bored with one
another. The barbarians, whose existence was simpler than ours, were even more bored than we are.
They killed and pillaged to divert themselves.
To-day we have clubs, dinners, books, newspapers,
and theatres, which amuse us a little. Our pastimes
are more varied than theirs. Flaubert seemed to
believe that the personages of antiquity enjoyed
the impression of strangeness which they give us.
That is a rather ingenuous but a very natural
illusion. At bottom, I do not believe that Flaubert
was as unhappy as he had the air of being. He was,
at least, a pessimist of a particular species ; he was a
pessimist with an enthusiasm for a section of human
and natural things. Shakespeare and the East
threw him into an ecstasy. Far from pitying
him, I proclaim him happy : he had the better
part in the things of this world, he knew how to
admire.

I do not speak of the happiness he experienced
in realising his literary ideal by writing excellent
books, because I am unable to decide if the joy
of the result equalled in his case the pain and anguish,
of the effort. It is an open question which tasted the
purest satisfaction, Flaubert when he wrote the last
line of " Madame Bovary," or the sailor of whom
M. de Maupassant tells us, when he put the last
bit of rigging on the schooner which he was patiently
constructing in a water-bottle. For my own part
I have only known in this world two men who were

happy in their work: one is an old colonel, the
author of a catalogue of medals; the other is an
office attendant who made a little model of the
Madeleine church out of corks.   One does not
write masterpieces for one's pleasure, but under the
pressure of an inexorable fatality.   The curse on Eve
strikes at Adam as well: man also brings to birth in
pain.   But if to produce is bitter, to admire is
pleasant, and this pleasure Flaubert tasted to the
full; he drank it in large draughts.   He admired
with rage, and his admiration was full of sobs,
blasphemies, shrieks, and gnashings of teeth.

I find my Flaubert again in his " Correspondance,"
the first volume of which has recently appeared, just
as he was when I saw him fourteen years ago in the
little Turkish drawing-room of the Rue Murillo:
rough and kind, enthusiastic and laborious, a poor
theorist, an excellent worker, and a fine, upright
man.

All these qualities do not make a perfect lover,
and we must not be too much surprised if the
coldest letters in this general correspondence are the
love-letters.   These are addressed to a poetess who
had, it is said, already inspired a long and ardent
love in an eloquent philosopher.   She was beautiful,
fair, and talkative.   Flaubert, when he was chosen
by this Muse, had already, at the age of twenty-
three, acquired a taste for work and a horror of
constraint.   Add to this that the man was always
incapable of the least falsehood, and you can judge
of his difficulties in being a good correspondent.
However, at first he composed excellent letters; he
applied himself to his task so thoroughly that he
succeeded in attaining nonsense.   He wrote on
August 26, 1846:

" I have definitely marked out for my own use two parts in the world and in myself : on the one hand, the external element, which I desire varied, many-coloured, harmonious, immense, and from which I accept nothing except to enjoy the spectacle of it ; on the other, the internal element, which I concentrate in order to render it denser, and into which I allow the pure rays of the mind to penetrate in full exhalations through the open window of the intelligence."

This tone was not natural to him. He quickly wearied of it, and composed his letters in a clearer, but hard, and even somewhat brutal, style. In his moments of tenderness, which are rare, he speaks to his beloved almost as he would to a good dog. He says to her : " Your good eyes, your good nose." The Muse had believed that she would inspire more harmonious tones.

I note this epistle, of December 14, as an excellent model of ill-grace :

" Yesterday," Flaubert says in it, " I had a small operation in the cheek on account of my abscess ; my face is wrapped up in linen and is grotesque enough ; as if all the putrefactions and all the infections that have preceded our birth and that will resume possession of us after our death were not enough, we are, during our life, nothing but successive corruption and putrefaction, alternating with one another and encroaching upon one another. To-day we lose a tooth, to-morrow a hair ; a wound opens, an abscess is formed, you are blistered or prodded with needles. Add to this corns on your feet, vile natural odours, secretions of every sort and of every flavour, and there you have no very exciting picture of the human person. And to think that people love this ! Even that people love themselves, and that I myself, for example, have the effrontery to look at myself in the glass without bursting into a fit of laughter. Has not the mere sight of an old pair of boots something profoundly sad and bitterly melancholy about it ? When we think of all the steps we have taken in them to come or go we know not where, of all the grass we have trampled down, of all the mud we have gathered, the gaping leather seems to say to you : ' Fool, buy others, varnished, shining, and creaking, they will come to be like me, like you one day, when you shall have stained many boot-trees and sweated in many uppers'."

B 2

We cannot, at any rate, accuse him of repeating insipid common-places. He admits further on that " the skin of his heart is hard," and in truth he can ill comprehend certain refinements of feeling. On the contrary he is sometimes strangely candid. He assures Madame X. of the *quasi-virginity* of his soul. In truth, that is indeed a confession that ought to touch a blue-stocking. Moreover, he has not the least vanity, and he admits that he does not understand the finer shades of love. What we must praise him for is his frankness. He is asked to promise to love for ever. And he never promises anything at all. Here also he is a very upright man.

The truth is that he had but one passion— literature. One could place beneath his statue, if a statue were raised to him, this verse which Auguste Barbier addressed to Michael Angelo :

"Art was thine only love and held thine entire life."

At the age of nine he wrote (February 4, 1831) to his little friend, Ernest Chevalier :

" I will write some novels which I have in my head ; they are 'La Belle Andalouse,' 'Le Bal Masqué,' 'Cardenio,' 'Dorothée,' 'La Mauresque,' 'Le Curieux impertinent,' 'Le Mari prudent'."

From that moment he had discovered the secret of his vocation. All the days of his life he walked in the way wherein he was called. He worked like a horse. His patience, his courage, his honesty, his probity, will ever remain exemplary. He is the most conscientious of writers. His correspondence bears witness to the sincerity, the persistence, of his efforts. He wrote in 1847 :

" The further I go, the more I discover difficulties in writing the simplest things, and the more I perceive the emptiness of those I had thought the best. Happily, my admiration for the masters increases in proportion, and far from despairing at this crushing comparison, on the contrary, it kindles the unconquerable fantasy I have for writing."

One must admire and venerate this man of great faith, who by resolute labour and zeal for beauty rid himself of the natural clumsiness and confusion of his mind, who slowly and perspiringly produced his superb books, and who gave to letters the methodical sacrifice of his entire life.

M. GUY DE MAUPASSANT
CRITIC AND NOVELIST

GUY DE MAUPASSANT gives us to-day, in the same volume,* thirty pages of æsthetics and a new novel. I shall surprise no one when I say that the novel is of great value. As for the æsthetic, it is of the kind one might expect from a practical and resolute intellect, naturally inclined to find the things of the mind simpler than they are in reality. One discovers in it, together with good ideas and better instincts, an innocent tendency to take the relative for the absolute. M. de Maupassant lays down the theory of the novel as the lions would lay down the theory of courage if they knew how to speak. His theory, if I understand it rightly, comes to this: there are all sorts of ways of writing good novels, but there is only one way of estimating them. He who creates is a free man, he who judges is a helot. M. de Maupassant shows himself equally imbued with the truth of both these ideas. According to him there exists no rule for producing an original work, but there exist rules for judging one. And those rules are stable and necessary. "The critic," he says, "ought only to appreciate the result according to

* "Pierre et Jean."

the nature of the effort." The critic ought " to
search for everything which least resembles the
novels already written." He ought to have no
" school prejudices " ; he ought not " to preoccupy
himself with tendencies," and yet he ought " to
comprehend, distinguish, and explain all the most
opposing tendencies, the most contrary tempera-
ments." He ought. . . . But what ought he
not ? . . . I tell you he is a slave. He can be
a patient and stoical slave like Epictetus, but he
will never be a free citizen of the republic of
letters. And yet I am very wrong in saying that,
since, if he is good and docile, he will elevate
himself to the destiny of that Epictetus who
" lived poor and infirm and dear to the immortal
gods." For that sage retained in slavery the
dearest of treasures, inward liberty. And that is
precisely what M. de Maupassant takes away from
the critics. He takes from them even " feeling."
They must understand everything ; but he absolutely forbids them to feel anything. They will
no longer know the troubles of the flesh nor the
emotions of the heart. Bereft of desire, they will
lead a life sadder than death. The notion of duty
is sometimes terrifying. It unceasingly troubles us
by the difficulties, the obscurities, and the contradictions that it brings with it. I have experienced
this in the most diverse conjunctions. But it is
whilst receiving M. de Maupassant's commandments
that I recognise the full rigour of the moral law.

Never did duty appear to me at once so difficult,
so obscure, and so contradictory. In truth, what is
more difficult than to appreciate a writer's effort
without taking into consideration whither that
effort tends ? How can one favour new ideas and

at the same time hold the balance evenly between the representatives of originality and those of tradition ? How can one at the same time single out and ignore the tendencies of artists ?   And what sort of a task is it to judge by pure reason of works that spring only from feeling ?   This, however, is what is demanded of me by a master whom I admire and whom I love.   I feel, in truth, that it is too much, and that so much ought not to be exacted from human and critical nature.   I feel myself over-whelmed, and at the same time—shall I say it ?—I feel myself exalted.   Yes, like the Christian on whom his God enjoined labours of charity, works of penitence, and the immolation of his whole being, I am tempted to exclaim: " I must be something since so much is asked of me."

The hand that humiliated me uplifts me at the same time.   If I am to believe the master and teacher, the germs of truth are laid up in my soul. When my heart is full of zeal and simplicity, I shall discern literary good and evil, and I shall be a good critic.   But this pride totters as soon as it is uplifted. M. de Maupassant flatters me.   I know my own irredeemable infirmity and that of my colleagues. For the study of works of art we shall never possess —neither they nor I—anything more than feeling and reason, that is to say the least precise instru-ments that are in the world.   Therefore we shall never obtain certain results, and our criticism will never elevate itself to the rigorous majesty of science.   It will always float in uncertainty.   Its laws will never be fixed, its decisions will never be irrevocable.   Far different from justice, it will do little ill and little good, if indeed to amuse refined and eager spirits for a moment is to do little good.

Leave it then unfettered, since it is innocuous. It has some right, it seems, to the freedom you so haughtily refuse it while you grant that freedom with a just liberality to works called original. Is it not the daughter of imagination like them ? Is it not in its own way a work of art ? I speak of it with absolute disinterestedness, being by nature very detached from things, and inclined to say each evening with the author of " Ecclesiastes " : " What profit hath a man of all his labour ? " Moreover, I do hardly any criticism, properly speaking. That is a reason for remaining impartial. And perhaps also I have still better ones.

Well, without, as you see, allowing myself to fall into the least illusion in regard to the absolute truth which it expresses, I hold criticism to be the most certain mark that distinguishes truly intellectual ages ; I hold it to be the honorable sign of an instructed, tolerant, and polite society. I hold it to be one of the noblest branches with which the aged tree of letters decorates itself in the autumn of its days.

Now, will M. Guy de Maupassant permit me to say, without following the rules he has laid down, that his new novel, " Pierre et Jean," is very remarkable, and discloses a very vigorous talent ? It is not a purely naturalist novel. The author knows this well. He is conscious of what he has done. This time—and it is not for the first time— he has set out from an hypothesis. He said to himself : " If such an event took place in such circumstances, what would be the result ? " Now, the starting-point of the novel of " Pierre et Jean " is so singular, or at least so exceptional, that observation is almost powerless to show its consequences.

To discover them it is necessary to have recourse
to reasoning and to proceed by deduction. That
is what has been done by M. Guy de Maupassant,
who is, like the devil, a great logician. Here is
what he has *imagined*: A sentimental jeweller's
wife of the Rue Montmartre, whose husband, to
whom she had borne a little boy, was a very common-place tradesman, pretty Madame Roland felt
painfully the emptiness of her existence. A stranger,
a customer, who had come to the shop by chance,
fell in love with her and told her so with delicacy.
He was a M. Maréchal, a civil servant. Divining
in him a tender and prudent soul like her own,
Madame Roland loved and gave herself. She soon
had a second child, another boy, of whom the
jeweller believed that he was the father, but whom
she knew to have been born under a happier influence. Between this woman and her lover there
were profound affinities. Their intimacy was prolonged, harmonious, and concealed. She only broke
with him when the tradesman, retiring from
business, took his wife, now past middle-age, and
the children, already grown up, to Havre. Madame
Roland, tranquil and pacified, lived on her secret
memories, which had in them nothing bitter,
for bitterness, they say, only belongs to faults
committed against love. At forty-eight she could
congratulate herself on an episode that had rendered
her life charming, without costing her anything
of her honour as a respectable middle-class woman
and mother of a family. But suddenly we learn
that Maréchal has died and appointed the second of
the Roland boys as his sole legatee.

Such is the situation, I was going to say the
hypothesis, from which the novelist has started.

Am I not right to affirm that it is a strange one ?
Maréchal had, during his lifetime, shown the same
affection for the two little Rolands.   Doubtless he
could not, in the depths of his heart, love them both
the same.   Nothing was more natural than that he
should prefer his own son.   But he felt that his
preference could not be disclosed without indiscretion.   Why did he not understand that this
same preference would be even more indiscreet
if it burst forth suddenly in a posthumous and
solemn act ?   Why was it not evident to him that
he could not favour the second of these children
without exposing their mother's reputation to suspicion ?   Moreover, would not the most natural
delicacy inspire him to treat both brothers with
equality, out of consideration for the fact that
they were alike the children of her whom he had
loved ?

No matter !   M. Maréchal's will is a fact.   That
fact is not improbable ; we can, we should, accept
it.   What will be the consequences of that fact ?
The novel has been written, from the first line to the
last, to answer this question.   The lover's too
expressive legacy suggests no reflection to the
husband, who is a simple-minded man.   The
worthy Roland has never understood or thought of
what there might be in the world save jewellery and
gudgeon-fishing.   He attained at a stroke and
perfectly naturally to supreme wisdom.   At the
time of her love-affair, Madame Roland, who was
not an artificial creature, could deceive him without
even lying.   She has nothing to fear on that side.
Jean, her younger son, also finds natural a legacy by
which he benefits.   He is a quiet, ordinary boy.
Besides, when one is preferred to another, one does

not bother oneself much by asking why.   But Pierre,
the elder, accepts less easily a disposition which is
to his disadvantage.   It appears, to say the least,
peculiar to him.   At the first mention of it to him
outside his home, he thinks it odd.   He is painted for
us as an honest enough soul, but hard, discontented,
and jealous.   He has, above all, an unhappy temperament.   When suspicions have entered, there is no
more rest for him.   He piles them up whilst wishing
to dissipate them ; he makes a regular inquiry.
He gathers indications, he collects proofs ; he
troubles, frightens, overwhelms his unhappy mother
whom he adores.   In the despair of his betrayed
piety and his lost religion, he spares that mother
no contumely, and he proclaims to his adulterine
brother the secret he has surprised and ought to
keep.   His conduct is cruel and monstrous, but,
given his nature, it is logical.   I have heard it said :
" Since he commits the unpardonable wrong of
judging his mother, he ought at least to excuse her.
He knows what old Roland was, and that he was a
fool."   Yes, but if he had not had the habit of despis-
ing his father, he would not spontaneously have made
himself his mother's judge.   Besides, he is young and
he suffers.   These are two reasons why he should
be pitiless.   And do you ask what is the issue ?
There is none.   From such a situation there can
be no issue.

The truth is that M. de Maupassant has treated
this unthankful subject with the sureness of talent
which he possesses so fully.   Strength, flexibility,
proportion, nothing is lacking in this robust and
masterly story-teller.   He is vigorous without effort.
He is consummate in his art.   I do not insist.   My
business is not to analyse books : I have done enough

when I have implanted some worthy curiosity in the well-disposed reader ; but I ought to say that M. de Maupassant deserves every eulogy for the manner in which he has drawn the figure of the poor woman who pays cruelly for a happiness that went unpunished for so long. He has shown, with sure and rapid touch, the somewhat vulgar but not unattractive grace of that " tender book-keeper's soul." He has expressed with a subtlety that has no irony in it the contrast of great feeling in a petty existence. As for M. de Maupassant's language, I shall content myself with saying that it is true French, for I know not how to give higher praise.

" HAPPINESS " *

SAID Candide, " There are no longer any Manicheans," and Martin answered, " I am one." We say in the same way to-day that there are no longer poets who write long works, and M. Sully-Prudhomme replies by publishing a philosophic poem in twelve cantos on " Happiness."

We must first of all admire the audacious novelty of the enterprise. Is it not, in truth, a singular and admirable effort to set out in verse an ample succession of thoughts, to forge in cadence a long chain of ideas, at a time when poetry, which seems to have definitely renounced the old heroic and didactic forms, has been satisfied, for the past three generations, with the ode and the elegy, and as regards epic poetry, willingly limited herself to experiments or fragments ? The sonnet has again found the favour which it enjoyed in the days when the " Pléiade " shone. It is regarded as not offering too narrow a frame for the poet's thought, and M. Sully-Prudhomme has himself written a collection of sonnets of a beauty at once intellectual and concrete. Several of those little poems which compose the collection of " Épreuves " express the profoundest thought in the most fragrant language. Such

* " Le Bonheur." A poem by Sully-Prudhomme.

undoubtedly are the sonnets on " La Grande Ourse " and on " Les Danaïdes." Such is the sonnet which begins with this delicious strophe:

> "S'il n'était rien de bleu que le ciel et la mer,
> De blond que les épis, de rose que les roses,
> S'il n'était de beauté qu'aux insensibles choses,
> Le plaisir d'admirer ne serait point amer." *

It is above all by his little poems, by his stanzas and his elegies, that M. Sully-Prudhomme is widely known and deeply loved. His first long poem, " La Justice," added to the admiration with which so sincere a poet inspired those who care for literature, without greatly adding to the sympathy which flows on all sides from refined and gentle souls towards the author of " Solitudes." It was for his elegies that M. Sully-Prudhomme was first of all loved and blessed. And what love and what blessings does he not deserve for having poured forth for us that balm, unknown before his time, that exquisite mixture, in which intelligence joins with feeling to refresh the heart and to fortify the mind? It was a miracle to find a poet at once so sensitive and so intelligent. As a rule, miracles last only for a short time. This one ended too soon. The perilous equilibrium of two contrary faculties which had astounded us was lost. In M. Sully-Prudhomme intelligence conquered feeling. The intellectual faculties, so rich in his nature, developed with a tyrannical power. To the poet of " Solitudes " succeeded the poet of " Justice." To rapid and profound impressions, M. Sully-Prudhomme

---

* " If nothing were blue save the sky and the sea, were fair save the corn, or rose but the roses, if beauty were found only in inanimate things, the pleasure of admiring would not be a bitter one."

preferred pure thoughts linked in a long succession
to one another. He ceased to be elegiac and became
philosophical. I am far from rejoicing at this.
But I cannot blame him for it. Even when one
secretly prefers the delicious troubles of the first
hour of the day to the serenity of evening, one should
be silent about one's vain regrets, and cheerfully
admit that if there is an end of smiles and tears,
it is perhaps a good thing to meditate, and that
in the end the kneeling Polymnia has also irresistible
grace.

The poem of " Bonheur " is a philosophical poem.
One learns in it the extra-terrestrial adventures of
Faustus and Stella. Like the Eiros and the Char-
mion, like the Monos and the Una of the American
visionary, Faustus and Stella form a couple set free
by death. Together they enjoy, far from this
humble and miserable earth, peace in desire and
joy in immortality. When he evokes them, the poet
adjures them to tell us what is ineffable. And that
is a formidable adjuration. Faustus and his gentle
Stella return from the unknown, at the poet's
command, only to make dark sayings clear to us,
and to reveal to us those secrets that are buried
deepest in our hearts. To tell the truth, this is
a task in which your Faustus and your Stella will
eternally fail. The poet knew it. He fell into no
illusion for a single moment regarding the authority
of his personages. He does not flatter himself that
the speeches of Faustus will put an end to human
uncertainty. If Faustus proclaims what is true,
as he himself says in his preface, "if this dream
borders upon reality, upright and steadfast hearts
would have no reason to repine, but it is to chance
above all that they should attribute the credit."

Alas! it is then true, the adventure of Faustus
and Stella is only a beautiful dream. This is that
dream:

Faustus and Stella, who had loved one another
on Earth without being able to be united, rediscover
each other, after death, on a new planet. Faustus
is welcomed there by Stella, who had died before
him. In this planet, different from ours, the poet,
as one might expect, shows us nothing that is not
terrestrial. It is impossible, in truth, to invent
anything. Our whole imagination is made up of
memories.

We have even manufactured Heaven out of
materials taken from earth. The myrtles of the
Elysian fields are to be found in our gardens, and the
angels' harps come from our lute-makers. The
nameless planet to which the poet carries us is more
beautiful and pleasanter than ours, but it contains
nothing which Earth does not contain.

M. Sully-Prudhomme must at least be praised
for not having peopled unknown worlds with inco-
herent visions as Swedenborg did. We do not
know what the planets illuminated by Sirius and
the Polar Star are like. We shall never know.
We must content ourselves with knowing that the
distant sun which gave them birth is composed of a
gas that is known to us. The unity of the composition of the heavenly bodies is certain. It may well
be that the universe is upon the whole monotonous
enough, and that it does not deserve the insatiable
curiosity with which it inspires us.

In the planet inhabited by Faustus and Stella,
there are winged horses. It is true that none of
these are found on Earth, but there are wings and
there are horses, and without these the Greeks would

not have formed the idea of Pegasus. A Pegasus, one of these horses of the air, carries the two restored lovers through the new world they inhabit, and deposits them at the entrance to an ancient forest. They plunge into it, and soon there opens before them a valley in which flowers and fruits of every species delight the taste and the smell. These flowers and fruits are the sole food of the inhabitants of this planet.

"No being exists there to the detriment of others."

The struggle for life is unknown there. Murder not being the necessary condition of existence, the spirits there are naturally peaceable and kindly. Just as life is established on our earth in such a manner as constantly to engender crime and pain, existence in the nameless planet has nothing but gentle and lenient necessities. People are not wicked there, since they do not suffer, and wickedness is inconceivable without pain; but for the same reason they are unable to display their good qualities. For it is impossible to imagine beings possessing at the same time goodness and beatitude. Virtue necessarily supposes the faculty of sacrifice; a being that cannot cease to be happy is condemned to a perpetual moral mediocrity. That causes some embarrassment. When one thinks of it, one does not know what to desire, and one dare not wish for anything, not even universal happiness.

Faustus and Stella meet a numerous troop of cavaliers of all races, formerly slaves on the earth, but now free and enjoying their freedom with rapture. They admire in them the beauty of the different human types. And this is not without reason: liberty beautifies those strong enough to embrace it, and this natural truth has served as a foundation for the aristocratic prejudices so deeply rooted in all human societies. I shall only remark here that Faustus and Stella have still before their eyes the outward appearances of the earth, since they represent to themselves so vividly the image of liberty. For liberty could not exist in a world where servitude did not exist. The vision of the two lovers is, properly speaking, only a mirage. The planet of the happy cannot carry in its flowery bosom the warrior-maiden Liberty, the virgin with the blood-stained arms. She only reveals herself in combat: happy planets do not know her. The more I think of it, the more I am persuaded that happy planets know nothing.

In their new abode, Faustus and Stella are charmed by its sounds, its forms, and its colours. I should never have believed that, being immortal, they could enjoy the pleasures of sight and hearing. Is not to see, to hear, or to smell to use up something of one's self, is it not to die a little ? And what is to live as we live on earth but to die continually and to spend every day a part of the totality of life that is in us ? But the poet's vision is so pure and his art is so subtle that we are transported and delighted.

Stella reveals to Faustus the highest expression of music. He enjoys the charm of the voice in a happy ecstasy which makes him forget his past life. Stella, who had hitherto appeared to him in a terrestrial shape, assumes before him her perfect beauty. They exchange their love in a sublime communion.

That is their happiness ! But how can they enjoy it if they are immortal ? We have love on earth, but it is at the price of death. If we were not destined to perish, love would be something inconceivable. Scarcely has Faustus embraced Stella in his rejuvenated arms than he becomes abstracted and thoughtful. Has his happiness lasted a day or thousands of millions of centuries ? We do not know, and he himself is equally ignorant. An unalloyed happiness cannot be measured. Even he who possesses it does not enjoy it or feel it. However this may be, curiosity, satiated for a moment by the delights of Paradisiacal life, awakens again in Faustus. He aspires to comprehend the nature he is enjoying. He wants to know. Immortal yesterday,

> " Une vague inquiétude,
> Le souci de savoir, que nul front fier n'élude,
> Le mal de l'inconnu l'avait déjà tenté." *

By this sign also, I recognise him as one of our brethren. He has not put off the old man ; he remains in mind a citizen of the little old planet on which some Latin schoolman once wrote this maxim : " We tire of everything except of understanding things."

Faustus evokes, in his disquiet, the distant memory of human knowledge. At first he recalls to his memory the philosophical systems of Greek antiquity ; then he passes in review the Alexandrians and the schoolmen. At last he braves the moderns, Bacon, Descartes, Pascal, Spinoza, Leibnitz, Locke, Berkeley, Hobbes, Hume, Kant, Fichte, Hegel, Schopenhauer, Comte. . . . This latter stops him, forbids him metaphysical speculations, and imposes on him a general view of human knowledge. But that philosophy does not lead to the knowledge of

* " A vague disquiet, the care to know, which no proud brow eludes, the misery of not knowing had already tempted him."

the origin and end of things ; the resignation which it imposes on his unsatisfied curiosity is not less repugnant to him than the rashness of metaphysical conceptions. Faustus, despairing of finding the truth in the teaching of terrestrial thinkers, abandons their deceptive aid.

He has thenceforth exhausted the joys of feeling and those of intelligence. Now, whilst he was enjoying his unconscious felicity, the chorus of human lamentation, incessantly growing larger since the most distant ages, was going up from earth to Heaven. It at last reaches the planet inhabited by Stella. Faustus hears those laments, recognises them, and feels awakening within him the consciousness and sympathy of brotherhood.

Oh ! what a dolorous eloquence swells the voice of Earth !

> " Lamentable océan de douleurs, dont la houle
> Se soulève en hurlant, s'affaisse et se déroule,
> Et marche en avant sans repos !
> N'est il donc pas encore apparu sur ta route
> Un monde fraternel où quelque ami t'écoute :
> N'auras-tu nulle part d'échos ? " *

Faustus, as he listens to the cries, promises himself that he will descend again to the earth, to bring to men the resources of his knowledge ; Stella will follow him and share his sacrifice. Obedient death will come to take them again.

How little man is made for immortality ! Faustus and Stella seemed to breathe it as if it were a suffocating fluid. Their death has the joyous sweetness

---

* " Lamentable ocean of griefs, whose waves uplift themselves in moans, subside and fall, and onward press unresting ! Has there not yet appeared upon thy way any fraternal world in which some friend may listen to thee : shalt thou know no echo ? "

of a re-birth.   One feels that it will give back to the
lovers their true destiny.   The poet has found rare
and exquisite tones in which to sing it, something
refined, flowing, subtle (one must recur to that word).
He has extracted the quintessence of his poetry :

> " La tombe est toute faite et, pour l'heure fatale,
> L'aube leur a tissé des suaires d'opale.
> Ils regagnent leur couche et se livrent tous deux
> En silence, à l'asile aujourd'hui hasardeux
> Que leur ouvre ce lit, odorante corbeille,
> Où depuis si longtemps leurs bonheurs de la veille
> Au fidèle matin renaissaient rafraîchis.
> Étendus sans bouger, droits, les bras seuls fléchis
> Pour rapprocher leurs mains et les unir, il semble
> Que le trépas déjà les ait glacés ensemble.
> Ils n'ont pas vu la mort achever leur repos :
> Leurs yeux, à leur insu, par degrés se sont clos ;
> Leurs fronts n'ont plus pensé, décolorés à peine,
> Et tout bas, ralentie, a cessé leur haleine.
>
> *   *   *   *   *
>
> Quand le soleil du monde abandonné par eux
> Embrassa tout à coup l'horizon vaporeux,
> Une abeille rôdeuse, explorant les prairies
> Sur un amas foulé de milles fleurs meurtries
> S'arrêta pour y faire un butin pour son miel,
> Comme avec la douleur se fait la joie au ciel." *

* " The tomb is quite prepared, and for the fatal hour the dawn
has woven for them its opal shrouds.   They gain their couch and be-
take themselves in silence to the refuge, hazardous to-day, which their
bed offers them, that fragrant repository in which so long their joys
of eve awoke renewed each faithful morning.   Outstretched, straight
and motionless, only their arms bent to join and link their hands,
it seems that death already has frozen them together.   They have not
seen death putting an end to their rest : Their eyes, unknown to them,
have slowly closed ; their brows no more know thought, they scarce
have lost their hue, and softly growing less, their breath has ceased.

*   *   *   *   *

When the sun of the world they had left lit up suddenly the misty
horizon, a wandering bee, exploring the meadows, stopped upon a
trampled heap of dying flowers to gather booty for its hive, so in
Heaven is joy distilled from pain."

Death has borne their unconscious forms to the earth. At the moment they touch the ancient planet whence there arose so great a cry of pain, the reanimated Faustus and Stella recognise their first home, but they perceive that there are no longer any men in it; the human species has long been extinct upon it. No matter; they will descend into this evil world. They will devote themselves to creating a happy race on the soil that formerly nourished so much suffering. Whilst they are making this decision, Death, obeying a Divine order, carries them towards the highest abode, which they have deserved by their incomparable devotion. Alas! what will they do in that glorious abode? Since we know, from their example, that even outside the earth there is joy only in sacrifice, we fear that in that seventh heaven where Death deposits them, they will enjoy but an insipid felicity. What is the true name of that sublime abode which the poet does not name? Is it not Nirvana that one finds there? And does not the poet's happy dream end with the irreversible absorption of the two souls in the Divine nothingness?

Such is the subject, or rather the bald argument, of this fine poem, at once one of the most audacious and agreeable of philosophic poems.

MÉRIMÉE *

Y publishing a biographical study of the author of "Colomba," M. d'Haussonville has once more proved that he can be just even towards those whose ideas and feelings he does not share. We know that M. d'Haussonville cares for nothing so much as for justice. His religious faith, his political convictions, his literary tastes, separate him from Mérimée. But still he has not refused his sympathy to a mind which, while disconcerting him by an apparent coldness, won him over by a sort of hidden generosity.

M. d'Haussonville was able to recognise in Mérimée, not without some respect, " one of those natures which, bruised by contact with life, give to their experience the form of a rather bitter cynicism, and which carefully conceal ardours, sometimes convictions, and always refinements, of which they are never suspected by the ruder probity of those whom they scandalise."

We must say that the unpublished letters printed by M. d'Haussonville in this study, reveal a Mérimée whom the correspondences with Panizzi and the two Unknown Ladies did not permit us to suspect,

* " Prosper Mérimée." A biographical and literary study. By the Comte d'Haussonville.

a Mérimée, tender, affectionate, faithful, and good. Those letters—there are about a score of them—are written, some to an English lady full of grace and wit, Mrs. Senior, the daughter-in-law of Mr. William Senior, who has left a collection of reminiscences; others to "the daughter of a soldier, doubly illustrious, both by the name he bore, and by the high rank he had attained in our army." Mérimée shows himself natural, trustful, affectionate, with both. We know that he was ready to give his confidence to women. Friendship, which he judged to be quite chimerical between men, did not seem to him absolutely impossible between a man and a woman. He regarded it in that case only as difficult, even "devilishly difficult, for the devil mixes himself up in the business"; but he flattered himself that he had had two friends.

Age helping him, he loved women with a spiritual and perfectly charming affection. Such an intercourse is the last joy of the voluptuary. Whatever theologians may say, souls have a sex as well as bodies. Mérimée knew it. He had always liked and understood women. His mistake was following the example of his master, Stendhal, to affect a systematic immorality. Stendhal and Mérimée expressly put certain audacities, certain violences, into the rank of the most imperious duties of the gentleman. I wish that at least he left us free and permitted us sometimes to be respectful. There are hardly any agreeable duties, and inverse duties are sometimes more painful than the others. But the brutality was only a mask. Mérimée was hiding his wound. He had plumbed the deeps of anguish, yet he betrayed his suffering only when

speaking of the passion of others. Thus he wrote
to Mrs. Senior :

" I believe that there is no lung disease in Spain, but there is disease
of the heart, an organ unknown or shrivelled up north of the Pyrenees.
I have amongst my memoranda several lamentable cases of such
maladies, among others an instance of two people who loved one
another, and who died within a week. What will surprise you greatly
is that it was not a husband and wife, or to speak more correctly,
it was a husband married to another wife and a wife married to
another husband. They were so worthless as to love one another in
spite of their position ; so they were punished. Let us hope they
will roast in a place which I shall not name, and which has been
established for such great criminals."

Do you not feel that beneath this irony there is
an ardent sympathy ? Mérimée was always sincerely
convinced of the legitimacy of the passions. He
required of them nothing but that they should
be true and strong. And this conviction inspired
him here and there with maxims on marriage and
chastity that would certainly have shocked Mrs.
Senior if she had been less of a modest woman, for
modest women are not as easily shocked as others.
Mérimée said to her :

" They have taken it into their heads to make a sacrament of what
should never have been more than a social convention."

This seems very irreverent. But everything is
permitted to philosophic doubt. As M. Berthelot
says, there is no longer any territory protected from
discussion. Did I not hear one of the greatest
philosophers of our time maintaining in the same
way the other day that marriage was a transitory
form, and that without doubt some substitute
will be found in five or six thousand years at latest ?
Merimée said further :

" I do not regard chastity as the most important virtue. It is not of such value that it should be put above everything."

On this occasion he obviously yielded to the pleasure of shocking his estimable friend a little. We need not take a whim of this sort too gravely. We need only say that there are men who have attached a great value to women's chastity. Every European, it is true, cares personally only for the chastity of one woman, or at most for the chastity of two or three women. He would even be very displeased if they remained chaste to his detriment, but this is enough to form opinion.

Whilst he spoke in this abrupt and flippant style, Mérimée was suffering cruelly. " I have become incapable of working," he said, " since a misfortune befell me."

And he continued:

" When I wrote I had an aim ; now I no longer have one. If I wrote, it would be for myself, and I should bore myself even more than I do. There was once a madman who believed he had the Queen of China (you are not ignorant of the fact that she is the most beautiful princess in the world) shut up in a bottle. He was very happy to possess her, and he exerted himself a good deal so that the bottle and its contents would have no reason to complain of him. One day he broke the bottle, and, as one does not find a princess of China twice in one's life, from being a lunatic he became a fool."

This agreeable madman was none other than himself. He one day tells Mrs. Senior how he lost his enchanted bottle, with an intentional dryness, attributing the adventure to " a friend of his." M. d'Haussonville guarantees in a note the truth of this disguised confidence.

" Imagine to yourself two people who love one another very truly for a long time, for so long that folks cease to trouble about it. One fine morning the woman takes it into her head that what has made her happiness and another's for ten years is wrong. 'Let us separate ; I love you still, but I don't want to see you any more.' I do not know, madame, if you can conceive what a man may suffer who has placed the whole happiness of his life in something that is suddenly taken away from him."

There he is, this strong man ! this despiser of tenderness and fidelity ! He loves for ten years, and he has placed his life's happiness in a gentle, serious, and prolonged intimacy. Thus the mask of cynicism and insensibility concealed a tender and serious countenance which the world has never seen.

Mérimée, born proud and timid, withdrew into himself all too soon, and, from his early youth, assumed the rigid and sarcastic attitude with which he went through life. Saint-Clair in the " Vase Étrusque " is himself.

" Saint-Clair was born with a tender and loving heart ; but at an age when one easily receives impressions that last throughout life, his too expressive sensitiveness had attracted the raillery of his companions. He was proud and ambitious ; he thought much of public opinion, as children do. Thenceforth he made it a study to suppress all appearances of what he regarded as dishonouring weakness. He succeeded, but his victory cost him dear."

Such was Mérimée at twenty, such he remained at forty, when he wrote to Madame du Parquet :

" My friends have often told me that I did not take enough care to display what good there might be in my nature ; but I have never troubled myself except for the opinion of certain persons."

This attitude did not deceive Mrs. Senior, who wrote to her friend that he was naturally a good-natured man. He agreed :

" I am charmed that you believe me *a good-natured man*. I believe it is true. I have never been wicked ; but as I have grown old, I have tried to avoid doing evil, and it is more difficult than people think."

Then, by a very human contradiction, regretting that he appeared as he had shown himself and that he had succeeding in hiding his good qualities, he complained of being wrongly judged, of being unjustly condemned by public opinion. He attributed solely to his candour the moral solitude that his pride, his timidity, and his superiority had made around him.

" If I had to begin my life over again with the experience I have acquired, I should apply myself to being a hypocrite and to flattering everybody. Now the game is not worth the candle. On the other hand, there is something sad in pleasing people under a mask and in thinking that if one unmasked one would become odious."

His keenest and most constant regret was that he had not a child, a little girl, to bring up. He wrote in 1855 to Mrs. Senior :

" I am too old to marry, but I should like to find a ready-made little girl to bring up. I have often thought of buying a child from a gipsy, because, if my method of education turned out badly, I should not in all probability have increased the unhappiness of the little creature I should have adopted. What do you think of this ? And how can a little girl be got ? The worst of it is that gipsies are too dark, and that they have hair like a horse's mane. Why have you not a little golden-haired girl to hand over to me ? "

The same regret some time later :

" The world overpowers me, and I do not know what will become of me. I think I have no longer a friend in the world. I have lost all those I loved ; they are dead or have changed. If I had the means I would adopt a little girl ; but this world, and above all, this country, is so uncertain that I dare not give myself that luxury."

The years pass, and this regret remains. He complains of his solitude. He sadly verifies the impossibility of keeping a friend, and he expresses anew his desire " to have a little daughter."

" But," he adds, " it might well happen that the little monster, after some years, might fall in love with some whipper-snapper, and leave me in the lurch."

However, this dream pursued him even in old age and illness. In 1867, at Cannes, where he was imprisoned by the affection of the lungs from which he was soon to die, he saw M. Prévost-Paradol's three children, one of whom was a perfectly beautiful child of thirteen: then regret at not having a child swelled up in his half-frozen heart. Mérimée wrote to a lady with whom he corresponded for several years:

" I should have loved greatly to have had a girl to bring up. I have many ideas on education, and particularly on the education of girls, and, I believe, talents which will unhappily remain unemployed."

Already for a long time he had suffered from the spleen, and was a victim to *blue devils* which Mrs. Senior was not able to conjure away. M. d'Haussonville has sought for the cause of this melancholy. He believes he has found it in " the confused instinct of an ill-directed life, given up to many allurements, the memory of which left more bitterness than pleasure." For my own part, I doubt whether Mérimée ever had a moral feeling of this sort. Of what would he have repented? He never recognised anything as virtues save energies nor as duties save passions. Was not his scepticism rather that of the sceptic for whom the universe is only a succession of incomprehensible images, and who equally fears life and death, since neither have any meaning for him? In a word, did he not experience that bitterness of mind and heart which is the inevitable punishment of intellectual audacity, and did he not drink to the lees what Marguerite of Angoulême so well denominates as the boredom common to every well-intentioned man?

OUTSIDE LITERATURE *

THE title of M. Georges Ohnet's new novel expresses a good deal by means of a single word.

Its title is a whole philosophy. "Will," that is what speaks to the heart and the mind! " ' Will,' by Georges Ohnet ! " How one feels the man of principle who has never doubted! " ' Will,' by Georges Ohnet, seventy-third edition ! ' What a proof of the power of will! Locke did not believe that the will was free. But his " Essay on the Human Understanding " did not reach seventy-three editions in a single morning. Here we have Locke victoriously refuted! The will is not an illusion, for M. Georges Ohnet has willed to have seventy-three editions, and he has achieved them. In truth the oftener I re-read this title, the more interest I find in it. It is beyond contradiction the finest page that has left M. Georges Ohnet's pen. Its style is sober and firm, its thought felicitous, clear, and profound. " ' Will,' by Georges Ohnet, seventy-third edition," how excellently thought, how well written !

I confess that the rest of the book has seemed to me inferior. From the philosophical point of view, this new work by the author of " Serge

* " Volonté." By Georges Ohnet.

Panine " is open to criticism, and gives rise to numerous objections. The problem of the will has not yet been solved to the satisfaction of all thinking humanity. There are metaphysicians who say that the will is nowhere. I should be rather tempted to see it everywhere, and to regard all the phenomena of the universe as the effects of an eternal and fatal will.

M. Georges Ohnet, who has refuted Locke so well in two words on the cover of his production, has not maintained the same superiority in the course of that production itself. He has neglected to tell us what he understands by will. That is a mistake. He has not told us either whether he believes that animals have will. For my own part, I am persuaded that they have it like us. If they have not, they must be machines. Moreover, what is will, in the vulgar sense of the word, if not the internal power by which man resolves to act or not to act ?

Animals act, therefore they will. Once when I was at table by the side of M. Darlu, I begged that eminent professor of philosophy to allow a little will to the vegetables. M. Darlu refused in the most absolute fashion ; I respectfully represented to him that if an oak grows it is because it wants to grow, and that if it was unwilling, nobody could force it to do so. M. Darlu refused to be persuaded. That evening I went away greatly perplexed. M. Georges Ohnet has taken away my uncertainty. Not content with affirming, without proofs, that the will is free, M. Georges Ohnet maintains that it is supreme. That is going too far and giving back to Locke the advantage he had won from him. For, indeed, it is clear that it would be useless for me to will, like M. Ohnet, to push my works into seventy-

three editions. I could not do it. As a philosopher, M. Georges Ohnet does not satisfy me.

In that capacity I find him ineffective. I wish it
were not my task to "appreciate" him from any
other point of view, for I am desperately anxious
to recite to you forthwith some stirring ballad of the
time when the world was young. But since M. Ohnet
writes novels, it is right and necessary to treat him as
a novelist. It is what I am going to proceed to do
with all the discretion of which I am capable. I
am disposed to moderation and indulgence. Those
who read me know that my criticism is friendly,
and that I perform an agreeable duty by always
expressing the most broad-minded opinions in the
most agreeable form. Well then, since I must
judge M. Ohnet as an author of novels, I shall say,
with the most placid of souls and the serenest of
consciences, that, from the point of view of art, he
is miles below the worst of the craft.

I had the honour last winter of being presented to
M. Georges Ohnet, and I am convinced, like everybody who has met him, that he is the worthiest of
men. He speaks in a very interesting manner, with
a most agreeable good humour. He inspired me
with sympathetic feeling. I recognise in him
qualities that do him honour, and I esteem him
profoundly, but I know no books that I dislike more
than his. I know nothing in this world more
displeasing than his notions or more ungraceful
than his style.

I confess that hitherto I have had little experience
of him as an "author." I have taken small notice
of the novels with which he has filled the universe.
They inspire me with an unavowed but indisputable
mistrust; I felt that they were not made for me,

and I had an instinct that they were antipathetic. If I had considered myself, I should have died without having read a line of M. Ohnet. I should have been spared that painful and dangerous ordeal. I take a great deal of trouble in avoiding through life what seems to me ugly. I should be afraid of becoming decidedly malicious if I were forced to live confronted by what shocks, wounds, and afflicts me. That is why I had resolved not to read " Will." But fate disposed of matters otherwise.

I have read " Will," and at first I was very unhappy. There is not a page, not a line, not a word, not a syllable of that book which has not shocked, offended, and saddened me. I was disposed to weep over it with all the Muses for company. I had never before read so bad a book: that gave it a certain consideration in my eyes, and I ended by conceiving a sort of admiration for it. M. Ohnet is detestable, and maintains a level and copious flow of badness ; he is consistent, and gives the idea of a species of perfection. There is genius in that. I do not say too much when I say that he has his own power, his own genius, and his own magic : everything that he touches, immediately becomes sadly vulgar and ridiculously pretentious. The miracles of nature and of humanity, the splendour of the heavens and the beauty of women, the treasures of art and the ravishing secrets of souls, in a word, everything that makes the charm and holiness of life becomes, as it passes through his thought, sickeningly vulgar. This then is what he sees, this what he feels ! And he cares to live ! It is incomprehensible ! What amazes me more than anything else, is the silliness of those perpetual caricatures in the midst of which he naturally lives and moves.

I have said he is detestable, flatterer that I am! The truth is that he is mediocre. As a writer he is a perfect *snob*. He lifts to the level of genius that species of comfortable silliness which the English call *snobbishness*, and that is why he is the ideal of the millions of snobs who swarm on the continents and islands of this planet.

All his ideas on life are worthy of the greatest thinker to whom snobbishness has given birth, to the undoing of simple, seemly, and lofty souls. He is, in the first place, a snob in his coarse love of luxury, when he shows us, as he does in " Will," " a victoria going down the Rue Boissy d'Anglas, drawn by two horses stepping with grace " ; when he makes us mount after him " a staircase of which the stone steps are covered with a sumptuous carpet ; " and when he introduces us into " the hall of a mansion enchantingly lighted by electric light," where we breathe " an intoxicating atmosphere composed of the perfume of flowers and the heady odour of women."

When Buridan, the captain, exclaims: " These are great ladies, very great ladies ! " one smiles with indulgence ; one is not too much shocked by the admiration that princesses inspire in this robust, naïve, and starveling scholar. Buridan shows his good-nature and his simplicity. But M. Ohnet's posturings when he presents to us his baronesses and his duchesses are positively nauseating ; I cannot read without exasperation this simple phrase : " Helen took a secret pleasure in touching that marvellous fabric. Her aristocratic nature showed itself in this taste for refined things." That is screamingly false and futile. There is nothing aristocratic in liking beautiful textures. What makes, or more correctly speaking, what did make, aristocracy was the long and hereditary habit of command. As for delighting in touching something pleasant, it can be the pleasure of a little shopkeeper's wife as well as of a patrician lady. But it is useless to dispute when one knows that one can never be understood. Let us criticise no more, let us only exhibit.

This Helen, who betrays her refined nature by her taste for refined things, is the heroine of " Will."

She is sublime. Loved by two men, one of whom has " fatal beauty," she prefers the other, out of generosity.

" ' Come, be frank,' interrupted Thauziat (Clement Thauziat is the man with the fatal beauty). ' Come, will you dare to confess before me that you love him ? '

" At this challenge, Mademoiselle de Graville (she is poor but she has breeding) feels a revolt within her.

" And, braving Thauziat with a look :

" ' Do you want me to tell you ? Well then, I will. Yes, I do love him.'

" ' What has he done to deserve it ? ' cried Clement bitterly.

" ' He is weak and in need of a defender.'

" ' Say he is cowardly and vicious.'

" ' Well, I will be his bravery and his virtue.'

" ' If he finds you superior to him, he will hate you.'

" ' Having done everything for the best, I shall suffer without complaining.'

" ' Do you think I will allow you to sacrifice yourself in this way ? '

" ' By what right would you intervene ? ' " (p. 213)

This concise and vigorous dialogue is indeed Corneille for snobs. But let us continue. This Clement de Thauziat, whom Helen withstands so proudly, also belongs to the highest aristocracy. " There was an exquisite moderation in his attire, which gave him a remarkable stamp of distinction." (p. 11). " In the fifteenth century he would have been one of those superb *condottieri* who," &c. (p. 12). " With him a woman's destiny would be great, would be happy, would be envied " (p. 201). " His embrace is warm and trembling " (p. 187). " He is pale and dark" (*passim*). " He seemed resplendent in Satanic beauty " (p. 362). He is killed by a bullet in the heart, in an honourable but terrible duel. After his death, he is still fatally beautiful. " He had fallen, elegant and correct, as he had lived " (p. 416).

By the side of this hero who has so much " cachet," M. Ohnet has been pleased to evoke a young Englishwoman, fair and perfidious, with a heart of marble, Lady Diana. " Her blond hair shone like a casque of gold " (p. 93). One could not endure the radiancy of "her blue eyes, as clear and as hard as steel " (p. 345). " Her skin and supple figure, moulded in her riding-habit, curved voluptuously " (p. 253). In piquant contrast, Lady Diana has for her rival, Émilie Lereboulley, a sprightly and tender, ironical and generous little hunchback. " This girl, so deformed by nature, seemed to have determined to compensate by the dazzling elevation of her mind for the miserable degradation of her body" (p. 11). You understand now what causes my sadness and my disgust, and you feel that everything, even the refined brutality of the realists, even the tortuous obscurity of the decadents, in a word, everything, is preferable to this wretched platitudinising.

These paltry rhapsodies find, I know, readers by hundreds of thousands. " Will " will delight a great number of people. That is worth reflecting upon, and ingenious persons will not fail to ask by what strange mystery the abominable rubbish which I have just quoted with a mixture of generous disgust and perverse joy, is transformed in innocent brains into romantic and touching poetry. Do not doubt it, there are women, charming women, who will think it all fine, and who will weep over it. Well, I shall not reproach them for that. On the contrary, I shall praise them for their candour and their simplicity. The mentally poverty-stricken must also have their ideal. Is it not true that the wax figures exposed in the windows of the hairdressers inspire schoolboys with poetical dreams ? Now M. Georges Ohnet's novels are in the literary order exactly what the wax figures of the hairdressers are in the plastic order.

BIBLIOPHILIA*

HAVE known many book-lovers in my life, and I am certain that the love of books renders life endurable to a certain number of well-born persons. There is no true love without some sensuality. One is not happy in books unless one loves to caress them. I recognise a true book-lover at the first glance by the manner in which he touches a book. The man who puts his hand on some precious, rare, lovable, or at the least, seemly volume, and who does not press it with a hand both gentle and firm, who does not voluptuously pass a tender palm over its back, its sides, and its edges, that man never had the instinct that makes Grosliers and Doubles. He may vainly say he loves books : we will not believe him. We will answer him : You love them for their utility. Is that love ? Does one love when one loves without disinterestedness ? No ! you have no fire and no joy, and you will never know the delight of passing trembling fingers over the delicious grain of a morocco-bound volume.

I call to mind two old priests who loved books and who loved nothing else in this world. One was a canon who lodged near Notre-Dame ; he had a

---

* " Bibliographie des principales éditions originales d'écrivains français du XVᵉ au XVIIIᵉ siècle." By Jules Le Petit.

charming soul in his little body. It was a perfectly round little body, the very padding and wrap for a canon's soul. He meditated writing the " Lives of the Saints of Brittany," and lived happily. The other, a curate of a poor parish, was taller, handsomer and sadder. The windows of his room overlooked the Zoological Gardens, and he slept to the roars of the captive lions. Both found themselves on the quays, before the secondhand booksellers' stalls, every day that God made. Their task on earth was to stuff calf-bound volumes with red edges into the pockets of their cassocks. These are doubtless simple and modest labours, well suited to the ecclesiastical life. I would even say that there is less danger for a priest in overhauling the stalls on the quays than in contemplating nature in the fields and in the forests. Whatever Fénelon may say, nature is not edifying. She lacks modesty, she counsels to combat and love; she is secretly voluptuous; she troubles the senses by a thousand obscure odours; one feels that she surrounds one with ardent breaths and kisses. Her very quiet is lascivious. A poet, who was sensitive to pleasure, has rightly said:

" Avoid
The recesses of the woods and their vast silence."

A walk along the quays from stall to stall presents none of these dangers: secondhand books do not trouble the heart. If some of them speak of love, they speak of it in an ancient language, with characters of the past, and they make one think of death at the same time as of love. My canon and my curate were very right to pass a great part of this transitory life between the Pont-Royal and the

Pont Saint-Michel. The spectacle which their
eyes oftenest encountered there was that of the little
gold floweret which the eighteenth-century binders
impressed between each bit of stitching on the calf
backs of their books. Oh ! the canon and the curate
were holy men ! I believe neither of them ever had
an evil thought !

As regards the canon, I would put my hand in
the fire in attestation : he was jovial. At seventy,
he had the soul and the cheeks of a little child.
Never did golden spectacles bridge a simpler nose to
give light to more candid eyes. The curate, with
his long nose and his hollow cheeks, was perhaps
a saint : the canon was assuredly a just man. Yet
this saint and this just man had their own sensuality.
They looked upon books in mottled calf with concupiscence, they fingered fawn-coloured calf with
voluptuousness. It is not that they placed their
joy and their pride in disputing with the princes of
the bibliophilic world for best editions of the
French poets, Mazarin or Canevarius bindings, or
illustrated works with two or three extra sets of
impressions. No, they were poor with joy, humble
with gladness. They brought into their love for
books the austere simplicity of their lives. They
only bought modest works, modestly bound. They
eagerly collected the writings of old theologians
which nobody any longer wants. They put their
hands with naïve joy on the despised curiosities
that strew the halfpenny box of the expert dealer.
They were satisfied when they found a " History of
Wigs " by Thiers or a " Masterpiece of an Unknown"
by Dr. Chrysostome Matanasius. They left morocco
bindings to the powerful of this world. Grained
calf, fawn-coloured calf, sheepskin, and parchment

sufficed for their desires, but those desires were ardent ; they were kindled with flame, and incited by goads : they were, in a word, those desires which Christian symbolism represented in the churches during the Middle Ages under the forms of little devils with birds' heads, goats' feet, and bats' wings. I have seen the canon with amorous hand caressing a fine copy in grained calf of the " Lives of the Fathers of the Desert." That is a sin. And what aggravates the fault is that it is a Jansenist book. As for the curate, he once received from an old maid a copy of the " Imitation," of the size called Elzevir, bound in purple cloth, on which the pious donor had embroidered a golden chalice with her own hand. He blushed with pleasure and pride, and exclaimed : " It is a present by which M. Bossuet himself would have been honoured ! " I like to believe that my curate and my canon have both worked out their salvation, and that they are now at the right hand of the Father. But everything has to be paid for, and in the Angel's book,

> " Wherein all hath been recorded,
> Whence shall judgment be awarded,"

the debt of the curate and that of the canon are inscribed. I think I read in that Book of Books :

" The canon : on such and such a day, on the Quai Voltaire, for taking delight in pleasant touching. On such and such another day, for having breathed the perfume of a bookseller's shop on the Quai des Grands-Augustins. . . . . The curate : " Imitation " in Elzevir small octavo : pride and concupiscence."

That, without doubt, is what is in the Angel's

Book, which will be read out on the day of the last judgment.

Oh ! the good curate ! Oh ! the excellent canon ! How many a time did I meet them with their noses in the boxes on the quays ! When you saw one, you were sure of soon finding the other. Yet they did not seek one another ; rather they avoided one another. It must be admitted that they were a little jealous of each other.

And how could it have been otherwise, since they both hunted the same ground ? Every time they met, that is to say every day, they exchanged a long unctuous salute during which they mutually spied at one another and sounded with a glance each other's pockets stuffed with books. Besides, their natures were not sympathetic. The canon had a devout and simple conception of the universe that could not satisfy the curate, whose soul was full of controversy and learned disputes. The canon enjoyed in advance here below the peace promised to men of good will. Like St. Augustine and like the great Arnault, the curate bared his brow to the storms. He spoke of the bishop with a freedom that made the good canon tremble in his overcoat.

The canon was not formed ror difficult situations. I met him one day in great distress. It was before the Institute, during a shower. In a wink, a squall had sprung up, and the wind carried into the Seine the pamphlets and papers that were displayed on the parapets. It also carried off the canon's red old umbrella. We saw it lifted up in the air and then fall into the river. The canon lamented it. He invoked all the Breton saints, and promised a penny to whoever would bring him back his umbrella. Yet the red umbrella sailed away to Saint-Cloud. A quarter of an hour afterwards, the weather had become fine again; beneath a pleasant sun, the excellent priest with his eyes still moist and his mouth already smiling, was buying an old Lactantius in Father Malorey's edition, and was joyously reading this phrase, printed in the fine italic type of the Alduses: *Pulcher hymnis Dei homo immortalis.* The Aldine italic had made him forget the loss of his red umbrella.

I knew on the quays at the same time a still stranger bibliomaniac. He had a habit of tearing out of books the pages that displeased him; and as he had a fastidious taste, there only remained in his library a single complete volume. His collection was composed of fragments and remnants which he had had magnificently bound. I have reasons for not giving his name, though he has been dead for a long time. Those who have known him will recognise him when I say that he himself wrote strange and sumptuous volumes on numismatics, and published them in parts. The subscribers were not numerous, but among them was one violent collector whose name has remained celebrated among the curious, Colonel Maurin. He had enrolled himself the first, and was very exact in claiming each part as it appeared. However, he had to make a fairly long journey. The other heard of this. He immediately published a new section and sent the following notice to the subscribers: " All copies of the last section that have not been claimed by the subscriber within fifteen days will be destroyed." He calculated that Colonel Maurin could not return in time to claim his copy. As a matter of fact, this was not possible. But the Colonel did the impossible and presented himself at the author-publisher's on the sixteenth day, at the moment when the latter was throwing the section into the fire. A struggle took place between the two collectors. The Colonel was victorious: he withdrew the sheets from the flames and bore them triumphantly to the house in the Rue des Boulangers where he accumulated all sorts of remnants of the ages. He owned boxes of mummies, Latude's ladder, stones of the Bastille. He was one of those men who wish to stuff the universe into a cupboard. This is the dream of every collector. And as that dream is unrealisable, true collectors have, like lovers, an infinite sadness even in their happiness. They know well that they can never put the world under lock and key in a glass case. Hence their profound melancholy.

I have also had intercourse with great bibliophiles, those who collect *incunabula*, the humble monuments of the xylography of the fifteenth century, and for whom the " Biblia Pauperum " with its crude illustrations, has more charms than all the seductions of nature joined to all the enchantments of art; those who collect royal bindings made for Henri II, Diane de Poitiers, and Henri III, and toolings of the sixteenth and seventeenth centuries, which Marius reproduces to-day with a regularity absent from the originals; those who seek morocco bindings bearing the arms of princes and queens; and finally those who collect original editions of our classics. I could have drawn for you portraits of some of these, but they would, I think, have amused you less than those of my poor curate and my poor canon. It is the same with bibliophiles as with other men. Those who interest us most are not the able and learned, they are the humble and simple-minded.

And then, however noble and beautiful be the copies in which a bibliophile rejoices, however admirable he considers a book, even if that book were " The Garland of Julia," in the caligraphy of Jarry, there is something that I place higher, and that is the tub of Diogenes. One is free in it, whilst the bibliophile is the slave of his collection.

At present we amass too many libraries and museums. Our fathers bothered themselves with fewer things and enjoyed nature better. Bismarck has a habit of saying so as to give weight to his arguments : " Gentlemen, I bring before you considerations inspired not by the green table-cloth, but by the green country." That image, a little strange and barbarous, is full of force and zest. For my own part, I enjoy it infinitely. Good reasons are those that living nature inspires. It is good to make collections : it is better to take walks.

So much being granted, I admit that a liking for good editions and fine bindings is the liking of an honest man. I praise those who preserve the original editions of our classics, of Molière, of La Fontaine, of Racine, and by such noble treasures make their houses renowned.

But, in default of these rare and famous texts, one can content oneself with the sumptuous book in which M. Jules Le Petit describes them exactly, and reproduces their titles in fac-simile. Our entire literature is represented in it by its *editiones principes*, from the " Romant de la Rose " to " Paul et Virginie." It is a collection which one does not run through without emotion. " This,

then," one says to one's self, "is the appearance
which the ' Lettres Provinciales' and La Fontaine's
' Fables ' had for their contemporaries when they
were new ! This quarto with a large vignette
representing a palm on a shield in the Renaissance
style is the ' Cid ' as it appeared in 1637 from the
house of Augustin Courbé, bookseller at Paris, in
the small hall of the Palais, at the sign of the Palm,
with the device : *Curvata resurgo*. These six little
duodecimo volumes whose title, intersected by an
escutcheon in the style of Louis XV is thus conceived : ' Lettres de deux amants habitants d'une
petite ville au pied des Alpes,' collected and published by J.-J. Rousseau, Amsterdam, Marc-Michel
Rey, 1761, is the ' Nouvelle Héloise ' as she made
our grandmothers weep. That is what the contemporaries of Jean-Jacques saw and touched ! "
These books are relics, and there remains something
touching in the image of them which M. Jules
Le Petit gives us. That excellent man has entirely
reconciled me to bibliophily. Let us admit that
there is no love without fetichism, and let us do
this justice to the lovers of old blackened paper, that
they are quite as mad as other lovers.

CRIMINALS *

HE story about which I am writing,
"Conscience," has been published
in this journal.† We have found
once again in this novel the probity
and seriousness that mark M. Hector
Malot's talent. I do not consider
myself entitled to judge this work
in the very place where it appeared. It is enough for
me to say that the name of Hector Malot recommends "Conscience" to readers who desire to be
respected even while they are amused. In writing
"Conscience," the author of "Victimes d'Amour"
and of "Zyte" has very intelligently accommodated
to our environment and our culture the drama that
Dostoïevsky conceived and executed with the
ingenuous atrocity of a Slav mind, when he wrote
that work of terror "Crime and Punishment."
Like the Moscow novelist's Raskolnikof, M. Hector
Malot's Saniel is young, intelligent, energetic.
He has given himself an end in life, and he says to
himself: In order to attain that end it is necessary
for me to suppress a human existence, that of a

* "Conscience." By Hector Malot.

† I take the liberty of reminding the reader that this article, like
all those that compose this volume, first appeared in the *Temps*
newspaper. I have avoided retouching it; naturalness is the only
merit of these chats.

contemptible and noxious being. He looks his crime full in the face and he commits it; he kills an old usurer. This Saniel, the son of a rough peasant of Auvergne, is as unconscious of hatred as of love. He is a stranger to all human sympathy, he lives only for science, and is absorbed in the physiological researches that have already led him to great discoveries. Such a soul is incapable of remorse. Also he has no horror for his crime. He even tells himself that what he has done is reasonable; yet it is impossible for him after the act to be what he was before. Like Raskolnikof also, he is seized with, he is possessed by, his crime. His mind obeys a logic that is as strange as it is implacable. There take place within him phenomena analogous to those that M. de Voguë has described so precisely in regard to Dostoïevsky's hero: " Through the irreparable fact of having suppressed a human existence, all the relations of the murderer with the world have changed; that world, looked at through the crime, has taken a new physiognomy and significance which shut out the criminal from the possibility of feeling and reasoning like other people, from finding his stable place in life " (" Le Roman Russe," by the Vicomte E. M. de Voguë, p. 248).

In that study, the Russian writer greatly outstrips the French novelist in atrocity. But who could distil terror like Dostoïevsky, of whom it has been said: " His power of terror is too superior to the nervous resistance of an average organism " ? Moreover, in treating such a subject, he had an advantage that M. Hector Malot will not envy him. He was an epileptic, and, owing to this, in direct communication with those souls whom an obscure malady devotes to crime, and whom a modern physiologist proposes to designate under the name of epileptoids. That nervous malady tormented him when he wrote " Crime and Punishment." During the composition of the book, he had terrible paroxysms. "The prostration into which they plunge me," he says, " is characterised by this : I feel myself a great criminal ; it seems to me that an unknown crime, an infamous action, weighs on my conscience." From this comes the sympathy which bound him to the unfortunate Raskolnikof.

Yes, unfortunate, for to be criminal is to be unfortunate. The wicked are very deserving of pity, and I can nearly understand the madness of that Catholic priest whose heart bled at the thought of the sufferings of Judas Iscariot. " Judas," he used to say, " has fulfilled the prophecies ; in betraying Jesus he did what was foretold, and he co-operated in the accomplishing of the mystery of Redemption. The salvation of the world is bound up with his crime. Judas did evil ; but that evil was necessary. Is it necessary that he should be damned to all eternity ? " That priest revolved this idea in his head for a long time, and he ended by being absolutely possessed with it. He suffered much on this account, for it was contrary to the faith of his soul, the faith of his life. In order to escape from the trouble that was growing upon him, he had recourse to fasting and prayer. But amidst his acts of faith and works of penitence, he asked of God only one thing, Judas's pardon. At this period of moral crisis, he was one of the curates of Notre-Dame de Paris. One night he went through a little door of which he had the key into the silent and deserted cathedral, vaguely lit up by the moon. He advanced to the foot of the high altar, and there, having prostrated himself on the floor, he uttered this prayer:

"My God, God of justice and goodness, if it is true, as I have an inner belief it is, that Thou hast pardoned the most unhappy of Thy Disciples, make known to me by a certain sign that ineffable marvel of Thy mercy. Send to Thy servant the Apostle Judas, who sits to-day at Thy right hand among Thine elect. Let Iscariot come from Thee, and let him lay his hand upon my prostrated brow! By that sign I shall be consecrated a priest of pardon, according to the order of Judas, and I shall proclaim to men the good news that Thou hast revealed to me."

Scarcely had the curate finished that prayer than he felt a cool and gentle hand laid upon his brow. He arose radiant and filled with tears.

As soon as it was day he went to the archbishop to tell him of his prayer of the night and the investiture that he had miraculously received. You can imagine the welcome that was given him. As for me, I am not an archbishop, I feel a keen and profound sympathy for the poor visionary, and I find a kindly wisdom in his madness. I am touched to hear him designate Judas with pity as the most unhappy of the Apostles. And notice that his mysticism borders upon natural philosophy. What that poor priest thought of the traitor of the Mount of Olives, the philosopher thinks of all criminals. Anthropology no longer sees in the criminal anything but a man suffering from incurable disease; it regards the scoundrel with tranquil pity; it says to the assassin what Jocasta said to Œdipus, when she had pierced through the mystery of that

blinded man's destiny. " Unhappy ! . . . That is
the only name with which I can name you, and I shall
never more give you another." Humane and prudent
thought !

Determinism has touched us all more or less.
The doctrine of responsibility is overthrown in the
most powerful minds. The wisest course is to
repeat to-day the words, so sweet and so mournful,
of the unhappy Queen of Thebes. But was there
ever an epoch when men believed fully in human
free-will ? I see none. Philosophers were always
divided on this point as on all others. As for
Christianity, it has always endeavoured to reconcile
free-will with the Divine fore-knowledge, and without ever succeeding.

Everything in man is a mystery, and we can
know nothing of what is not man. That is human
knowledge ! In truth the doctrine of the non-
responsibility of criminals is not a dangerous
novelty. Even practically, it has no very considerable
interest. If it should prevail, our laws would not
be sensibly modified by it. Why ? Because codes
of law are founded upon necessity and not upon
justice. They only punish what it is necessary to
punish. Philanthropic criminologists do not admit
that we should put a thief in prison ; that would be
punishing him, and we have no right to do so.
They propose to keep him in an asylum, behind
firm bolts. I do not see any great difference.
The punishment of death could even withstand the
triumph of the doctrine of non-responsibility ;
it would be enough to declare that, properly
speaking, it is not a punishment.

Shall we go further and maintain, with the new
anthropological school, that the non-responsibility of

the criminal has been physiologically and anatomic-
ally demonstrated ? Shall we say with Maudsley that
crime is in the blood, and that there are scoundrels in
a society, just as there are black-headed sheep in a
flock, and that the former are as easy to distinguish
as the latter ?   Shall we enter into the views of
one of the most convinced of anthropologists, an
Italian, the author of the " Uomo Delinquente " ?

Signor Cesare Lombroso flatters himself that he
has verified the existence of a human type, destined
to crime by its very formation.   There exists,
according to him, a born criminal, recognisable by
various signs, the most characteristic of which are
smallness and want of symmetry of the skull, the
development of the jaws, sunken eyes, thin beard,
abundant hair, ragged ears, a flat nose.   In addition,
criminals are, or ought to be, left-handed, colour-
blind, squint-eyed and debilitated.   Unfortunately,
these signs are wanting in the majority of criminals,
and are found, as an offset, in many very honest
people.   The skull of Lammenais and that of
Gambetta were very small ; Bichat's skull was not
symmetrical.   We all know excellent people who
suffer from colour-blindness, from squinting, from
debility, or who are flat-nosed, have projecting
jaws, &c.   Let Signor Lombroso put himself in a
position to declare with certainty, after examination,
that such and such a person will be a criminal, and
that such and such another will remain innocent, or
let him give up declaring that he is in possession of
the specific characteristics of the " criminal man."
Positive knowledge is recognised by the certainty of
the predictions that we draw from it.   To tell the
truth, I firmly believe that the able Italian anthro-
pologist will never succeed in reducing all criminal

men to a single type. And the reason for this is
that criminals are by nature essentially different
from one another, and that the name that designates
them presents nothing clear to the mind. Signor
Lombroso has not even thought of defining this
word, criminal. Therefore he takes it in the vulgar
acceptation. Vulgarly, we say that a man is a criminal when he commits a very grave infraction of the
moral code and of the laws. But as there are many
laws, and as morals are not fixed, the diversities of
crime are infinite. In reality, what Signor Lombroso
calls a criminal is a prisoner. All prisoners end by
resembling one another in something. The regimen
that is common to them determines in them certain
special anomalies by which at last they are distinguished from men who live in freedom. We can
say as much of priests and of monks whom we
recognise even when they have abandoned the habit
and the soutane. As for criminals, criminals in
the fullest sense of the word, murderers, it is impossible, I repeat, to reduce them to a single type,
either physiological or psychological: they are not
all of the same essence. What connection is there
to be established, for instance, between this Saniel,
whose history M. Malot tells us, this doctor who kills
in order to make sure of his discoveries, and that
brute who, the other day, led the girl with whom
he lived to the bank of the Seine and threw her into
the water to win a wager of a bottle of wine ?

Whatever Lombroso and Maudsley may say, one
can be criminal without being mad or diseased.
Humanity began altogether with crime. With
prehistoric man, crime was the rule and not the
exception. In our own days, it is still the rule
among savages. One can say that in its origin it

is confounded with virtue. It is not yet distinct
from it among the black tribes of Central Africa.
Mteza, king of Touareg, used to kill three or four
of the women of his harem every day. One day he
caused to be put to death one of his women who
was guilty of having presented him with a flower.
This Mteza, put into relations with the English,
showed much intelligence and a singular aptitude
for understanding the ideas of civilised peoples.

How can we avoid recognising it ? It is nature
herself that teaches crime. Animals kill their like to
devour them, or from a jealous fury, or without any
motive. There are many criminals among them.
The ferocity of ants is terrible ; female rabbits
often devour their young ; wolves, whatever one
may say, eat one another ; female orang-outangs
have been seen to kill a rival. These are crimes ; and
if the poor beasts that commit them are not responsible, then nature must be accused ; she has in
truth attached too many miseries to the condition
of men and of animals.

But, also, how sublime is that victorious effort of
man to free himself from the old bonds of crime !
How august is that slow building up of morality !
Men have little by little established justice. Violence, which was the rule, is to-day the exception.
Crime has become a sort of anomaly, something
irreconcilable with the new life as man has made it
by dint of patience and courage. Having entered
into an existence, crime gnaws and devours it :
crime is henceforth a radical vice, a morbid germ.
It was the old nursing-mother of the cave men ;
now it poisons the wretches who ask life of it. That
is what, following Dostoïevsky, M. Hector Malot has
shown us.

DEATH AND THE LITTLE GODS *

HERE is a poet whom I love all the more dearly as I am the only person to love him. In his life, which was gentle, obscure, and brief, he was called Saint-Cyr de Rayssac. Now he has no longer a name, for nobody mentions him. Italy was the true home of his soul. He loved gardens and museums. One day, as he left the Capitol, after having gazed at that Funeral Genius, so pure and so tranquil, the young and already dying poet wrote these delicious verses:

" De ses flancs ondulés, quand j'ai vu la blancheur,
Quand j'ai vu ses deux bras relevés sur sa tête,
Comme au sommet vermeil d'une amphore de Crète
Les deux anses du bord qui s'élèvent en chœur,

O mort des anciens jours, j'ai compris ta douceur,
Le charme évanoui de ton œuvre muette,
Lorsqu'insensiblement tu couvrais de pâleur
Un profil corinthien de vierge ou de poète.

Le calme transpirait sur l e front déserté,
Du sourire la grâce était plus molle,
Tout le corps endormi flottait en liberté :

* " La Nécropole de Myrina." Report of excavations made by the French School at Athens. Text and notes by Edmond Pottier and Salomon Reinach.

On eût dit une fleur qui distend sa corolle,
Tandis que de sa bouche une abeille s'envole,
Emportant ses parfums et non pas sa beauté." *

The Louvre possesses a good replica of the
Funeral Genius, and, before that fair immortal,
asleep in death, I have more than once repeated
the pagan sonnet of Saint-Cyr de Rayssac. The
poet, it seems to me, has well rendered the antique
thought: to sleep, to die. Death is only an endless
sleep.

It is not that death was in itself pleasing to the
Greeks. Death was at all times hideous and cruel.
In vain will it be said that it ought not to be feared,
and that to be dead is merely not to be; man will
reply that the idea of the last hour is full of horror
and terror. The Greeks also feared death. At
least they did not make it ugly; far from it. The
Hellenic imagination beautified everything, and even
gave grace to the supreme swoon. The Middle
Ages, on the contrary, have frightened us with the
fear of hell, with a lugubrious phantasmagoria of
devils snapping at the sinner's soul as it passes,
with funereal phantoms of sepulchres, with images of
skeletons and the worms of the coffin gnawing at the
corrupted flesh, and finally with ghastly dances.
Death was greatly aggravated by these.

* " When I have seen the whiteness of her curving sides, when I
have seen her two arms raised above her head, like the two handles
of a Cretan jar which rise harmoniously from the border to the vermilion top, O death of the ancient days, I have understood thy
sweetness, the vanished charm of thy silent labour when thou didst
insensibly cover with paleness the Corinthian profile of a poet or a
virgin. Calm breathed upon her lifeless brow, the grace of her
smile was softer, all her sleeping body floated free: One would
have said she was a flower extending her corolla whilst a bee flies
from her mouth, bearing away her perfume but not her beauty."

It was only in the eighteenth century that tombs
ceased to be horrible.   Surmounted by graceful urns
and flower-wreathed loves, they adorned the English
gardens and the fashionable parks.   When the fair
and good Madame de Sabran visited the tomb of
Jean-Jacques in the island of Ermenonville, she was
quite surprised at experiencing only agreeable and
peaceful sensations.   This tomb, she said to herself,
invites one to rest.   And she wrote immediately to
her friend Boufflers: "I had half a longing to be in
Rousseau's place; I found its calm attractive, and
I thought with mortification that I should not even
be free one day to enjoy that happiness, innocent
as it is.   Our religion has spoilt everything with its
lugubrious ceremonies, it has, so to speak, personi-
fied death; the ancients would not endure that
horrible image which our destruction presents to
us."   Madame de Sabran was right.   The ancients
died more naturally than we do.   They left life with
facility because they left it without fearing too much
or hoping too much.   Subterranean things scarcely
touched them, and they did not imagine that this
life was a preparation for the next.   They said:
I have lived.   The dying Christian says: At last
I am going to live.   The pagan idea of death is well
represented in the funerary monuments of the fine
Greek style, which represent the dead in a sitting
posture, beautiful, and peaceful.   Sometimes, a
living friend, a woman whom they had left on earth,
comes gently to lay a hand on their shoulders, but
they cannot turn their heads to see them.   They
are for ever exempt from joy and pain.   For the
ancient Greek, death is secure.

It is a sleep without dreams as without awaking.
Some   epigrams   in   the   "Anthology"   express
D

admirably the peace of the ancient tombs. One
sleeps well in them. And if the shades speak, they
speak only of things of the earth. They know no
others. Listen to these words exchanged two
thousand years ago on some myrtle-perfumed road,
bordered with white tombs, between a traveller
and the shade of a young woman:

" Who art thou, of whom art thou the daughter,
O woman who liest under this column of marble ?
—I am Praxo, the daughter of Calliteles.—Where
wert thou born ?—At Samos.—Who has built thee
this tomb ?—Theocritus who unbound my girdle.—
How did'st thou die ?—In the pains of child-birth.
—What age had'st thou ?—Twenty-two years.—
Didst thou leave a child ?—I leave a son of three
years, little Calliteles.—May he reach the age in
which his grey hairs will be honoured !—And thou
passer-by, may fortune give thee all that men
desire in this life ! "

These are kindly creatures ! And how the dead
and the living are still of the same world ! This
good Praxo, from the depth of her tomb, knows
only a single life, that of earth. Death, thus
understood, was extremely simple.

Thus we must not be surprised if the ancient
tombs do not present lugubrious images to the
eyes. Two young scholars of great merit, MM.
Edmond Pottier and Salomon Reinach, have during
the years 1880, 1881, and 1882, explored the necropolis of the ancient Myrina, one of the Amazonian
towns of Aeolis, on the soil of which there now
vegetates a wretched Turkish village. Myrina
was never very famous or very rich. Its citizens
lived obscurely before they went to sleep their
eternal sleep in the chalky tufa-stone where their

graves were dug. MM. Edmond Pottier and Salomon Reinach have excavated these tombs with a zeal that nothing could abate. A brilliant pupil of the School of Athens, Alphonse Veyries, who shared their labours and their fatigues, succumbed to them. He died at Smyrna on the 5th of December 1882. The survivors have just published the result of these fruitful excavations. The necropolis of Myrina, a great part of which they have explored methodically, received bodies during the two centuries that preceded the Christian era.

Many of those bodies were burned. Some were only partially burned, but the greater part were placed in the earth without having undergone the ordeal of fire. People have at all times readily buried the dead. It is not difficult, and it costs nothing. On the contrary, the pyre, the celebrated magnificence of which has been described for us by the Latin elegaic poets, was only elevated at a great expense. In the tombs of Myrina, the usual objects have been found, such as mirrors, spatulæ, and strigils ; ornaments and diadems, cups, plates, phials, coins, and statuettes of baked clay. Pious illusion ! The Myrinians pleased themselves by leaving to the dead, in his subterranean existence, the familiar objects among which he had passed his life. Thus they left to women in the tomb a mirror and a pot of rouge, persuaded that the shade of a woman still gazes at itself in the mirror and takes pleasure in giving " this cheek a little red." They encircled the dead with diadems of gold. It was, doubtless, not in order to displease them. But in honouring them, they deceived them a little. These sheets of gold were so thin that a breath would have reduced them to dust,

and the berries of the funeral laurels were only balls
of gilded clay.   The good Myrinians knew that the
dead were not hard to please, and that, provided
they are buried, they never come back.   That is
why they regulated accounts with them as cheaply
as possible.   They put into their mouths the obolus
for Charon.   It was a poor brass coin.   MM.
Pottier and Reinach have not found a single gold or
silver medal.

As to the custom of funeral offerings, there
remained some traces of it in the second and third
centuries before the Christian era.   Men in their
earliest and simplest days brought food and drink to
their dead friends.   In memory of these old rites
the Myrinians sometimes laid in the tombs tables
of baked earth, as large as the hollow of your hand,
on which were modelled cakes, grapes, figs, and
pomegranates.   To these they added little clay
bottles which were not even hollow.   These people
no longer believed that the dead were hungry or
thirsty, they regarded them as insensible, and yet
they could not imagine that beings which had felt
should have completely lost feeling.

The inhabitants of Myrina were men like us:
they fell into inextricable contradictions.   They
knew that the dead are dead, and they sometimes
persuaded themselves that the dead are living.
By a pious custom which we ought to bless, for it
has preserved for our curiosity some charming
vestiges of the potter's art, the Greeks cast into
the tombs of their beloved dead little figures of
baked earth, representing gods or merely men, and
sometimes even poor little deformed and ridiculous
men.   The meaning of this custom cannot be precisely ascertained.   We know that it was very

widely spread over the continent and in the islands. It can only have been a religious custom. It is true that we find, among the figures offered to the dead, comic masks, clowns, slaves, young women coquettishly tricked out. But, on the whole, it is the Oriental and Funeral Pantheon that is dominant in these delicate monuments of an art full of fantasy. Perhaps the limits between the divine and human were not very clearly marked in the mind of a Myrinian of the second century before the Christian era. However this may be, both religious and profane figures of baked earth are not rare in the necropolis explored by MM. Pottier and Reinach. These two scholars think that the Myrinians themselves smashed these offerings as they brought them. " In a great number of cases," they say in the account of their excavations, " the statuettes were lying face downwards on the earth, deprived of a head or limb, which were found on the opposite side ; a fact which seems clearly to indicate the movement of a person who, keeping on the brink of the grave, would break in two the object he holds, and would throw with each hand one of the fragments into the trench." What did this funeral rite signify ? Why did they thus mutilate those little human or divine images ? We do not know.

They are for the most part extremely curious. The Louvre possesses some of them. Several are charming ; almost all are pleasing. Yet they have lost their vivid colours. Originally all of them were painted. As they left the furnace, they were dipped in a bath of lime and then they were covered with bright tints among which blue and rose were predominant. Thus, harmonious and vivid in their

fresh newness, they realised that dream of coloured
statuary so dear in our days to that learned
sculptor, M. Soldi.

Very different from the Tanagra figures, which
retain a certain severity even in their coquetry, the
Myrina plasters express all the sensuality and all the
enervation of Asia. The artist loves to mark
uncertainty of sex with soft and gentle lines, and he
likes to model young men with feminine forms.
Such is the pretty Eros that can be seen at the
Louvre, with his hair curling on his brow and his
head covered with a sort of kerchief. He slightly
bends his charming head. He flies—for he has
wings. An open tunic gives a glimpse of his almost
male limbs which would suit a Diana. One would
say a voluptuous soul, or rather a very sensual
and very subtle mind, the perverse dream of a
fastidious artist. M. Pottier (whose notes, I may say
in passing, are excellent memoranda of archæology
and art) tells me that this Eros is bringing a pot of
rouge to his mother. But he himself is the rouge
and unguent of beauty : he is eternal desire. It is
through him that Venus is beautiful.

The potters of Myrina have a great liking for
winged figures. Their extremely sensual art is
at the same time very ideal. They excel in giving
a sublime movement to voluptuous forms. With a
strange fantasy, they mingle celestial grace and
mortal languor, so that this art is at once aphro-
disiacal and almost painful. It is the dream of the
senses, but it is still a dream. These Eroses, these
Atisses as beautiful as virgins, these naked Aphrodites,
these funeral sirens, these Victorys mingled with
Eroses in the procession of the divine lover of Adonis,
these Bacchuses and these Mænads, in a word, all

these little gods painted in fresh hues, I see them in imagination, ranged quite new, in the shop of the humble potter, like the Virgins and the Saint Josephs in the windows of the shops of the Rue Saint-Sulpice to-day. They must have been a source of joy to the good little girls and the old women of their time.

There is a striking analogy between the figures of baked earth of Myrina and the figures of painted plaster that are sold in the vicinity of our Catholic churches. It is a new divine personality which has been substituted for the other and one which answers to the same needs of souls. The little Aphrodite springing out of the wave, the Demeter and Cora of the ancient mysteries, have been replaced by Our Lady of Victory with the child Jesus, by the Immaculate Conception, whose opened hands scatter graces over the world, and by the youthful Our Lady of Lourdes, who wears a blue sash on her white robe. The Aphrodites were better modelled and in better tone, the Virgins are chaster. But Venus and the Virgins have equally brought ideals to the simple. Pious people have changed less than is believed. On both sides there is the same touching childishness, and the paganism of the Rue Saint-Sulpice yields nothing in candour and a sort of innocent sensualism to the potters of Myrina. From the one as from the other the great divine ideas are excluded. One no more finds Zeus at Myrina than one finds God the Father with the purveyors of Holy Virgins.

This is why it seems to me that a devout Myrinian, if she suddenly returned to life, would not be too much out of her element amidst the innumerable statuettes of piety which represent all the persons of Christian mythology. She would, doubtless, make some audacious identifications. But she would hardly be deceived, I think, in regard to the general sentiments of these shallow symbols. She would at once understand their touching grace.

THE GREAT ENCYCLOPÆDIA *

ERMANY and England possess good encyclopædias that are carefully kept up to date. Brockhaus's "Conversations-Lexikon" is especially an excellent repertory of human knowledge. France had nothing that approached Brockhaus. The "Didot Encyclopædia," begun in 1824 and finished in 1863, has grown very much out of date. Larousse's "Great Dictionary" is entirely lacking in criticism and solid learning. A new inventory of the arts and sciences was awaited by all those who need to study or who have a love for it. The mere formation of a plan takes up years, the execution of that plan requires a powerful organisation and the co-operation of many forces. That is why we should rejoice at seeing a new encyclopædia making its appearance, conceived in a truly scientific spirit. The oversight of this work has been entrusted to scholars like MM. Berthelot, Hartwig Derembourg, Giry, Glasson, Hahn, Laisant, H. Laurent, Levasseur, H. Marion, Müntz, A. Waltz. M. Camille Dreyfus has been appointed secretary, and presses the enterprise forward. Finally, the list of contributors already includes more than three hundred well-

* "Inventaire raisonné des sciences, des lettres et des arts." Par une Société de savants et de gens de lettres. Vols. I-V.

known and reputable names. The " Great Encyclopædia " is far from being complete. It has as
yet accomplished only a small part of the vast circle
it has traced out for itself ; it has reached its fifth
volume and attacked the letter B, which is, as you
know, one of the richest of the alphabet. That is
enough for us to be able to judge of the merit of
the work. This encyclopædia is carried on with a
good deal of method. Its editors and contributors
are working in a scientific fashion. They have
sought for exactness and impartiality. The practice
of this latter virtue has been troublesome to some
of them, but all have observed it. The general
secretary, M. Camille Dreyfus himself, has given an
example of it.

Some of the articles published in the first five
volumes are real monographs. It seems to me
that military questions, in particular, have been
treated with care and in great detail.

Illustrations render the text clearer where necessary, and good coloured maps accompany the geographical articles. Finally, what in my opinion
gives a special value to the work is the summary
bibliography placed at the end of each article.
Indications of this sort allow the curious to make
researches on points that interest them.

In order to show M. Lamirault that I have
glanced with interest through the five large volumes,
the material construction of which does him honour,
I shall offer two rather minute observations. The
first has reference to the article AVARAY (Comte d').
It deals with that Comte d'Avaray to whom the
Comte de Provence showed so much friendship.
The author of that article has omitted to indicate
in his bibliography the " Relation d'un voyage à

Bruxelles et à Coblentz," the author of which is none other than Louis XVIII himself. Yet that book forms the principal source for the biography of the Comte d'Avary. My second complaint is a little more serious. It has to do with the biography of the false Joan of Arc, the lady of Armoises. The contributor has confused two distinct persons. If he had read M. Simeon Luce's " Jeanne d'Arc à Domrémy " he would not have fallen into that error. These are very trifling cavils.

What a fine thing a well-executed encyclopædia is ! And what wealth this new inventory of our sciences will contain ! The circle of human knowledge has been marvellously increased during the past half-century. Our range to-day reaches phenomena that were not suspected before our day. Keeping only to the letter A, astronomy, the noblest of the sciences, has given us in succession some astonishing revelations ; it has shown us in the luminous sphere of the sun commotions of which we had no idea, we who live on a very small, and, upon the whole, fairly peaceful planet. Could they imagine, only five and twenty years ago, that on the gaseous texture that envelopes the sun, there occur rents a thousand times as large as the earth, and that these are repaired in a few minutes ? There no longer remains a vestige of that incorruptible sky described in the ancient cosmogonies. We know to-day that the ethereal spaces are the theatre of energies that produce life and death. We know that stars become extinct ; we even know by what signs the death of a star may be predicted. A star that no longer burns except with a red and smoky glare is soon going to die. But what is dying save being born again ? The death of a sun is perhaps only the

birth of a planet.   As for the planets, they are not
exempt from the universal decay.   They perish
at the destined hour, and the scattered fragments
of Kepler's planet have been observed, not far from
the earth.   Everything in the universe is in movement, or rather everything is movement.   The stars
which were believed to be fixed swim through the
air with the speed of a flash of lightning.   And yet
we do not see them stir.   How can that be ? Listen :
Here is a cannon-ball ; at the moment when it is
discharged from the mouth of the cannon, its
surface is modified by chemical agents of great
power, it is covered with fruitful germs ;   an
infinitely small flora and fauna are born on it :
that bullet has become a world.   After many efforts
and innumerable attempts, types of a superior
animal life are produced and tend to become fixed
upon it.   At last, intelligent beings see the light
on it.   They have a thirst for love and knowledge.
They measure their world, and the immensity of
that world astonishes them.   Their intelligence is
full of restlessness and audacity.   Armed with
powerful apparatus, they put themselves into communication with that part of the universe to which
they have been hurled.   They scrutinise space,
they discover unintelligible forms in the infinite,
they distinguish, without knowing their true nature,
some soldiers of two armies, a mill, and a steeple
towards which, unknown to them, they have been
directed.   They even achieve an approximate
measurement of some distances.   But they fancy
that the world, the surface of which they populate,
is suspended motionless in space, and that the
unknown figures which they scarcely distinguish
in the bosom of the infinite are equally motionless.

And how should they have any other impression, since the life of each of them is so short that with its joys and griefs and long desires it is completely ended before the cannon-ball, their world, has gone through an appreciable portion of space ?   What is a moment in the projectile's journey, is for them a long succession of centuries. However, as they are mathematicians, their learned men end by perceiving that the sphere they inhabit, though motionless in appearance, is in reality animated by a very rapid movement, and that the distant bodies they discover on the confines of their universe are equally animated by their own movement. Little by little, under the action of very complex causes, the cannon-ball becomes uninhabitable, intelligence, then life, become extinct on it, and it is no longer anything save an inert mass when it lodges with a crash in the steeple of a poor village church.   None of the innumerable generations who had inhabited it during its fruitful period had suspected either the starting-point or the destination, or the aim of the journey.   The philosophers of the cannon-ball had rightly said : " We must relinquish knowing the unknowable." But the anxious souls, thrown by blind destiny upon the moving projectile, had in turn worshipped and blasphemed God, believed, doubted, despaired. There, immemorial ages had unrolled themselves in a few seconds.   That cannon-ball is the earth, and the intelligent race that accomplished upon it its rich destiny of an instant, is humanity.   We are too small to behold the flight of the stars.   Yet they fly like sea-birds in harmonious circles.   We last too short a time to see the constellations change their shape.   The Great Bear seems to us for ever

motionless. Yet the Great Bear, in some thousands
of centuries, will present a new face to the inhabitants of earth. But the lovers of that time, who shall
behold it, as they clasp hands, will also salute it
shudderingly as the immutable witness of their
ephemeral joys. And humanity will have lived
without knowing whence come or whither go these
butterflies whose garden is the heavens.

For a short period past, astronomy has begun to
throw fresh terrors into men's imagination. It has
shown us a little star that wavers, and it has told
us : " That one at least is our neighbour, and the
closest to us of all. It is the *alpha* of the Centaur."
If the stars spoke to one another, our sun ought to
have hardly any secrets from that star : they
touch, so to speak. Well then, a ray from the
alpha of the Centaur, travelling with a speed of
79,000 leagues a second, takes three and a half
years to reach us. The other stars are more distant.
The beautiful red flame of Sirius spends seventeen
years in coming to us. Even Sirius is a neighbour.
But there is the case of a star which perhaps became
extinct centuries ago, and from which we still
receive light. Thus the innumerable lights that the
sky of night sends us are not contemporaries. All
those beautiful glances speak to us of diverse pasts.
Some speak to us of an unfathomable past. A ray
which comes to-day to caress our eyes was already
travelling in the sky when the earth did not yet
exist. Immensity of time and space ! Do you
distinguish that luminous point, so pale in that dust
of worlds ? It is a nebula, situated on the confines
of the visible universe. And here is a telescope
which decomposes it into thousands of stars. That
point is another universe, perhaps greater than ours.

That grain of sand is by itself as much as, and more than, all the stars of our nights.

Science will reduce that immensity to unity. Spectrum analysis will make known to us the chemical composition of the stars. It will teach us that the substances which burn on the surface of those distant luminaries are precisely those of which our sun is formed. Those substances are all found on the earth which is the daughter of the sun, flesh of his flesh. So that this drop of mud in which we live yet contains in itself the whole universe.

It was time that physical astronomy should bring us that revelation and show us our infinity when we no longer saw anything but our nothingness. Earth is nothing, but that nothing possesses the same riches as Sirius and the Polar Star. The very stones that have fallen to us from heaven have brought nothing unknown.

Contemporary chemistry has also fashioned a new idea and philosophy of things. Its subtle analysis has so thoroughly penetrated bodies that they have all evaporated. It has relegated matter to the rank of coarse appearances. It has shown that substance is nothing, that nothing exists in itself, that there are only states, and that what was called substance is only an unseizable Proteus. It has laid down the dogma of universal instability. It has said: " Heat, light, electricity, magnetism, chemical affinity, movement, are diverse appearances of the same unknown reality. Illusion, eternal illusion, alone reveals the hidden god. Nature only appears to us as a vast phantasmagoria, and chemistry is only the science of metamorphosis. There are no longer either gases or solids or fluids, there is only the smile of the eternal Maya."

Chemistry, giving its hand to physiology, has recognised that organic matter is not distinct in its principle from inert matter, or rather that there is no inert matter, and that life and movement are everywhere.

Philosophical physiology congratulates itself upon having reduced animal and vegetable life to the same type, by demonstrating that in the plant there are the faculties of motion, respiration, and sleep.

Man is to-day more intimately bound up with nature. Not to speak of the great hypotheses that have been formed regarding his origins, prehistoric archæology reminds him of his humble beginnings and his long progression. It shows him, wretched and naked, yet already ingenious, in the time of the mammoth, in the caves, for which he quarrelled with the big bear. We know now with scientific certainty what those Greeks so full of insight knew when they made beautiful stories about the satyrs and about Heracles, the conqueror of monsters. The science of languages, connected with the natural sciences, henceforward equals them in precision. New historical methods have been inaugurated. The study of microbes furnishes medical practice with new means of action ; the progress of physiology gives to surgery a terrifying yet happy audacity. Neurology excites and systematises nervous phenomena whose strangeness seems to belong to the miraculous. Great discoveries applied to industry change the very conditions of life.

" And what time was ever so fertile in miracles ? "

What wealth for the " Great Encyclopædia," and how we long to see an exact inventory of our knowledge drawn up at last !

M. HENRI MEILHAC AT THE FRENCH ACADEMY

N preferring M. Henri Meilhac to two perfectly *academisable* competitors, the Academy has made a bold, brilliant, felicitous choice, which pleases by its very bluster. The Academy risks nothing by resembling heaven, to which people go by different roads. The Church Triumphant welcomes by the side of the professional saints amiable saints predestined to eternal salvation. By this practice it gains an agreeable diversity among the elect. If there were only one sort of Academicians and only one sort of blessed, the Academy and Paradise would be monotonous.

Do not tell it, but in the bottom of my heart I feel a secret inclination for those predestined ones who, like St. Mary the Egyptian and like M. Meilhac, have been chosen by a dazzling outburst of grace when they were not thinking of it and even when they were thinking of something else.

And who does not feel that grace is better than justice ? Yes, the gentlemen of the Academy have made an excellent choice. Do they know how very excellent their choice is ? Do they know that the author of " Gotte " is a rare and charming spirit ; that he is Attic in his own way, and that that

way is one of the best, for it is natural ? Have
they said to themselves that M. Henri Meilhac, in
his fluent works, joined truth, fantasy, and comic
audacity, to just observation ?

That is a good choice. We want others like it.
We also want bad ones, we want detestable ones.
It is no paradox to affirm that the worst choices
are necessary to the existence of the French Academy.
If weakness and error did not play a part in its
elections, if it did not sometimes give the appearance
of taking at hazard, it would render itself so hateful
that it could no longer live. It would be in French
letters like a tribunal in the midst of the condemned.
Infallible, it would appear odious. What an affront
it would be for those whom it did not welcome, if
the elected candidate were always the best !
Richelieu's daughter ought to show herself a little
frivolous so as not to appear too insolent. What saves
her is that she has fancies. Her injustice makes her
innocence, and it is because we know she is capricious
that she can repel us without wounding us. It is
sometimes so advantageous to make a mistake that
I am tempted to believe she does it intentionally.
Selections of that sort disarm envy. Then, at the
moment when one is despairing of her, she shows
herself ingenious, free, and perspicacious. It is
very true that in all human affairs we must give
chance its share.

A FORGOTTEN POET

SAINT-CYR DE RAYSSAC

THÉODORE DE BANVILLE often says that men need poetry as much as bread. I am tempted to believe him: peasants who know nothing know songs, and the love of verses is natural to well-disposed persons. I had a proof of this the other day when I received twenty letters asking me who was the Saint-Cyr de Rayssac, whose fine sonnet I had quoted.* I felt then, I assure you, more joy than I had experienced before in my whole literary career. I said to myself: So it is not entirely vain to write! So those little black signs that we put down on paper go and spread through the world the emotion that moved us when we traced them. There are, then, minds that correspond with our mind, hearts that beat with our heart! What we say finds sometimes a response in other souls.

It is thus that I have had the happiness of causing fourteen unknown and practically unpublished lines to be enjoyed and loved. People have written from Paris, from Rome, from Bucharest, to ask me: Who then is this Saint-Cyr de Rayssac? Have his poems

* For the sonnet on the " Genius of Eternal Sleep " see p. 77.

97

been published ? I answer the second question
first. The poems of Saint-Cyr de Rayssac were
published in 1877 by Alphonse Lemerre, with a
preface by Hippolyte Babou. As for the poet
himself, I will gladly say what I know of him and
why I love him.

Saint-Cyr de Rayssac was born at Castres in
1837. His father, a younger son of an old Albigen-
sian family, as proud as Artaban and as poor as Job,
had, at the age of forty, after innumerable love-
affairs, married an innocent young girl, Mademoiselle
Noémi Gabaude. A royalist and a duellist by
inclination, outrageous fortune had made him a
postmaster. He was a prodigiously jealous husband.
His perpetual rages terrified the poor creature who
tremblingly worshipped him. When he saw that
she was *enceinte*, his suspicions redoubled. " Woe
to you," he used to cry to her, " if your child has
not blue eyes ! " and the poor woman, shuddering
and weeping, prayed to God to make blue the eye-
balls of the little child whom she was carrying in
her bosom.

" And that is why I have blue eyes," Saint-Cyr
used sometimes to say, with a melancholy smile.
" But that is also why I came into the world two
months before my time, and so frail that they
thought I should not survive."

Not having been able to bear him long enough,
his mother brooded over him so well that he lived.
He displayed from his childhood an ardent and
tender soul. At the age of twelve, transplanted
with his family to Saint-Chamond in the Lyonnais,
where his father had been appointed postmaster,
he devoured the public library that Saint-Chamond
owes to the posthumous liberality of Dugas-Montbel,

her most illustrious child. The good Dugas-Montbel, who translated Homer with simplicity, had collected monuments of ancient poetry and art. Amidst this noble wealth, Saint-Cyr felt the love of the beautiful swelling in his adolescent heart. It is said that at the same time living beauty began to trouble him and that he was thenceforward irrevocably destined to exquisite sufferings.

His studies ended, he came to Paris. But soon he was called to the bedside of his dying father. Almost at the same time he lost his younger brother, who returned mortally wounded from Mexico. Saddened by this double grief, he went to seek divine consolation in Italy. Italy received him like a mother. In the sun of Florence he sang. He only passed through it, but he took away with him glowing images of beauty. When he quitted Florence, he left behind as an adieu one of those sonnets at once precious and unstudied, into which his thought readily flowed:

> " Hôtesse aux bras ouverts, qui me jetais des fleurs,
> Toi, l'amante d'un jour que jamais on n'oublie,
> Qui, dès les premiers pas, fais aimer l'Italie,
> Son ciel et sa beauté, sa gloire et ses malheurs,
>
> Oh ! sans doute le temps a fané tes couleurs :
> Mais tu garde encor sous ta mélancolie
> Ce parfum d'élégance et d'amitié polie,
> Qu'on cueille sur ta bouche et qu'on emporte ailleurs.
>
> Pour tous les souvenirs tu tiens une merveille.
> Ton enceinte viante est comme une corbeille,
> Les festons sur le bord, les perles au milieu.
>
> Bref, ton charme est si doux, colline de Florence,
> Que je trouvai des pleurs, et je venais de France,
> Des pleurs pour te bénir en te disant adieu." *

---

* " Hostess with open arms, who threw me flowers, thou, the lover of an unforgettable day, who from the beginning dost cause Italy,

He remained longer at Rome, whose splendours
and ruins he loved. The desolation of the Roman
campagna gave him infinite delight:

> " A peine à l'horizon voit—on sur un coteau
> Quelques buffles errants, que le pâtre abandonne
> Pour se coucher en paix sur un fût de colonne
> Et dormir au soleil, drapé dans un manteau.
>
> . . . .
>
> Au ciel, pas un soupir, pas un battement d'ailes :
> C'est bien la majesté des douleurs éternelles
> Que n'ont plus rien à dire et plus rien à pleurer." *

It was in Rome that Saint-Cyr de Rayssac found
the most abundant revelation of beauty. His soul
overflowed with enthusiasm. Sometimes he piously
visited the Raphael rooms at the Vatican and
became elated by the contemplation of ideal art:

> " Sages sous le portique, apôtres au concile,
> Tous ils portent au front la lumière subtile,
> Le voile transparent de l'immortalité." †

Sometimes he adored the Venus of the Capitol,
" that white drop of foam," perfectly pure in
its sky and its beauty, its glory and its misfortunes, to be loved, oh,
doubtless time has faded thy colours ; but beneath thy melancholy
thou dost still retain that perfume of elegance and of polished
friendliness which we gather from thy mouth and bear away elsewhere. Thou holdest a wonder for all memories. Thy laughing
expanse is like a bridal casket, festoons without and pearls within.
Thy charm is so sweet, hill of Florence, that my tears flowed, though
I came from France, tears to bless thee in bidding thee farewell."

* " One can just discern on a hillock on the horizon some wandering
oxen, whom the shepherd deserts that he may lie in peace on the
shaft of a column, and draped in his mantle, sleep in the sun. In
the sky, not a breath, not a beat of wings. It is indeed the majesty
of eternal grief that has nothing more to say and nothing more to
weep for."

† " Sages beneath the portico, apostles in council, they all wear
on their brows the subtle light, the transparent veil of immortality."

the purity of her form, which has nothing carnal,

> " Save her immodest gesture and her unbound hair,"

and which harmony and grace cover as with august garments. Saint-Cyr de Rayssac, at Rome, wanders with intoxication from the antique marbles to the frescoes of the Renaissance. He equally admires Greek and Christian art. Yet he perhaps reserves his deepest tenderness for those statues that have issued from or been inspired by the Hellenic spirit and that have brought into the world that incomparable thing—divine naturalness. What force used to drag him towards the Venus of the Capitol and the Genius of Eternal Sleep ? The very same which in his adolescent years made him feel love and beauty beneath the dust of the books gathered by old Dugas-Montbel, the fruitful union of sensuousness and idealism, the generous ardour that makes the genius of the Prud'hons and Chéniers. The meditative soul of Saint-Cyr de Rayssac was served by exquisite senses. That is why he felt so strongly the caress of lines and the divinity of forms. There was also in his genius a dignity, a reserve, which Hellenic art alone fully satisfied. He was thankful to the ancient sculptors for their sublime impassibility :

> " If their souls were sad or their brows were radiant,
> They never told it to the Attic marbles."

So when at last he must leave his beloved Rome, he returns to grow tender for a last time in that hall where the Muse is so fair : He exclaims :

> " Oh, if her dear arms could open wide at last ! "

I believed for a moment, he adds:

> " I believed her melancholy and tender glance
> To meet with mine had just flamed into life."

Then, startled, ashamed of his generous blasphemy, he fears he has offended the Muse:

> " Pardon, pardon, I was mad with love,
> And through my loving thee I saw thee smile ! "

On his return from Italy, Saint-Cyr de Rayssac frequented the studio of a Lyons artist, to-day completely forgotten, Janmot, who was honoured by the friendship of Ingres, of Flandrin, and of Victor de Laprade. He was a mystical painter of great distinction. He used to paint angels. He took pleasure in giving them the features of one of his pupils, a sixteen-year-old girl, a ward of Madame Janmot (*née* de Saint-Paulet). This young girl, an ardent royalist and Catholic, zealously studied music and painting in that studio where the calm of the sanctuaries presided. Saint-Cyr de Rayssac, full of images of Italian art, saw in her one of those angels who descend from heaven to pick up the brush that has fallen out of Fra Angelico's hands, and who paint the fresco during the good monk's sleep. He loved her, married her, and still loved her.

All those who knew Madame Saint-Cyr de Rayssac bear witness to her rare beauty and charming intellect. Her husband has painted her in two lines :

> " French of the finest days, heroic and charming,
> With humid lip and with quick mocking glance."

He says elsewhere : " They praise your figure and your eyes. Nothing is more beautiful; but what charms me most in you is your voice." Madame de Rayssac had indeed a delightful voice. Some one who listened to that lady said: "When she speaks she sings a little, as the bird that alights on a perch still flies." From her early youth, according to another witness, she had a rich and well-stored memory. Taught by her father, who had seen a great deal, and by her godmother, one of the most brilliant women in Lyons society, she told a story with great charm and wealth of language. One day some one said to her:

"But, how old are you, then, to be able to speak in this way of Monsieur de Villèle and Armand Carrel, of Monsieur de Jouy and Victor Hugo, of Madame de Souza and Madame de Girardin, of Alfred de Musset and of Stendhal?"

And she answered:

"I am as old as my godmother, I am as old as my father, and sometimes I am as old as myself."

The love verses that Saint-Cyr de Rayssac wrote for her have happily been preserved. They inform us that Bertha (Madame de Rayssac was called Bertha) was jealous of the past. That is a great unhappiness to which proud and fastidious souls are subject. She suffered cruelly from the thought that he whom she loved had formerly given to others a part of the treasure which she now drank with delight. She could not restrain her laments. The poet wrote her a sonnet to console her:

> "Dans ce temps, j'épelais pour mieux savoir te lire,
> Et tout les vieux amours qu'il te plaît de maudire
> Enseignaient à mon cœur quelque chose pour toi.
> . . . .

Et j'ai mis à tes pieds, virginale maîtresse,
La brûlante moisson de toute ma jeunesse,
Le sauvage bouquet fait de toutes mes fleurs." *

He, in his turn, reproached her. He found reason to complain of her, for he loved her. Madame de Rayssac was an ardent painter and musician. She sang for hours, and used to go to her studio to paint. " I am alarmed at this expenditure," the poet would say in an accent of tender reproach:

" Are you convinced, dear child,
That all one gives to poetry
Is not a loss for love ? "

Such were the cares of these two good and happy beings. But one day the poet awoke pale and ill. Phthisis had seized upon him; it made rapid progress. Saint-Cyr de Rayssac died at Paris on May 15, 1874, in his thirty-seventh year.

His poems were published four years afterwards through the care of Hippolyte Babou. The public did not care for them. Poets by trade, I ought to add, cared but moderately for them. Saint-Cyr de Rayssac is a careless poet. That was not to be forgiven in 1878. His sonnets are not regular. They are not rhymed with exactness. That was perceived, but it was not perceived that their feeling is rare and often exquisite.

He was not forgiven for being of the school of Musset and for defending the author of the " Nights." Musset was looked on as frivolous,

* " At that time I was spelling, so that I might be the better able to read thee, and all the old loves which it pleases you to curse taught my heart something for thee. . . . And I have placed at thy feet, virginal mistress, the burning harvest of all my youth, the wild bouquet made of all my flowers."

people despised him ; Saint-Cyr only admired him all the more.

> "Oh ! léger ! quelle gloire.—Amis, soyons légers,
> Légers comme le feu, les ailes et la plume,
> Comme tout ce qui monte et tout ce qui parfume,
> Comme l'âme des fleurs dans les bois d'orangers." *

I admit it. Saint-Cyr de Rayssac has many faults : his expression is often feeble and uncertain. But he is simple, natural, harmonious ; he has excellent taste, a pure style, easy and musical verse. Is all that nothing ? He is profoundly, deeply a poet. He has fresh images. Had he only written these three lines on Correggio's Magdalene I would have loved him with all my heart :

> "La voilà donc, pieds nus, la belle pécheresse,
> Pieds nus, cheveux en pleurs, et la tiède paresse
> Gonfle, en les déroulant, les anneaux de sa chair." †

How expressive that is, and what feeling !

I quoted the other day the sonnet "On the Funeral Genius of the Capitol," and the morbid grace of those fourteen lines delighted the choicest of my readers. Here is another sonnet, in a graver and less touching tone :

> "Oh ! non, pas un blasphème et pas un désaveu ;
> Mais je tombe, Seigneur, et je me désespère,
> Mais quand ils ont planté le gibet du calvaire,
> C'est dans mon cœur ouvert qu'ils enfonçaient le pieu !
>
> Crois-tu que je t'aimais, moi dont le manteau bleu
> T'abrita quatorze ans comme un fils de la terre ?

---

* "Oh ! slightness ! how glorious !—Friends, let us be slight, light as fire, as wings, as a feather, like everything that ascends and everything that perfumes, like the soul of flowers in orange woods."

† "Here then is she, barefooted, the beauteous wanton, barefooted, her hair in tears, and tepid languor swells, as they unloosen the ringlets of her flesh."

Oh ! pourquoi, juste ciel, lui donner une mère ?
Qu'en avait-il besoin, puis qu'il était un Dieu ?

L'angoisse me dévore ; au fond de ma prunelle,
Roule toujours brûlante une larme éternelle
Qui rongera mes yeux sans couler ni tarir.

Seigneur, pardonnez-moi, je suis seule à souffrir.
Ma part dans cette épreuve est bien la plus cruelle,
Et je peux bien pleurer sans vous désobéir." *

I do not know, but it seems to me that the poetry of Saint-Cyr de Rayssac is original in its simplicity, and that in it one feels a peculiar mingling of idealism and sensuousness. I imagine that this poet may please some fastidious minds. He is quite unknown. I shall be very happy if I have induced a few gifted people to dip into him. They will think of me from time to time and say, " We owe a friend to him."

A PIETA

* "Oh, no, not a blasphemy and not a denial ; but I fall, Lord, and I despair, for when they set up the Rood on Calvary it was in my open heart that they plunged the stake ! Dost Thou believe that I loved Thee, I whose blue mantle sheltered Thee for fourteen years as a child of earth ? Oh, why, just Heaven, give Him a mother ? What need had He of one since He was a God ? Anguish devours me ; in the depths of my eyes there flows ever burning an eternal tear which will sear them and yet never fall and never dry up. Lord, pardon me, I am alone with my suffering. My part in this trial is far the cruellest, and I may indeed weep without disobeying Thee."

THE ERRORS OF HISTORY *

PHILOSOPHERS, as a rule, have small liking for history. They are ready to cast on it the reproach of proceeding without method and without an aim. Descartes held it in contempt. Malebranche used to say that he attributed no more importance to it than to the gossip of the neighbourhood. In his old age, he recognised the merit of the young d'Aguesseau and favoured him with some conversations on metaphysics ; but one day, having surprised him with a Thucydides in his hand, he withdrew his regard ; the frivolity of such reading scandalised him. The very day before yesterday I was lucky enough to have a chat with M. Darlu, a philosopher whose conversation is always profitable to me, and I had a great deal of trouble in defending history against him, for he regards it as the least honourable of the works of the imagination.

Thus I did not experience too much surprise this morning when I opened the very solid and powerful book in which M. Louis Bourdeau relegates the works of historians to the rank of fables akin to the stories of Mother Goose. According to M. Bourdeau, as according to Dr. Johnson, history is

* " L'Histoire et les Historiens." A critical essay on history considered as a positive science. By Louis Bourdeau.

an old almanac, and historians cannot claim any higher dignity than that of makers of almanacs.

"History," says M. Louis Bourdeau, "is not, and could not be, a science." The reasons he gives for this do not fail to make an impression on my mind ; and there is perhaps some reason for that. To be quite candid, I had tried to indicate them myself before him. Ten years ago I threw them lightly and jestingly into a little book entitled "The Crime of Sylvestre Bonnard." I did not dwell on them. But now that I see they are worth something, I hasten to resume possession of them.

"And first of all," I said in that little book, "what is history ? History is the written representation of past events. But what is an event ? Is it any fact whatsoever ? No. It is a notable fact. Now, how does the historian judge whether a fact is notable or not ? He judges arbitrarily, according to his own tastes and caprice, his own ideas, in a word as an artist ! for facts are not divided by their own nature into historical facts and non-historical facts. But a fact is something extremely complex. Will the historian represent facts in their complexity ? No, that is impossible. He will represent them denuded of the greater part of the special circumstances that constitute them, and consequently truncated, mutilated, different from what they were. As to the inter-relation of facts, let us not speak of it. If a so-called historical fact is brought about, as is possible, by one or several non-historical, and on that account, unknown facts, how can the historian mark the relation of those facts ?

"And I am assuming that the historian has certain evidence beneath his eyes, while in reality he bestows his confidence on this or that witness only from reasons of feeling or interest.   History is not a science, it is an art, and a man succeeds in it only by imagination."

These are precisely, if I am not mistaken, the fundamental ideas on which M. Louis Bourdeau bases his refusal of all scientific value to history.   He quotes this definition from the Dictionary of the Academy : " History is the recital of things worthy of remembrance."

And he adds :

" A definition of this sort, though it corresponds well enough with the works of historians, could not suffice for the foundation of a science, and the deeper we dig into it, the less it satisfies the reason.   What do ' things worthy of remembrance ' represent in the sum of the developments of human life ?   Have they a special essence, fixed characters ?   By no means.   That qualification results from an arbitrary appreciation which escapes all rule.   How far ought the adjacent boundaries and limits of celebrated things to be extended in detail ?   That has not been indicated.   The frontier remains undecided.   Every one fixes the limits according to his own fancy."

Then, coming to examine the value of evidence and the credence due to tradition, M. Bourdeau easily establishes that the verification of facts by the historian is always a difficult operation and one of doubtful success.

We are thus in perfect agreement, M. Bourdeau and myself.   I am proud of this, for I regard M. Bourdeau's mind as resolute and convinced.   Therefore there is not, properly speaking, a science of history.

But can that truth, which we pursue in vain when

it is a question of establishing an old event, be reached if we confine ourselves to verifying a contemporary fact ? If the past escapes us, can we lay hold of the present ? M. Bourdeau does not believe it. He forbids the chroniclers and the writers of memoirs to tell lies, and in relation to this subject he tells the adventure of Walter Raleigh. That statesman, shut up in the Tower of London, was engaged in writing the second part of his " History of the World." One day he was interrupted in this work by the noise of a quarrel that broke out beneath the windows of his prison. He followed the incidents of the brawl with an attentive glance, and believed that he had taken an exact account of it. The next day, chatting about the scene with a friend of his who had also witnessed it, and even taken an active part in it, he was contradicted by him on every point. Reflecting then on the difficulty of knowing the truth about distant events when he could be mistaken about what took place under his eyes, he threw the manuscript of his history into the fire.

It is none the less to be remarked that this difficulty of knowing the truth about recent events has struck all historians, and all of them have not burnt their writings. Among the minds penetrated by this universal uncertainty, M. Renan is distinguished by a special feeling of resigned mistrust. He has never had illusions regarding the irremediable uncertainty of human testimony.

" Let us attempt in our own days," he has said, " with our innumerable means of information and publicity, to know exactly how any great episode in contemporary history has taken place, what occurred in connection with it, what were the precise views and intentions of the actors in it, and we shall not succeed. For my own part, I have often attempted, as an experiment in historical criticism, to form a complete idea of events that have taken place almost quite under my eyes, such as the days of February, of June, &c. I have never succeeded in satisfying myself."

Indulgent minds put up with the betrayals of history. That Muse is false, they think, but she no longer deceives us as soon as we know that she does deceive us. Constant doubt will be our certainty. We shall prudently go forward from error to error towards a relative truth. Even a falsehood is a sort of truth.

As for M. Bourdeau, he does not want to be deceived, even knowingly, and he absolutely repudiates history. He chases her away as deceptive, immodest, dissolute, sold to the powerful, a courtesan in the pay of kings, an enemy of the people, unrighteous and false. He replaces her by statistics, which are properly " the science of social facts expressed in numerical terms." No more fine recitals, no more moving narratives, only figures.

The historians of the future will especially have the task of interpreting statistical data concerning the facts of common life. The activity of reason always resolves itself into acts, and the sole manner of rendering an account of them is, after having classified them according to definite functions, to document them at the moment they take place, to tabulate them under prearranged headings of population, place, and period, then to compare these simultaneous or successive returns, to note the variations of function, and to draw from them the deductions of which they admit. Thus only shall

E

we one day be able to know what the multitudes
of whom humanity is composed, do."

Henceforth the only historical documents will be
tables of population, Customs tariffs, commercial
registers, bank balance-sheets, railway reports.
M. Bourdeau flatters himself that they will be less
deceptive than the evidence appealed to by historians such as Tacitus or Michelet. He may be
right, although statistics themselves are subject to
a good deal of uncertainty. It is not only the Muses
who lie.

M. Bourdeau desires that history, hitherto exclusively devoted to illustrious personages and
extraordinary events, should henceforth interest
itself in the daily life of peoples. In this respect, it
must be admitted that the price of iron or the rate of
interest is more instructive than the story of a battle
or of the interview between two sovereigns.

M. Bourdeau desires that we should know how
the millions of obscure beings have lived, whose
harmonious energy makes the life of a people. He
desires that that great activity should be analysed,
studied bit by bit, noted, summarised.

"That," he says, "is the history that should
henceforth be written, not only for young States
which, like Australia, New Zealand, Canada, La
Plata, are founded under such new conditions, but
even for the old societies of Europe which also
aspire to rule themselves in accordance with an
ideal of order, of labour, of peace and' liberty.
From the point of view which we have reached, any
other way of studying history is inexact and puerile.
A reform is enjoined, and it will be made either by
the historians or against their will. The age of
literary historiography is reaching its end ; that of

scientific history is about to begin. When it shall
be capable of retracing the life of a people in the
sense indicated, we shall see that no recital offers so
much interest, instruction, and grandeur."

I do not contradict this. Create the science of
history, and we will applaud it. But leave us the
charming and magnificent art of men like Thucydides
and Augustin Thierry.

M. Bourdeau himself feels that he is cruel. He
takes away from us our beautiful histories, but he
takes them with regret. " Since we must choose
between beauty and truth," he says, " let us without
hesitation prefer the second." For my own part,
if I had to choose between beauty and truth, I should
not hesitate either : it is beauty that I should keep,
certain that it has in it a higher and deeper truth
than truth itself. I will dare to say that there is
nothing true in the world except beauty. Beauty
brings to us the highest revelation of the divine
that we are permitted to know. But why choose ?
Why substitute statistical history for narrative
history ? It is replacing a rose by a potato ! Can
we not have side by side the flowers of poetry and
those " nourishing roots that make souls learned,"
as the good M. Lancelot said ? I know as well as
you that history is false, and that all the historians
from Herodotus to Michelet are narrators of fables.
But that does not disturb me. I am quite willing
that an Herodotus should deceive me in an agreeable manner ; I shall let myself be dazzled by the
sombre radiancy of the aristocratic thought of
Tacitus ; I shall enter again with joy into the
dreams of that great blind man who saw Harold
and Fredegonde. I would even regret it if history
were exact. I willingly say with Voltaire : reduce

it to truth and you ruin it : it is Alcinous robbed of his enchantment.

It is only a succession of images. That is why I love it ; that is why it suits men. Humanity is still in its childhood. Men have recently determined, or believed they have determined, in an approximate manner, the age of the earth. The earth is not old. She has existed in a solid state only for twenty-five millions of years at the most, and it is hardly more than twelve millions of years since she gave life to marine plants and to shell-fish. A slow evolution has produced plants and animals. Man has come last : he was born yesterday. He is still in the fire of youth. We must not ask him to be too reasonable. He has need of being amused by stories. Do not take away from him history, which is the finest intellectual amusement. If humanity needs stories, M. Bourdeau will answer : Have we not the poets ? They are more amusing than the historians, and they are not much falser. M. Bourdeau, who is so severe towards the annalists, the chroniclers, and generally towards all the writers of memoirs, stores in his heart, on the contrary, treasures of indulgence for the poets. As they do not draw inferences, he forgives them everything. I have noticed that philosophers as a rule live on good terms with the poets. The philosophers know that poets do not think; that disarms, softens, and delights them. But they see that historians think, and that they think differently from the philosophers. That is what the philosophers do not forgive. M. Bourdeau sends us back to the " Iliad " and to "Mother Goose." They are fine stories. But we hardly believe in them any longer. We want stories in which we can believe—the history of the French

Revolution, for example.   Leave us the romance of
the universe.   If it is not entirely true, it contains
some truth.   I will even say that it contains truths
which your statistics will never contain.   Old
history is an art ; that is why she retains, in her
beauty, a spiritual and ideal truth far superior to
the material and tangible truths of the sciences of
pure observation : she paints man and the passions
of man.   That is what statistics will never do.
Narrative history is essentially inexact.   I have said
as much, and I do not unsay it ; but it is still, along
with poetry,the most faithful image that man has
traced of himself.   It is a portrait.   Your statistical
history will never be anything but an autopsy.

ON SCEPTICISM *

I SPENT many happy years of life before I was seized with the inclination to write. I led a contemplative and solitary life, the remembrance of which is still infinitely pleasant to me. Then, since I studied nothing, I learnt much. It is indeed on our leisurely strolls that our great intellectual and moral discoveries are made. On the other hand, what we discover in a laboratory or a study does not, as a rule, amount to very much, and it is to be remarked that scholars by profession are usually more ignorant than most other men. I recall that one morning during that happy time I was walking haphazard along the winding alleys of the Zoological Gardens amidst the deer and sheep who stretched their heads over the shrubs to beg bread of me, thinking as I walked that this old garden peopled by animals, was not so unlike the terrestrial Paradise of the old engravings, when suddenly I saw coming towards me the Abbé L——, who, his breviary in his hand, was walking along with the virile gladness of an unspotted soul. The Abbé L—— was, in truth, a saint; but he was also a scholar. His heart was peaceful but his mind never ceased disputing. You needed to know

* " Les Sceptiques Grecs." By Victor Brochard.

him to understand how the pride of a priest can be
united to the simplicity of a saint. Having said his
mass, he argued for the rest of the day. He had
read all the theology, morality, and metaphysics
that is to be found in calf bindings and red edges
on the stalls of the secondhand booksellers. Innumerable are the books whose margins he covered
with notes and with snuff. He spent the eloquence
of an incomparable doctor in conversation along
the quays or in the public gardens. Moreover, he was
not looked upon favourably by the bishop. His
superiors esteemed the purity of his conduct,
but they feared the pride of his intellect. Perhaps
they were not altogether wrong.

That morning the Abbé L—— addressed me in
these terms :

" John the Deacon relates that St. Gregory,
having wept at the thought that the Emperor
Trajan was damned, God, who takes pleasure in
giving what we venture to ask of Him, exempted the
soul of Trajan from eternal punishment. That
soul remained in Hell but thenceforward it felt no
pain. It is not forbidden us to imagine that the
adopted son of Nerva wanders in those pallid
pastures where Dante saw the heroes and the sages
of antiquity. Their glances were slow and grave ;
they spoke in a gentle voice. The Florentine
recognised Anaxagoras, Thales, Empedocles, Hera-
clitus, and Zeno. Why did he not also see Pyrrho
among those souls guilty only of having lived in
ignorance of the divine law ? Of all philosophers of
antiquity, Pyrrho was the wisest. Not only did
he practise the virtues which Christianity has
sanctified, not only was he humble, patient, and
resigned, a lover of poverty, but also he professed

the truest doctrine of all profane antiquity, the only one which is in exact accordance with Christian theology. Born in the darkness of paganism, he knew that he was without light, and he deserves the highest praise for having remained undecided and uncertain. Even to-day, for one who has suffered the misfortune of not having been born a Christian, wisdom lies in Pyrrhonism. What do I say ? In everything that is not an article of faith, Christian philosophy is itself Pyrrhonism ; it remains in suspense. Everything which has not been revealed is subject to doubt. It is even questionable whether the Christian religion itself has not furnished scepticism with new arguments, and whether faith in the mysteries as well as in the miracles has not rendered nature more incomprehensible and reason more uncertain."

The Abbé stopped a moment before the zebra's house. He struck his breast.

" For me," he added, " it is the invisible world which reveals the visible. I believe in the reality of man only because I believe in the existence of God. I know that I exist solely because God has told me so. The Eternal has spoken to me, *locutus est patribus nostris, Abraham et seminis ejus in sæcula*—' as he spake to our forefathers, Abraham and his seed for ever ! ' And I have answered, ' Here I am since Thou called'st me.' Outside of revelation, everything, physical as well as moral, is open to doubt ; nothing is distinct, consequently nothing is interesting, and religion alone, lifting me up in its luminous hands, delivers me out of the Pyrrhonic ataraxy. Without the love of God I should have no love ; I should believe in nothing if I did not believe in the impossible and the absurd. That is why I hold Pyrrho for the wisest of the pagans."

Thus spoke the Abbé L——.

I call to mind his words literally for they made a profound impression on me. I had never heard such words from the mouth of a priest, and I have never heard their like since. I do not believe that I am deceived in saying that the Church distrusts apologists who, like the Abbé L——, push onwards with excessive logic. She remembers in time the memorable saying of the devil: "I also am a logician." The devil did not flatter himself in speaking thus. He definitely remains the only doctor who has not yet been refuted. For my part, it was in front of the zebra's house, listening to the Abbé L——, that I began to doubt many things which until then had appeared to me credible.

Alas! the Abbé L——, who died parish priest of a little village of La Brie, rests now in an untended and flowery cemetery in the shelter of a slender thirteenth-century church. The stone that covers his remains bears this inscription in witness of his ardent faith, *Speravit anima mea.* As I read these words, I thought of the epitaph in dialogue which a witty Greek of Byzantium composed for Pyrrho:

"Art thou dead, Pyrrho?"—"I do not know."

And I began to think that, except on one point, the philosopher and the priest thought alike.

All these memories came back to me presently in a single flash, while I read the study that M. Victor Brochard devotes to Pyrrho in his excellent book on the Greek sceptics. It is in the highest degree interesting. Those ingenious Greeks invented innumerable philosophic systems. The schools entertained themselves with a showy display

E 2

of disputations, men's minds were pestered and deafened, and then scepticism was born. It appeared just after the death of Alexander during that military orgy whose monstrous crimes sullies the classic land of truth and beauty.

Demosthenes and Hyperides are dead. Phocion drinks the hemlock. There is no longer anything to hope from men or from gods. Liberty and the antique virtues are done with. It is true that the political state of a people does not of necessity determine the private condition of its members. Life is sometimes tolerable enough amidst public calamities, but, in truth, the times of Cassandra and of Demetrius were execrable. Besides, it must be borne in mind that tyranny, even in its gentlest form, was for a long time repugnant to the Hellenic soul.

Pyrrho was a native of Elis in Elidos. At first a painter and a poet, he was born with an active imagination and an irritable temperament. But later in life his character underwent a striking change. Having embraced philosophy, which was at the time in Greece a sort of monachism, under the guidance of his master Anaxagoras he joined in Alexander's expedition. In India he saw the magi, called by the Greeks gymno-sophists, who lived naked in their hermitages. Their contempt for the world and for vain appearances, their motionless and solitary life, their thirst for annihilation and forgetfulness, all these marks of a gentle and resigned pessimism struck the young Pyrrho, and certain characteristics of the doctrine of the philosopher of Elis are of Hindoo origin.

After the death of Alexander, Pyrrho returned to his native town. There on the charming banks of the Peneus, in that flowery vale where each evening nymphs come to dance in chorus, he led the existence of a holy man. He lived piously ($εὐσεθῶς$), his biographer tells us. He kept house with his sister, Philista, who was a midwife. It was he who took the poultry and young pigs to the town to market ; he swept the house and dusted the furniture.

That is the example that this philosopher gave to his disciples, so that his life bore testimony to his doctrine of renunciation and indifference. He taught that all things are alike uncertain and controvertible. Nothing, said he, is intelligible. We ought to trust neither our senses nor our reason. We must doubt everything and be indifferent to everything. There was nothing subtle in his teaching. His doctrine was, above all, M. Brochard tells us, a moral doctrine, a rule of life.

According to Pyrrho, " to have no opinion about either good or evil is the only means of avoiding the causes of trouble. For the most part, men render themselves unhappy through their own fault ; they suffer because they are deprived of what they believe to be a good, or because, possessing it, they fear to lose it, or because they are enduring what they believe to be evil. Suppress all belief of this nature and all evils will disappear."

For Pyrrho, as for Democritus, the supreme good is good humour, absence of fear, tranquillity.

" To retire within one's self," says M. Victor Brochard, " so as to give the least possible hold to misfortune, to live simply and modestly, like the humble, without any sort of pretension, to let the world go and to resign one's self to those evils that are in nobody's power to prevent ; that is the ideal of the sceptic." Pyrrho maintained that it is of no more account to live than to die or to die than to live.

" Why then do you not die ? " he was asked.

" For the very reason," he answered, " that life and death are equally indifferent."

In a great peril of shipwreck he was the only one whom the tempest did not alarm. As he saw the other passengers filled with fear and sadness, he told them with a tranquil air to look at a pig that was there eating its food as usual.

" That," said he, " is what the insensibility of the philosopher ought to be."

Marvellous ! The pig was a philosopher, but that was little to its credit ! It is difficult to be insensible when one thinks vividly, and the serenity of a pig is a discouraging example for most men. May I repeat what a disciple of Lamettrie once said to the beautiful Mrs. Elliott, whom the patriots of Versailles had put in prison as an aristocrat ? The jailer put into the young Scotswoman's cell an old doctor of Ville-d'Avray, who was obsessed by materialism and atheism. He was weeping. The tears moistened the dust with which his long cheeks were covered, and the poor philosopher's face was all besmeared. Mrs. Elliott took a sponge and wiped her companion's face, murmuring to him these consoling words :

" Sir," said she to him, " it is probable that we are both going to die. But whence comes it that you are sad while I am gay ? In losing life do you lose more than I do ? "

" Madam," he answered her, " you are young, you are rich, you are beautiful and healthy, and in losing life you lose a great deal ; but you are incapable of reflection, and you do not know what you lose. As for me, I am poor, I am old, and I am ill, and to take away my life is to deprive me of little ; but I am a philosopher and a physician ; I have a conception of existence which you are without, and I know exactly what I lose. That is the reason, Madam, that I am sad while you are gay."

That old doctor of Ville-d'Avray was far less of a sage than Pyrrho, but he was more impressive, and, in truth, his tears though a little too imbecile, are more human than the virtuous insensibility of the sage of Elis. A striking example of that insensibility is related. We are told that having seen his master Anaxarchus fall into a ditch, Pyrrho passed on without deigning to stretch out a hand to help him. And not only did the master refrain from complaining, but he praised the indifference of his disciple. Bayle, who relates the fact, adds, " What is there more surprising that one could do under the discipline of La Trappe ? "

M. Brochard rightly calls Pyrrho a " Greek ascetic." It is in the lives of the fathers of the desert that we see examples of a similar effort to despoil man of all humanity.

The holy life that Pyrrho led at Elis rendered him venerable in the eyes of his fellow-citizens, and they elevated him to the priesthood. He performed his functions of high priest with exactitude and decency, as a man who respected the gods of the republic. By showing this respect he in no way abandoned his philosophy, for scepticism never denies that it is necessary to conform to the customs, and to practise the duties of morality. He made up his mind on these questions without waiting for certainty. Similarly, our Gassendi could profess theology without believing in God, and was indeed a very worthy man.

P.S.—It was not and could not be my intention to give the reader an idea of M. Victor Brochard's book. That book has been awarded a prize by the Academy of Moral Science. You will find a fitting appreciation of it in the report addressed to that Academy by M. Ravaisson in 1885. My chat barely touches on it. But I should not like to appear to ignore the great merit of that work, which unites originality of outlook to critical accuracy. Carneades and Pyrrho are presented in it in a new light. There are a dozen pages in a little story that I have just published in the *Revue des Deux Mondes*, which I could never have written had I not read M. Brochard's book. That is an avowal which M. Brochard can have no interest in hearing, but it is my duty to make it.

EURIPIDES *

LECONTE DE LISLE gives us to-day a lyrical drama, "L'Appollonide," which is a study from the antique. You know that, following Goethe's example, the author of the "Poèmes Antiques" and of the "Poèmes Barbares" has on several occasions with consummate art employed in our own language the Greek poetic form, notably when, twelve years ago, he gave us a tragedy the feeling and colour of which were derived from Æschylus.

The "Apollonide," which appears to-day in the booksellers' shops, is a study of the same nature. But the model is very different. This time it is no longer Æschylus but Euripides. The "Apollonide" is the "Ion" of the third tragic poet of Athens.

M. Leconte de Lisle, who had shown so much vigour in wrestling with the Titan of Greek drama, gives a proof of his versatility when he has to measure himself with a fluid and caressing genius like Euripides. He has found for this encounter treasures of gentleness, grace, and tenderness. He, robust and violent when it pleases him, has here shown himself harmonious and pure. In truth, one

* "L'Apollonide." A lyrical drama in three acts and five scenes from the "Ion" of Euripides). By Leconte de Lisle.

could not push the magic art of verse further than
this master has done.   His new work, like its pre-
decessors, amazes one by its unfaltering perfection.

I have said that the grace of " L'Apollonide "
was a pious grace.   There is, indeed, in the Greek
original a savour of the sanctuary, and this the
French poet has carefully preserved.   The hero is
a priest who has just reached man's estate, the
scene a temple, each chorus a prayer, the ending of
the play an oracle.

Euripides was not religious.   He was an atheist.
But he was atheist and mystic combined.   He
excelled in painting young priests who, like Ion and
Hippolytus, unite the purity of asceticism with the
beauty of youth.

At dawn, this young Ion, clothed in white and
crowned with flowers, descends the steps of the
temple of Apollo, and repeats, as he plucks a branch
of symbolic laurel :

" O laurier, qui verdis dans les jardins célestes,
    Que l'aube ambroisienne arrose de ses pleurs !
    Laurier, désir illustre, oubli des jours funestes,
    Qui d'un songe immortel sais charmer nos douleurs !
    Permets que, par mes mains pieuses, ô bel arbre,
    Ton feuillage mystique effleure le parvis,
    Afin que la blancheur vénérable du marbre
        Eblouisse les yeux ravis !

O sources, qui jamais ne serez épuisées,
    Qui fluez et chantez harmonieusement
    Dans les mousses, parmi lès lis lourds de rosées,
    A la pente du mont solitaire et charmant !
    Eaux vives ! sur le seuil et les marches pythiques,
    Épanchez le trésor de vos urnes d'azur,
    Et puisse aussi le flot de mes jours fatidiques
        Couler comme vous, chaste et pur ! " *

---

* " O laurel that bloomest in the celestial gardens, which the
ambrosial dawn waters with its tears ! Laurel, illustrious desire,

O magic of beautiful verse ! Here we are transported by enchantment to the holy Athens of the poets, the sculptors, the architects, and philosophers.

That little rock of Cecrops was for a long time rugged, covered with stiff and painted idols who smiled mysteriously. On it lived men at once rude and magnificent, who wore golden grasshoppers in their long plaited hair, and a whole maritime population nurtured on garlic and songs. The women, still barbarous, tore into pieces on the public places the messengers of disaster. An heroic and barbarous genius dominated the little city and lay upon the squat form of the old Parthenon that the Median wars were to destroy.

The finest of human phenomena, the Attic genius, burst forth suddenly. Marathon and Salamis were won, Greece was preserved by the Athenians, treasure was wrested from the Persians, Victory doffed her golden sandals to seat herself in the city of her choice ; so swift a glory and so great a joy transformed Athens, made of her the city with the white pediments, and the colossal chryselephantine statues, the opulent protectress of the Ionian cities, the beautiful rival of Sparta, in a word, the land whose harmonious genius is

oblivion of the ill-omened days, who knowest how to charm away our sorrows by an immortal dream, permit, O fair tree, that thy mystic foliage may strew the pavement by my hands, so that the venerable whiteness of the marble may dazzle the ravished eyes ! O founts that will never be exhausted, which flow and sing harmoniously through the moss amid the dew-laden lilies on the slope of the charming and lonely mount ! Living waters ! Sprinkle the treasure of your azure urns on the threshold and on the Pythian steps, and may the stream of my fate-revealing steps flow like you, chaste and pure."

reflected in the tragedies of Sophocles. But those radiant hours will not last long. They will quickly pass, the days of moderation in power, of simplicity in wealth, of obedience to the gods, of serene peace, in the course of that Attic life so rich and so rapid. When harmony, when perfect accord, shall be silenced, when the troubles of the philosophic temper shall agitate the sons of the soldiers of Marathon, when the rights of the individual shall be imprudently proclaimed, when knowledge shall bring useful prejudices to ruin, when the gods of the city shall be attacked by reason and the law shall vindicate them with the poison-cup, who shall be the poet of these restless days ? What anxious and melancholy figure shall express the new thought ? Euripides is he.

If we are to credit a story which begins like a nurse's fable, Mnesarchus, the son of Mnesarchus, was a tavern-keeper, and his wife Clito was a vendor of herbs in the island of Salamis, where they had taken refuge from the Persians of Xerxes. Clito became a mother, and the poor couple placed great hopes on the expected child. Mnesarchus went to consult the god on so dear a subject, and the god answered that the existence which was about to begin in a tavern would close in honour, " with peaceful and consecrated crowns." The child was born in the first year of the seventy-fifth Olympiad, the day of the glorious battle that stained the Euripus with blood, and he was named Euripides. To aid the accomplishment of the oracle, the poor parents made their son an athlete. The crowns of the arena were the only ones that they could imagine. Besides, Greece honoured the athletes. Could the manly beauty of the wrestlers

have been other than dear to a people who adored
the human form ? The philosophers alone dis-
esteemed the glories of the boxing-match, the
contest of the five exercises, and the foot-race.

" The athlete," they said, " cannot be compared
with us, for our wisdom is above the strength of men
and horses."

Euripides was inclined to philosophy. However,
if he abandoned the arena, if he ceased to anoint his
limbs with oil, it was to paint in wax on wooden
tablets, and to endeavour to draw, according to the
Hellenic taste, pure forms, presented without
foreshortening and without perspective. But he
did not for long employ the cestrum and the rods
charred in the fire. Turning to another art, he
studied rhetoric under Prodicos. This master taught
that nothing is absolute, that we call what is agreeable good, and what is displeasing evil. A denier of
the gods whom the vulgar worshipped, he paid
with his life for his rational impiety: he drank the
hemlock. When he entered the house of Prodicos,
Euripides found there friendly minds, intellectual
relatives. The pride of thought, the love of
subtle reasoning, a gentle impiety, in a word, his
own nature, had been revealed to him. But the
true master of Euripides was Anaxagoras of Cla-
zomenæ, who taught Ionian doctrine at Athens.
Conformably with the spirit of the schools, he sought
the origin of things, and he believed he had found
it in what he called νοῦς, that is to say, mind.
Animals, plants, the world, everything, he said,
are in diverse manners penetrated by mind. By it
the plants know and desire: they rejoice to bear
leaves, and grieve when they feel them die. Mind,
which determines all form and all thought, has

given dominion to man by giving him two hands. The contemplation of nature, a sad and proud submission to the eternal laws, the feeling of the power of things and the weakness of man—these are what young Euripides was trained to comprehend in the school of this philosopher, profound in his observation of phenomena, and great in the freedom of his mind. The physical system of Anaxagoras was perfectly rational. Out of the son of Hyperion, out of " the unwearied Helios, who, drawn by his steeds, gives light to mortal men and the immortal gods," it made an incandescent block, larger than the Peloponnesus. For it the winds were no longer divine, and were caused by a sudden rarefaction of the air. Anaxagoras revealed the cause of eclipses to the Athenians, whom he thus deprived of a fond and ancient terror. Accused of impiety, he was saved from death by the tears of Pericles. The Athenians exiled him, or rather, as he said, they exiled themselves from him. He retired to Lampsacus. His last thought was benevolent, and reveals a smiling old man: he asked that the anniversary of his death should be a holiday for schoolboys. He died at the age of seventy-two, and we believe he willingly left this world in which he had thought so much.

His disciple, still very young, revealed himself as a poet. In the first year of the eighty-first Olympiad, he had his first tragedy played in the theatre of Bacchus which, standing against the rock of Cecrops, was lighted by the direct rays of the sun.

The pupil of Anaxagoras showed in it human actions in a new aspect. He infused the philosophy on which he had been nurtured into his drama.

Hitherto destiny brooded over tragedy, and enveloped it with an obscure terror. An incomprehensible, unintelligible power, external to men whom it delivers as a prey to one another ; gigantic heroes awaiting in proud immobility, in tranquil horror, for the fatal hour in which to slay or perish, hereditary murders, slaughterings pompous as hecatombs, such are the images with which old Æschylus appalled the spectators' eyes and stifled their breasts. Sophocles himself, the most perfect of poets, the purest of tragedians, had conceived of destiny as a force independent of man. Euripides came and placed man's destiny in man himself. He fixed the springs of action. He was the first to show all the interest of the labours of life, all the beauty of those diseases of the soul that are a thousand times dearer and more precious than health, I mean the passions.

When he married Choerina, the daughter of Mnesilochus, he lived on good terms with his father-in-law, who was an excellent and learned man, but he suffered cruelly from his wife's bad conduct. When he lost her, he married another wife, who made him suffer in the same way. Her name was Melito. A tinge of sadness overspreads the whole life of Euripides. He sometimes went to meditate upon his tragedies in his native island. There has since been shown, at Salamis, a grotto where the oldest of the poets of melancholy used to brood in the shade. An Alexandrian has said of him with elegant brevity:

" The disciple of the noble Anaxagoras was not a very agreeable companion : he laughed little, and did not even know how to jest at table, but everything he has written is honey and a song of sirens."

Although he liked to converse with certain friends, his chief pleasure was in books.

He possessed a library, a new and rare thing in that epoch, when every one took only as much from poetry, science, or philosophy, as floated in the perfumed and bee-laden air. So keen was his fondness for reading that he considered it one of the benefits of peace to be able " to unfold those pages which speak to us, and which form the glory of the sages." His long face, which ancient busts represent to us, bore the furrows of weariness and grief, a high rather than a broad forehead, hair thin on the crown of his head and falling in curls below his eyes, large pensive eyes, the corners of his mouth a little turned down, everything in him bespoke a sad and gentle man whom life had now spared.

He was linked in friendship with Socrates, who at the time used to teach wisdom in the barbers' shops. The son of Phænarete, who rarely went to the theatre, was nevertheless present at the performance of all the tragedies of Euripides. It is even said that he had a share in the composition of some of those poems. We shall never know what part Socrates took in composing the dramas of Euripides. But it is not impossible to recognise, with M. Henri Weil, traces of the Socratic teaching in several maxims of the poet, and particularly in the contrast, which he drew in his " Medea," between physical love and that other far preferable love (so he said) which beautiful souls inspire, and which is a school of wisdom and of virtue.

It is known that Anaxagoras was afterwards claimed by the sceptics. He at least belongs to them in some sort by the philosophical indifference

with which he regarded what the vulgar call benefits
or injuries. He placed his wisdom in impassibility.
Such was also the philosophy of Euripides. He held
meditation to be the sovereign good.

" Happy," said he, " is he who possesses knowledge ! he does not seek to usurp power from his
fellow citizens, he does not meditate an unjust
action. Contemplating eternal nature, the unalterable order, the origin, and the elements of
things, his soul is stained by no shameful desire."

These are fine and noble maxims. But like
Prodicos, like Anaxagoras, like Socrates, Euripides
held concerning the gods opinions that were contrary to the old maxims of the city. That scientific
and modern spirit constituted a dangerous impiety
in the eyes of observers. Everything in Euripides
betrayed contempt for the divine and heroic conceptions of Hellas. This caused hatreds, outrages,
perils. At last, it was necessary either to flee like
Prodicos, or to die like Anaxagoras. The poet of
philosophy left Athens and went to seek under a
tyrant that liberty which democracy did not give
him. He died in the royal dwelling of Archelaus.

Thus I have imperceptibly related to you the life
of Euripides. I do not tell you, like the man who
shows the magic lantern, that if I had to begin
again I should relate it to you in the same way.
I believe, on the contrary, that I should relate it
in a somewhat different fashion. I would not say
that Euripides had been an athlete and a painter,
because in reality we do not know that this was the
case. An ancient gem shows him to us hesitating
between two women who represent, the one Palæstra
the other Tragedy. But it would be necessary to
know if that stone is ancient, if it really represents

Euripides, and, finally, whether the engraver had not been inspired by a legend. M. Heuzey, with his unwavering and charming knowledge, could tell us. But I do not know. At Megara were shown pictures, painted, it was said, by Euripides ; but was it said with truth ? Certainly one must have a mania for story-telling to tell stories as uncertain as that. How much better I should have done had I simply sent the readers to an introduction which M. Henri Weil has placed at the beginning of a selection of seven tragedies of Euripides ! There knowledge speaks. But, after the example of the Greeks, I like stories, and take pleasure in what the poets and the philosophers say. Philosophy and literature are the " Thousand and One Nights " of the West.

M. SIGNORET'S MARIONETTES

SIGNORET'S marionettes are playing Cervantes and Aristophanes, and I think they will also play Shakespeare, Calderon, Plautus, and Molière. Did not English marionettes play the tragedy of " Julius Cæsar " in the time of Queen Elizabeth ? And was it not at a performance of the true history of Doctor Faust, represented by articulated puppets, that Goethe conceived the great poem on which he worked down to his latest day ? Did you imagine, then, that it is impossible for marionettes to be eloquent or poetical ?

If those of the Vivienne gallery heeded me, they would also play Gustave Flaubert's " Temptation of St. Anthony," and an abridgment of the Orleans " Mystery " with which M. Joseph Fabre would love to furnish them.

The little marionette who played the Maid would be naïvely carved, as if by some good image-maker of the fifteenth century, and in such a fashion that our eyes would see Joan of Arc almost as our hearts see her when they are pious. Finally, since it is the nature of man to desire without limits, I formulate a final wish. I shall therefore say that I am very anxious that the marionettes should play one of those dramas of Hroswita, in which the virgins of the Lord speak with so much simplicity. Hroswita was a Saxon nun of the time of Otto the Great. She was a very learned person, with a mind at once subtle and barbarous. She bethought herself in her convent of writing comedies in imitation of Terence, and it turned out that those comedies resembled neither those of Terence nor of anybody else. Our abbess had a head full of flowery legends.

She knew in detail all about the conversion of Theophilus and the repentance of Mary, Abraham's niece, and she put these pleasing things into Latin verses with the candour of a little child. That is the drama I want. The drama of to-day is too complicated for me. If you want to please me, show me some piece of Hroswita, that, for example, in which we see a venerable hermit, disguised as an elegant cavalier, going into an evil place to take out of it a female sinner predestined to eternal salvation. In order to accomplish his design, the hermit at first makes a pretence of carnal desire. But— candour of the incorruptible Hroswita ! the scene is of exemplary chastity. " Woman," says the hermit, " I would like to enjoy thy body." " O stranger, it will be according to thy desire, and I am going to deliver myself up to thee." Then the hermit repulses her and exclaims, " What ! art thou not ashamed . . . . ? " &c.

That was the abbess of Gandersheim's notion of how to handle a situation. She had no wit. She was as innocent as a poet, that is why I like her. If I ever obtain the honour of being presented to the actress who plays the leading parts in the marionettes' theatre, I shall throw myself at her feet, I shall kiss her hands, I shall touch her knees, and

I shall beg her to play the part of Mary in my abbess's comedy. I shall say : Mary, the niece of Abraham, was an anchoress and a courtesan. These are great situations which are expressed by a small number of gestures. In them a beautiful marionette like you will surpass the actresses of the flesh. You are quite small, but you will appear great because you are simple, whereas a living actress would in your place appear small. Besides, there is nobody but you left to express religious feeling nowadays.

That is what I shall say to her, and perhaps she will be persuaded. A truly artistic idea, an elegant and noble thought, should enter into the wooden head of the marionette more easily than into the brain of a fashionable actress.*

In the meantime I have seen the marionettes of the Rue Vivienne twice, and I have enjoyed them very much. I am infinitely thankful to them for having replaced living actors. If I must speak my whole mind, actors spoil comedy for me. I mean good actors. I might perhaps come to terms with the other sort ! but decidedly I cannot endure excellent actors such as are to be seen at the Comédie-Française. Their talent is too great : it overwhelms everything. There is nothing but them. Their personality effaces the work they represent. They are important. I would like an actor only to be important when he has genius. I dream of masterpieces played in a slap-dash style in barns by strolling players. But perhaps I have no idea of what the

---

* Through the intercession of M. Maurice Boucher, my prayer has been heard. M. Signoret's marionettes have since played Hroswita's " Abraham." That performance will be spoken of in a later chat.

theatre is. It is much better for me to leave to
M. Sarcey the task of speaking of it. I only want
to speak of marionettes. It is a subject which suits
me, and on which M. Sarcey would not be much
good. He would treat it rationally.

It needs an extreme liking and a touch of veneration. The marionette is august : she emerges from
the sanctuary. The marionette, or *mariole*, was
originally a little Virgin Mary, a pious image. And
the Rue de Paris where these figures were formerly
sold was called the Rue des Mariettes or des Marionettes. Magnin says so, Magnin the learned historian of marionettes, and it is not entirely impossible
that he speaks truly, though that is not the habit of
historians.

Yes, the marionettes came forth from the sanctuary. In old Spain, in the ardent home of Madon-
nas clad in beautiful dresses like lamp-shades made
of pearls and gold, the marionettes acted in mystery-
plays and performed the drama of the Passion.
They are clearly designated by an article of the
Synod of Orihuela, which forbids the employment
in the sacred representations of these mobile little
figures : " Imajunculis fictilibus, mobili quadam
agitatione compositis, quos titeres vulgari sermone
appellamus." [*]

Formerly, during the great religious festivals at
Jerusalem, puppets were made to dance piously on
the Holy Sepulchre.

Similarly, in Greece and Rome, jointed dolls had
at first a part in the ceremonies of religion ; then
they lost their religious character. In the decline
of the drama, the Athenians were seized with such

---

[*] " Little moulded images, arranged with a certain active movement, which in the vulgar tongue we call *titeres*."

a fancy for them that the archons authorised little wooden actors to appear in that theatre of Bacchus, which had resounded to the lamentations of Atossa and the furies of Orestes. The name of Pothinos, who erected his stage on the altar of Dionysos, has come down to us. In Christian Gaul, Brioché, Nicolet, and Fagotin have remained famous as displayers of marionettes.

But I do not doubt that M. Signoret's dolls are superior in style and grace to all those of Nicolet, Fagotin, and Brioché. They are divine, those dolls of M. Signoret, and worthy of giving form to the dreams of the poet whose soul, Plato says, was " the sanctuary of the Graces."

Thanks to them, we have an Aristophanes in miniature. When the curtain has risen on an aërial landscape and we have watched the two semi-circles of birds taking their places on either side of the sacrifice, we have formed some idea of the theatre of Bacchus. What a delightful representation ! One of the two leaders of the birds, turning towards the spectators, utters these words :

" Feeble men, like unto the leaf, vain creatures fashioned out of clay and wanting wings, unhappy mortals condemned to an ephemeral and fugitive life, shadows, baseless dreams. . . ."

It is the first time, I think, that marionettes have spoken with this melancholy gravity.

MOTHER AND DAUGHTER *
MADAME DE SABRAN AND MADAME DE CUSTINE

 BARDOUX rarely fails to withdraw himself into the past each time that the duties of public life allow him to indulge in that agreeable retreat. He then willingly chooses the gardens and salons of the end of the last century as a place in which to allow his mind to ramble. He dreams of a room with white wainscotting where Gluck's " Orpheus " is open on a harpsichord, whilst a cashmere scarf trails over the lyre-shaped back of a mahogany chair. Or better still, he sees in thought an English garden with a Greek temple over against a labyrinth, and a tomb set around with poplars. For it is amid such surroundings that dwelt those women of former days whose memory is dear to him, those women whose keen intellects and fragrant tenderness imparted to life a delicate flavour that was unknown until their day—those middle-class beauties, those polished aristocrats, who, brought up in the softness of luxury, love, and art, faced the prisons and scaffolds of the Terror without the loss of any of their pride and grace ; those heroines, full

* " Madame de Custine." By M. A. Bardoux.

of courage and of weakness, who were incomparable
friends. How well M. Bardoux knows and understands them ! He admires them ; he does better,
he loves them. It was in order to be loved that they
were beautiful. He has surprised and has revealed
to us all the secrets of that Pauline de Beaumont
who had the soul of a philosopher and the heart of
a lover. He has made a whole volume out of the
intimate history of that friend of Chateaubriand.
And here he is now studying Delphine de Sabran,
who in 1793 became the widow of the youthful
Custine, a hero and sage of twenty-six years of age,
condemned to death by one of the most iniquitous
judgments of the Revolutionary Tribunal. Like
Pauline de Beaumont, Delphine de Custine took up
life again in a restored and victorious France in the
incomparable years of the Consulate. She was
then in all the radiance of her lovely youth. She
loved, and he whom she loved was the man—what
do I say ?—he was the god whom Pauline de
Beaumont adored, he was the same immortal René.
M. Bardoux, who is publishing his new work in the
Revue des Deux Mondes, has as yet issued only the
first part of it, which does not go beyond the year
1794; but at the outset he has summed up in a
few lines the episode he proposes to narrate fully from
unpublished documents. I mean the intimacy between his heroine and Chateaubriand. " Begun," he
says, " in 1803, at the time when René was appointed
secretary to the Embassy at Rome, it was soon in
the full swing of intoxication. Chateaubriand's
letters, which have been obligingly entrusted to me,
are proof of this ; they will even help to explain
that stormy and restless soul. Keen as was the
attraction he felt, his fickle affections could not be

fixed and held for long. Madame de Custine continued to be his friend for twenty years, down to
the hour of her death." Even then she still remained
the lover in spite of age and desertion, and showed
herself more jealous for the great man's reputation
than for her own. A little before her death, as she
was showing one of the rooms in her house to a
friend :

"That," said she, "is the room in which I used
to receive him."

"It is here, then," said the friend, "that he has
been at your knees ! "

She answered : "Perhaps it was I who was at his."

We shall avail ourselves of the study on Madame
de Custine when it is published in full. To-day,
since M. Bardoux lingers agreeably over his heroine's
first years, and shows us Delphine beside her mother,
let us also speak of that mother who deserves
immortal eulogy. Let us summon her enchanting
shade from the depths of the past. No one is
pleasanter to meet. There is none of a more agreeable conversation, not even those shades which the
Florentine poet saw so buoyant upon the wind
that he had a great wish to speak to them. He
disclosed his desire to his guide, who answered
him :

> "Vedrai quando saranno
> Piu presso a noi : e tu allor li prega
> Par quell'amor che i mena, e quei verranno." *

It is also in the name of love that we must entreat
Madame de Sabran. To love was, in this world, the
great affair of her life, and if she does anything

* "Wait a little until they be closer to us; entreat them then
by that love that leads them, and they will come."

to-day in the other world, it should be exactly what she did in this.

I

Madame de Sabran without love would not be Madame de Sabran. She only loved once on this earth, but it was for life. That happened to her in 1777. She was then twenty-seven, and had been for several years the widow of a husband who, whilst he lived, was fifty years older than she was. A widow with two children, she believed that she was no longer lovable because the flower of her beauty had already departed. But she was exquisite. The publishers of her correspondence have given a portrait of her from a painting by Madame Vigée Le Brun. A more lovable creature cannot be imagined. She has fair hair, puffed out round her head, with thick eyebrows and dark eyes. As for her mouth, it is a wonder. Its arch is at once smiling and melancholy ; the voluptuous and firm lips take on an exquisite refinement as they approach the corners. A plump chin, a fragile neck, a supple figure in a dress striped according to the fashion of the time, delicate wrists, there is something gentle, caressing, soft, and magnetic in her whole person— she has no need of beauty to make her adorable.

She was twenty-seven, as we said, when she met the Chevalier Boufflers, who was thirty-nine. He was a fine soldier, a graceful poet, a very honourable man, and, above all, a most graceless scamp. She wanted to please him for she was coquettish. A woman of heart is not coquettish with impunity. This one made herself loved, but she loved still more.

Twenty-five years later, the Comtesse de Sabran,

F

having become the Marquise de Boufflers, wrote this quatrain :

> " De plaire un jour sans aimer j'eus l'envie ;
> Je ne cherchais qu'un simple amusement.
> L'amusement devint un sentiment ;
> Ce sentiment, le bonheur de ma vie."

She loved the Chevalier with her whole heart and for life. " After ten years of tenderness," she wrote to him, " I love you madly, in spite of Fate that spins the web of my days, Time that laughs at my misfortunes, and the winds that bear away all our memories."

And when she sought the reasons for so deep a feeling, she did not find them. She said :

" It is certainly not the effect of my charms (for they no longer existed when you met me) that have kept you by me; and it is not your Red Indian ways either, your moody and absent-minded air, your great appetite, and your profound slumber when one wants to chat with you, that have made me love you to madness."

Thus one loves truly only when one loves without reasons.

The passion that came to her in the flowering of her youth gave her all the happiness that one can expect in this world, that is to say, that perpetual anguish and that infinite solicitude which make one forget one's self and feel that one no longer exists in one's self, and which render life tolerable by making us forget it.

A great passion does not leave a moment of repose ; that is its benefit and its virtue. Anything is better

---

" Once I wished to please without loving ; I only sought a simple pastime. The pastime became a feeling ; the feeling became my life's happiness."

than to be too careful of one's life.   The Chevalier,
when she began to love him, was, as we said, a graceless
scamp and a very worthy man.   She had an excellent
influence over him.   She taught him to prefer
happiness to pleasure.   It was under Madame de
Sabran's inspiration that Boufflers, in his pretty tale
of " Aline," declared : " Happiness is stable pleasure.
Pleasure resembles a drop of water ; happiness is
like a diamond."

It was the same man too who wrote to the woman
who had captured his heart :

" On comparing my lot before I met you with
my lot after meeting you, it is clear to me that I
have been much happier since I reached forty than
in the years before.   Yet this is not ordinarily the
age of pleasures ; but true pleasures have no
age : they are eternal children like the angels ;
they are like you, who will always charm and love.
Let us not be sad then, or, if our reflections affect
us in spite of ourselves, let us at least draw consoling
reflections from the thought that such happiness as
we have lost was illusory, that the true still remains
with us, that our minds are capable of discerning it,
and our hearts worthy of enjoying it."

There was in this man of light and frivolous
appearance a great fund of energy and constancy.
Boufflers had a vigorous soul and a generous heart.
He is no vulgar voluptuary, this man, who, when he
was starting for Senegal, wrote to Madame de
Sabran : " My fame, if ever I acquire any, will be
my dowry and your ornament. . . . If I were
handsome, if I were young, if I were rich, if I
could offer you everything that renders men happy
in their own eyes and in the eyes of others, we would
long ago have borne the same name and shared the

same fate.   But there is nothing save a little honour
and consideration that can cause my age and my
poverty to be forgotten and can adorn me in the
eyes of all who observe us in the same way that
your tenderness beautifies you in my eyes."

"Proud! cruel! senseless!" answered Madame
de Sabran, who adhered to the moral of the two
pigeons in the fable.

She was right.   But in the Chevalier's reasons
there are a pride and a nobility which we especially
admire when we think how he kept his word ; how,
in the three years that he spent in Africa he gave
proof of the most serious qualities, and signalised his
administration by deeds of energy, of wisdom, and
of kindness.   He was an excellent man.   " The
basis of his character," says the Prince de Ligne,
who knew him intimately, " is an unbounded kindness.   He could not endure the idea of any living
thing in pain.   He would go without bread to feed
even a scoundrel, above all if he were his enemy.
' That poor rascal ! ' he used to say."

He was opposed in his administration by a poor
rascal whose career and destiny he could have
broken by a stroke of the pen.   In spite of his
anger, he did not wish to crush the man.   " When
I think," he said, " that I can only avenge myself
with a club, all my resentment is calmed."

His journal from Senegal bears as much witness
to his good heart as to his pretty wit.   During the
voyage he wrote to Madame de Sabran :

" In the midst of my inaction and the quieting
of all my violent passions I love to turn my thoughts
towards that dear house, and to see you in the midst
of your occupations and recreations, writing, painting, reading, sleeping, arranging and disarranging

everything, extricating yourself from great matters, disturbing yourself about small ones, spoiling your children, spoilt by your friends, always different and always the same, and, above all, always the same to this poor old husband who loves you so well, who will love you as long as he has a heart."

He has a horror of grandiloquence, and he gives a familiar turn to the most delicate feelings : .

" When I have not you near me, my poor head is like an old house whose porter is absent and where everything is soon topsy-turvy."

He keeps his good humour amidst all physical and moral trials :

" My life is spent in privations, in impatiences, in accidents, in uneasinesses ; all this is proof enough that your poor pigeon is far from you. Prepare yourself to console him well when you see him again. I have left my happiness with you, as we leave our money at our lawyer's."

M. Bardoux is inclined to believe that a secret marriage had united him to Madame de Sabran before his departure for Senegal. In that case, the marriage celebrated in 1797, at Bresiau, during the emigration, was only a public consecration of that union.

Such souls, at once frivolous and strong, ironical and tender, could only be produced by a long and practised processs of culture. Old Catholicism and young philosophy, dying feudalism and nascent liberty contributed to form them with their piquant contrasts and their rich diversity. Such as they were, a Boufflers, a Sabran, do honour to humanity. Those proud and charming beings could only have been born in France and in the eighteenth century.

Many things in them had doubtless become atrophied, many good and useful things; notably, belief in and respect for the old human ideal. But also how many things that are infinitely precious to us had their origin in them and through them! I mean the spirit of tolerance, the profound feeling for the rights of the individual, the instinct of human liberty.

They were able to free themselves from vain terrors; they had open minds, and that is a great virtue. They knew neither intolerance nor hypocrisy. They wished well to themselves and to others, and they conceived the idea, then new and strange, that happiness was a desirable thing. Yes, those gentle heretics were the first to think that suffering is not good and that it ought to be dealt out to men as sparingly as possible. Let a violent feudal genius, let a De Maistre, pursue them with his hatred and anger. He is right. Those amiable ladies, those benevolent landowners, slew fanaticism. But is it our part to count that a crime? Ought we not rather to smile at their indulgent astuteness? They knew that life is a dream, and they wanted it to be a pleasant dream. They replaced faith by tenderness and hope by kindness. They were benevolent. Their life was, upon the whole, innocent, and their memory is of good report.

II

M. Bardoux has just published in book form the study he has made of Madame de Custine from unpublished documents. " These documents which serve as the web of our story," he says in his preface, " will, we hope, interest the reader. They will

certainly enable him to know and esteem the better
those souls of old France, at once philosophical and
loving, who have taught us liberty of spirit as well
as the two virtues of which our epoch has most
need, practical tolerance and an indulgent prudence."
Yes, I shall answer him, if he permits me, as one
of his most attentive readers, yes, exact and delicate
chronicler of the mental and moral graces, yes, your
work interests us, not only on account of the documents it contains, but also by the charm of its
narrative, the sureness of its criticism, and the
elevation of its sentiment. You love your subject
and you make it lovable to us. You irradiate all
the outlines of your model with a pleasing and
caressing light. Your portraits are true ; they
preserve the glance and the smile, and now that
you have painted for me this lovely Delphine I can
almost believe that I knew her. I see her, crowned
with her beautiful fair hair, wandering deep in
melancholy through the glades of Fervacques,
beneath those trees she loved so much and to which
she gave the names of her absent friends. It is to
you I owe that pleasing picture. How many times
have you not had a kindred vision ! And how you
are to be envied for having lived with such charming
ghosts ! You have returned from those Elysian
fields of old France imbued with a quiet restraint :
you pity generous failings ; you value good taste,
disinterestedness, liberty of spirit, stoutness of heart,
and kindly tolerance, as the dearest treasures of life.
You think that your books will make old France
loved all the better. I think so too. I think that
a country in which the finest society in the world
was formed is the finest in the world. I said to
myself as I read your book : France is in Europe

what a peach is in a basket of fruit ; it is what is finest, sweetest, and most exquisite. What an amazing culture that was which produced a Delphine de Custine !

She was brought up as girls were then brought up, without pedantry, soberly, and with circumspection. At fifteen years of age she appeared in the world. Taken to Madame de Polignac's on a night that the Archduke and Archduchess of Austria supped there, she was very frightened, and being separated for a moment from her mother, she did not know how to act. The Archduke took it into his head to come and speak to her. She was so disconcerted that, hearing nothing of what he said and not knowing what to answer him, she adopted the plan of rushing to the other end of the room, mightily red and rumpled. All through the evening the guests amused themselves at the little savage's expense. But her mother, noticing that the disorder became her, was not annoyed.

This shyness was to remain to the end bound like a charm to Delphine's moral nature. Conformably with the destiny of great lovers, Madame de Sabran's daughter was devoted to solitude.

Delphine married in 1787 young Philippe de Custine, a son of the general. She was eighteen years old. The wedding took place in the country, at the house of Monsignor de Sabran, the bride's uncle. There was a week of rural festivities. Madame de Sabran relates that at one of these festivals, " covered lamps like those at Trianon, gave so soft a light and such faint shadows, that the water, the trees, and the people, all seemed aerial." The moon had also resolved to be at the festival ; she was reflected in the water and " would have put

dreams into the mind of the most indifferent."
And Madame de Sabran adds : " Music, songs, a
crowd of very gay and very pleased peasants followed
our steps, and grouped themselves here and there for
the pleasure of our eyes.   In the most lonely part of
the depths of the wood there was a hut, a humble
and chaste abode.   Curiosity took us there, and
we found Philemon and Baucis bent under the
weight of years and still lending one another their
mutual support as they approached us.   They
gave excellent lessons to our young couple, and the
best of these was their example.   We seated ourselves
for some time with them, and as we left them we
were melted to tears."

There is in this a new feeling for nature.   All
those fair ladies were in some degree daughters of
Jean-Jacques.   It was the pastoral on the eve of
the Terror.   Three years afterwards, old General
de Custine was arraigned before the Revolutionary
Tribunal.   His daughter-in-law, who, however, had
reason to complain of him, supported him before
the judges, and was, as has been said, his most
eloquent defender.   She was at the Palace of
Justice at six o'clock every morning ;   there she
waited until her father-in-law came out of prison ;
she threw herself on his neck and gave him news of
his friends and his family.   When he appeared
before his judges, she looked at him with eyes
bathed in tears.   She sat in front of him on a stool
beneath the tribunal.   As soon as the cross-
examination was suspended, she hastened to offer
him the cares his condition required.   Between each
session she spent the hours in secretly soliciting the
favour of the judges and the members of the com-
mittees.   Her charm availed to touch the rudest

F 2

hearts. The public prosecutor, Fouquier-Tinville, was alarmed at it.

At one of the last hearings he caused the " Septembriseurs," who were collected on the steps of the Palace of Justice, to be incited against her. The general had just been led back to prison; his daughter-in-law was preparing to descend the steps so as to regain the hackney-coach that was waiting for her in a secluded street. Timid, a little shy, she always had an instinctive fear of human crowds. Frightened by the multitude of men with pikes, and the " knitters " who shook their fists and screamed at her, she stops at the top of the steps. An un-known hand passes her a note warning her to redouble her prudence. This obscure advice puts the finishing touch to her terror; she is afraid that she will fall into a faint; she already sees her head on the end of a pike, like the head of the unhappy Princesse de Lamballe. However, she ad-vances. As she descends the steps the crowd becomes thicker and thicker, and follows her with its shouts.

" It is Custine ! It is the traitor's daughter ! "

Naked sabres are already raised against her. One sign of weakness, one false step, and all was ended. She afterwards related that she bit her tongue until the blood came so that she might not turn pale.

Spying about for a chance of safety, she looks around her and sees a woman of the people holding a little child against her breast.

" What a fine child you have, madame ! " she says to her.

" Take him," answers the mother.

Madame de Custine takes the child in her arms and crosses the courtyard of the palace through the midst of the motionless crowd. The innocent infant protected her. She could thus reach the Place Dauphine, where she gave back the child to the mother who had so generously lent him. She was saved.

You know that General de Custine ended on the scaffold and that Philippe de Custine soon followed his father. He died with the calm of an innocent man and the constancy of a hero.

A widow of twenty-three, Madame de Custine resolved to leave France with her young son, but she was arrested as an intending emigrant, and led to the prison of the Carmelites. She there awaited death with that tranquil pride which race and tradition bestow. The 9th Thermidor saved her. She was young, she was a mother; she lived; she took up again the thread of her life. Time is like a stream that bears everything away with it. A widow by the executioner's hand, she regarded her widowhood as sacred. But all the voices of youth sang plaintively in her heart, and sometimes she felt bitterly the emptiness of her soul.

In 1797 she wrote to her mother:

"I should like to find a good, reasonable, and sensible husband, one having the same tastes as I have, and possessing all the sentiments of which my existence is composed; a husband who would feel that in order to live happily it is necessary to be with you and who would lead me to you, who would find himself happy there and would love my son as his own; a husband gentle in opinions as in character, philosophical, well-informed, not fearing adversity, even acquainted with it, but who would regard it as a compensation for his ills to have a companion like your Delphine—that is the being I should like to find and whom I greatly fear I shall never meet."

No, this dream of peaceful happiness was never to be realised. Delphine de Custine was fore-doomed to the tempests. A few years more and her destiny will be fixed. It is not a reasonable and sensible husband she will meet, but an impetuous and discontented master, and she will pay with the repose of her life for an hour's happiness.

It was in 1803. She was thirty-three years old. Her blond complexion had remained as fresh as in the time when Boufflers used to call her the queen of the roses. Gentleness and pride blended seductively in her delicate countenance. She joined to the refractoriness of youth the resignation of those beings who have had a wide experience of life. The fair victim saw Chateaubriand. He was in the full radiance of his youthful fame and already he was consumed with boredom. She loved him. He allowed himself to be loved. At first he showed some passion. This letter was written whilst his feeling was fresh :

"If you knew how happy and unhappy I have been since yesterday, you would pity me. It is five o'clock in the morning. I am alone in my cell. My window is open on the gardens that are so fresh, and I see the gold of a beautiful rising sun which shows itself above the district where you live. I think that I shall not see you to-day, and I am very sad. All this is like a novel ; but have not novels their charms ? And is not all life a sad novel ? Write to me so that I may at least see something that comes from you ! Adieu, adieu until to-morrow.

"Nothing new about the accursed journey."

The journey is that to Rome, whither René, having been appointed secretary to the Embassy, was to accompany the dying Madame de Beaumont.

He set out ; at the first trees on the road he had already forgotten Delphine de Custine. On his return to France in the following year he brought her back an absent-minded, eloquent, and sullen love. She received him at the estate of Fervacques, which she had recently bought, and it is said that the old castle, enlivened by the memory of the fair Gabrielle, still possessed Henry IV's bed.

It was after one of these visits that Delphine wrote this note to him:

"I have received your letter. It has filled me with what feelings I leave you to think. It was worthy of the public of Fervacques, and yet I have refrained from reading it to them. I might well be surprised that in the midst of your lengthy enumeration there was not the smallest word about the grotto and the little room decorated with the two fine myrtles. It seems to me that they ought not to be forgotten so quickly."

One feels that in writing those lines the delicate creature was still moved by a gentle tremor. She had the memory of the heart and of the senses, this poor woman who was condemned from that moment to live only upon remembrances. Nothing was to efface from her soul the grotto and the two myrtles. Chateaubriand did not even leave her the illusion of happiness. On March 16, 1805, she wrote to Chênedollé, her confidant:

"I am not happy, but I am a little less unhappy."

Eleven days afterwards she said:

"I am more insane than ever; I love more than ever, and I am more unhappy than I can tell."

René, who sought nothing in the world but metaphors, was preparing for his journey in the East.

Madame de Custine wrote fron Fervacques on June 24, 1806:

.   .   .   .

"The 'Genius' (Chateaubriand was the 'Genius') has been here for a fortnight; he starts in two months, and it is not an ordinary departure, nor is it for an ordinary journey either. That dream of Greece is at last realised. He starts to gratify his wishes and to destroy all mine. He is at last going to accomplish what he has desired for so long. He will return in the month of November, according to what he assures me. I cannot believe it. You know how sad I was last year; think, then, what I shall be this year! I have, however, the assurance of being the best-loved; the proof of it is not very striking.

.   .   .   .

"Everything has been perfect for the past fortnight, but also everything is ended."

Everything was ended. Her instinct did not deceive her; René, in that pilgrimage, went to seek another victim. Madame de Mouchy awaited him at the Alhambra.

Madame de Custine outlived herself for twenty years. She had the courage to remain the friend of the man who no longer loved her. The world, which she had never cared for, became odious to her. She remained shut up in Fervacques.

M. Bardoux has published the charming letters that she wrote in 1816 to her friend, the celebrated Rahel de Varnhagen. These letters let us see the clearness of Delphine's soul.

She writes:

"I still love the trees! Heaven has had pity on me in leaving me 1least that affection. I turn to every one the best face I can, but annot do much, because I suffer in the depth of my soul."

And again:

"You say in a charming manner 'that one should not be alone when one is no longer young'! At least one ought to be old! But one has been no longer young for so long a time before one becomes old that therein lies all the bitterness. What consoles me is the rapidity of everything. Time passes with terrifying speed, and in spite of the sadness of the days one sees them escaping like the waters of a torrent."

She had been for a long time suffering from a malady of the liver which distress had stimulated.

In the summer of 1826 she went to Bex to breathe the air of the mountains and also to be

nearer Chateaubriand, who had accompanied his
wife, who was ill, to Lausanne. There Delphine
de Custine died without pain on July 25, 1826, in
the fifty-sixth year of her age. Chateaubriand
watched by her death-bed. He wrote these cold
and brilliant lines in his " Memoirs " :

" I have seen the woman who faced the scaffold with the greatest
courage, I have seen her, whiter than one of the Fates, clothed in black,
her figure shrunken by approaching death, her head adorned with only
her own silken hair, smile upon me with her pale lips and beautiful
teeth when she left Sécherons, near Geneva, to die at Bex, at the
entrance to the Valais.

" I heard her coffin passing in the night through the lonely streets
of Lausanne to go to its eternal abode at Fervacques."

Certainly, Madame de Sabran's daughter had
given everything and received nothing. What
matters it, since true happiness in this world consists
not in receiving but in giving ? She had the share
of joy that on earth devolves upon folk of a kindly
nature, since it was in loving that she dreamed the
dream of life. It was for her and her like that it
was written, " Blessed are they that weep ! "

P.S.—As I read over the proofs of this article I
am attacked by doubts and anxieties : I hear it
vaguely said that M. Bardoux has discovered papers
belonging to Madame de Custine, and that the
romance of that amiable lady's life receives some
hurt from them. People even go so far as to
whisper that Delphine, who wrote love letters so
well, made them do duty several times. I do not
yet wish to believe anything of this. There is always
time enough in which to become disillusioned.

M. JULES LEMAÎTRE *

JULES LEMAÎTRE has just pub-
lished his articles on the drama
under the title of "Impressions de
Théâtre." In them we may savour
something ingenuous that comes
from the heart and something
strangely experienced that comes
from the mind. That is very proper. It is well that
the heart should be ingenuous and that the mind
should not. The angels, who are all frankness,
would certainly produce very bad literature, and
one does not imagine a seraph in possession of
philosophic irony.

In dealing with human affairs M. Jules Lemaître
does not always remain serious. But his fantasy is
so charming that we are grateful to him for sometimes failing in gravity. This lettered man, who
has taken all his degrees, sometimes gaily throws his
doctor's cap into the air and amuses himself here
and there with schoolboy frolics. It is Fantasio
angling for the most venerable periwigs. It is
piquant and delightful thus to see a spice of mischief
accompanying so much learned and poetic talent;
we enjoy it as a rare spectacle. Pedantry being the
ordinary habit of important people, we are amazed
when a man of distinction pushes naturalness to

* "Impressions de Théâtre." By Jules Lemaître.

the verge of impudence. What forgetfulness of
self is revealed in this, what simplicity, and also
what philosophy! But what is perhaps most
engaging in M. Lemaître is the sudden remorse
which seizes upon him for having been cruel or
pitiless in his frolics. These are his sudden relent-
ings. For everything, even melancholy, exists in
that mobile, fluid, light, and charming soul which is
like that of some Puck who has taken his degree in
literis.

M. Jules Lemaître has a very prudent and very
subtle mind whose happy perversity consists in
incessantly doubting. That is the state to which
reflection has brought him. Thought is a frightful
thing. It is not astonishing that men should
naturally fear it. It led Satan himself to revolt.
And yet Satan was a son of God. It is the acid
that dissolves the universe, and if all men set themselves to think simultaneously, the world would
immediately cease to exist; but that misfortune is
not to be feared. Thought is the worst of things.
It is also the best. If it is true to say that it
destroys everything, one can also say that it has
created everything. We only conceive of the
universe through it, and when it demonstrates to
us that the universe is inconceivable, it but bursts
a soap-bubble that it had itself blown.

This is essentially what M. Jules Lemaître does
every Monday with diabolical grace. He tells
everything and would fain have told nothing. His
weakness is to understand too much. What authority
would he not have acquired if he were only half as
intelligent as he is! But he sees the reverse side of
ideas. Such perspicacity is not easily forgiven.
He reconciles what at first seems irreconcilable; he

instinctively carries in his charming and mobile soul the rich philosophy of Hegel: if he encounters hostile ideas he reconciles them by embracing all of them together. Then he sends them forth for an airing. That certainly is wisdom: people do not forgive it. In politics as in literature what we prize most in our friends is the partiality of their minds and the narrowness of their views. When one belongs to a party, it is first of all necessary to share its prejudices. M. Jules Lemaître belongs to no party. His intelligence is absolutely free. I regard him as a true philosopher who contemplates the world, and if he has taken a liking for the theatre, it is doubtless because he has seen in it a sort of microcosm. In truth, the theatre is the world in miniature. What is a comedy but a succession of images formed in the mystery of a single thought? Now this definition equally suits a dramatic piece and the visible universe. The images strike us; we overlook the thought that assembles them: it must be pointed out to us. This is the occupation of the philosopher or of the dramatic critic, in accordance with whether it is a question of the divine plan or one of the plans of M. Alexander Dumas.

M. Jules Lemaître occupies himself with the theatre even in his dramatic articles, and M. Francisque Sarcey has congratulated him on this. But M. Jules Lemaître occupies himself with many other things in those studies, ever diverse and ever new, or rather, he only occupies himself in them with a single thing, and that is the human soul.

It is to this that he brings everything back. Hence the interest of those pages written from day to day and bound together as if with a golden thread by philosophical feeling.

M. Jules Lemaître has no doctrine, but he has a
moral philosophy. That philosophy is bitter and
sweet, indulgent and cruel, and, above all, good.
Wisdom of the bee who makes her sting felt, yet
yields her honey ! I am very sure that, if one could
love without hating, M. Jules Lemaître would never
hate. But he is a voluptuary who never forgives
ugliness for saddening the feast of life. He loves
men, he wants them to be happy ; he believes that
there are more species of virtue than those generally
numbered in the manuals of morality. He is one
of those men who wish ill to nobody, who are
tolerant and kindly, and who, having no faith of
their own, yet hold communion with the believers.
These people are called sceptics. They believe in
nothing ; that creed compels them to deny nothing.
They are, like others, under subjection to all the
illusions of the universal mirage ; they are the playthings of appearances ; sometimes of vain forms
that make them suffer cruelly. It is useless for us
to discover the emptiness of life : a flower will
sometimes be enough to fill it up for us. It is thus
that M. Jules Lemaître, sometimes sensuous and
sometimes ascetic, amuses himself with the diversions
of the stage and enjoys at the theatre the illusion of
an illusion. He brings us exquisite impressions
which, I assure you, echo and re-echo within me in a
perfectly delightful fashion.

I have an infinite fondness for the theatre every
time he speaks to me of it. He has made me enjoy
Meilhac as I have not been able to enjoy him
unassisted, and he helps me to find a mystical and
supernatural sense in Gyp's dialogues. He also
assists me greatly in understanding Corneille and
Molière, for no one surpasses him in classical culture.

Lastly, he has revealed to me new aspects of Racine's genius, fairly familiar though I was with it.

Without flattering myself, I regard that as meritorious. But what M. Jules Lemaître shows best in his gallery is himself. He shows himself under different masks. Far from blaming him for this, I congratulate him on it. On the whole, criticism is of value only through him who writes it, and the most personal is the most interesting.

Criticism is, like philosophy and history, a sort of romance designed for those who have sagacious and curious minds, and every romance is, rightly taken, an autobiography. The good critic is he who relates the adventures of his soul among masterpieces.

I believe I have already tried to say that there is no objective criticism any more than there is any objective art, and all those who flatter themselves that they put anything but themselves into their work are dupes of the most fallacious philosophy. The truth is that we can never get outside ourselves. That is one of our greatest misfortunes. What would we not give to be able for a moment to see heaven and earth through the many-faceted eye of a fly, or to comprehend nature with the rude and simple brain of an orang-outang! But to do this is absolutely forbidden us. We cannot, like Tiresias, be a man and remember having been a woman. We are shut up in our own personality as in a perpetual prison. The best thing for us, it seems to me, is to admit this frightful condition with a good grace, and to confess that we speak of ourselves every time we have not strength enough to remain silent.

Criticism is the last in date of all literary forms; it

will perhaps end by absorbing them all. It is
admirably adapted to a very civilised society whose
memories are rich and whose traditions are already
age-long. It is particularly suited to a curious,
learned, and polished race of men. In order that it
may prosper, it demands more culture than all other
literary forms. It had for its creators Saint-
Evremond, Bayle, and Montesquieu. It derives at
once from philosophy and from history. It needed,
in order to develop, an epoch of absolute intellectual
liberty. It replaces theology, and if we look for
the universal doctor, the St. Thomas Aquinas of the
nineteenth century, is it not of Sainte-Beuve that
we must think ?

1814 *

E have already had, on 1814, without counting innumerable Russian and German works, the elegant sketch by Baron Fain, the Emperor's secretary,Commandant Koch's book, and the volume by Thiers in which the French campaign is related with patriotic emotion. M. Henry Houssaye, who had hitherto applied his remarkable gifts as an historian to ancient Greece, retraces for us to-day the civil and military events of 1814 with more precision and at greater length than his predecessors have done. He has exclusively made use of original documents: letters, orders, protocols, reports of generals and prefects, police-bulletins, newspapers of the time, memoirs : a hundred thousand documents and five hundred volumes. He has studied the chief actions of the campaign on the spot. He has carefully compared the evidence of the two opponents in each combat. He has been the first to give the exact numbers of the effective forces engaged on both sides, as well as the number of killed and wounded. His accounts of the battles are new in many respects. Moreover, they are clear and animated : M. Henry Houssage has the military feeling. He knows how to specify the decisive " moments " of actions

* " 1814." By Henry Houssaye.

and to follow masses in movement; he enters into
the mind of the soldier. But he has not limited
himself to a statement of the facts of the war; he
has studied the political situation of France and
sketched the state of the public mind, and this part
of his book is entirely new and arouses immense
interest. Never have the miseries of France in that
cursed year been painted with such bitter truth:
the Continental blockade, the fields lying fallow,
the closed factories, the complete stoppage of
business and public works, the keeping back of 25 per
cent. of non-military salaries and pensions, the
enormous increase of taxes, the Funds fallen from
87 fr. to 50 fr. 50; Bank stock worth 715 francs then
quoted at 430 francs; the exchange on bills advanced
to 12 per thousand in silver, and to 50 per thousand
in gold; metallic currency so scarce that usury
had to be tolerated and the law which fixed interest
at 5 or 6 per cent. suspended up to January 1,
1815.

Mobile columns ransacked the woods in search of
defaulters; bailiffs' men were quartered on the
mothers of those who did not surrender. In certain
districts it was the women and children who worked.
Soon the Minister of the Interior proclaimed
throughout the country, by means of the newspapers, an order that women and children could
usefully replace men in working in the fields, and
that spade tillage was to supply the place of plough
tillage which had become impossible from the lack
of horses.

The picture which M. Henry Houssaye draws is
terrible; its exactness cannot be denied, since every
feature is taken from an authentic document. It is
to be remarked, however, that the re-summoning

of the conscripts of the year XI and following years, the levy of 1815, the calling up of the mobile national guards only affected men from nineteen to forty years of age.

M. Henry Houssaye's impartial and at the same time generous labour shows us heroism and infamy side by side. In that cruel year France covered herself with glory and shame. The peasant soldiers were sublime. The royalists were abominable. These latter never saw Bonaparte undertake a war without hoping for his defeat. The invasion filled them with hope. "The Cossacks," they said, "are only brutal in the newspapers." More than twenty emissaries left Paris to give information to the hostile staff. The Chevalier de Maison-Rouge and many others guided the Russian and Prussian columns against the French army. On the entry of the Allies into Paris, the royalists displayed an impious joy and "changed that day of mourning into a day of shame."

In the Faubourg Saint-Martin, where the column of the Allies was at first stationed, men of the people, scattered and silent, looked on with sullen eyes. At the Porte Saint-Denis, where the crowd was thick, there were raised isolated cries of " Hurrah for the Emperor Alexander! Hurrah for the Allies ! " Soon the Royalists, who moved in a crowd at the head of the horse, mingled with these cheers cries of " Hurrah for the Bourbons ! Down with the tyrant ! "

As the sovereigns advanced towards the wealthy districts the boulevards took on the aspect of a triumphal way. Acclamations increased in number and strength. At the windows, on the balconies, from which there hung white flags made out of tablecloths

and sheets, elegant women waved their handker-
chiefs. Fine gentlemen wearing white cockades,
enraptured with joy, overcome with admiration,
shouted : " How handsome the Emperor Alexander
is ! How gracefully he bows ! "

When they reached the Champs-Élysées, where
the review of honour was to take place, the sovereigns
and the Prince of Schwarzenberg placed themselves
on the right side of the Avenue, as high up as the
Élysée. The troops defiled before them, whilst the
crowd, which had hastened from the boulevards,
prolonged its cheers. In order the better to see
the march past, the ladies of the aristocracy asked
the staff officers to lend them their horses a moment.
Others mounted on the cruppers behind the Red
Cossacks of the Guard.

> " J'ai vu, jeunes Francais, ignobles libertines,
>   Nos femmes, belles d'impudeur,
>   Au regards d'un Cosaque étaler leur poitrines
>   Et s'enivrer de son odeur." *

To put a worthy close to this festal day, the Vicomte
Sosthène de La Rochefoucauld, the Marquis de
Maubreuil, and certain other gentlemen conceived
the idea of casting at the feet of their conquering
foe the glorious effigy which crowned the column
erected in honour of the Grand Army. Working-
men enlisted in the drink-shops passed ropes round
the neck and trunk of the statue, whilst, in the square,
their wine-sodden comrades set to work at hauling it.
The bronze Victory which the Emperor held in his
hand was torn down. But Napoleon remained erect.
Then some wretch scrambled on to the shoulders of

* " Young Frenchmen, ignoble libertines, I have seen our women,
beautiful in their wantonness, expose their bosoms to the gaze of a
Cossack and intoxicate themselves with his odour."

the colossus and administered a couple of slaps on the bronze face.

What an ineffaceable disgrace and indignity, for which we may well blush even now ! But mark the unsullied glory and consolation of the deeds that atone for it. In defence of her violated territory our France, drained of her life blood, surrenders her last offspring, a handful of peasants, very young and very poor, almost all married, snatched pitifully from their home, their wives, and the lowly contentment of their native fields. They were nicknamed Marie-Louises. And the Marie-Louises were sublime. They scarcely knew how to sit a horse, and General Delort said of them, " I think the authorities have gone crazy to expect me to charge with such cavalry as this ! " Nevertheless they swept across Montereau like a torrent, overthrowing the Austrian battalions who were massed in the streets. They scarcely knew how to load a gun ; but at Bar-sur-Aube, one against four, they defended the woods of Lévigny with nothing but their bayonets ; and at Craonne they held out for three hours on the crest of the plateau within close range of the enemies' batteries, the grape-shot from which mowed down six hundred and fifty men out of nine hundred and twenty. With no overcoats, in eight degrees of frost, and badly shod, they marched through the snow, went without food, and still kept up their spirits.

There are glorious pages, too, about the National Guards in this Chronicle of Blood. The Spartans at Thermopylæ, the grenadiers at Waterloo, were not more intrepid than were these National Guards in their sabots and round hats at La Fère-Champenoise. M. Henry Houssaye has drawn a flaming picture of this battle from an unpublished account by one of the generals. The National Guards numbered four thousand; they convoyed two hundred waggons of ammunition. Attacked at the outset by six thousand cavalry; they pierced through this force and forged ahead. The enemy received reinforcements; four thousand Prussians, and then the whole cavalry of the two vast armies; twenty thousand cavalry surrounded the French, now reduced to less than two thousand and formed up in three squares. The National Guards refused to surrender. Their cartridges being exhausted, they received the charges at the point of their bayonets, sorely bent by the repeated shocks. Finally a fresh discharge of seventy cannon opened a breach in the living walls. The cavalry hurled itself into the gap. Scarcely five hundred of those heroes escaped. The Tsar was profoundly moved by this despairing resistance. Later on, when Talleyrand talked to him of the desire of the French for the return of the Bourbons, the Russian sovereign called to mind the National Guards at La Fère-Champenoise, falling before the grape-shot to the cry of " Long live the Emperor."

The Old Guard was admirable in its constancy and firmness. Those veterans, who had seen Marengo and Hohenlinden, " always grumbled and followed him." They did not desert their emperor.

After the capitulation of Paris, on the 3rd of April, at Fontainebleau, Napoleon placed himself in the middle of the courtyard and summoned the officers and non-commissioned officers of the Friant division. When they had formed a circle, he said in a loud voice: " Officers, non-commissioned officers, and soldiers of my old guard, the enemy has stolen

three marches on us.   He has entered Paris.   I have
offered the Emperor Alexander a peace bought at a
great sacrifice: restricting France to her old boundaries, renouncing our conquests, losing all we have
won since the Revolution.   Not only has he refused
it, he has gone further still: at the perfidious
suggestion of those emigrants to whom I granted
life and whom I loaded with favours, he authorises
them to wear the white cockade, and soon he will
want to substitute it for our national cockade.   In
a few days I shall attack him in Paris.   I count upon
you."   The emperor expected a burst of acclamation.
But the grumblers kept silence.   Surprised, uneasy,
he asked them:

"Am I right ? "   At that word they all shouted
with a single voice: "Long live the Emperor !
To Paris !   To Paris ! "—" We had kept silence,"
says General Pelet, with heroic simplicity, "because
we thought it unnecessary to answer."

M. Henry Houssaye has written an impartial
history in a sober style.   No phrases, no vain and
decorative words ;   everywhere the truth of facts
and the eloquence of happenings.   To give an
idea of his manner, I will quote a passage giving
a picture of the capital during the Battle of
Paris:

"The apprehension of danger caused more trouble and alarm than
the danger itself.   The Parisian population, which had been terrified
since the first days cf February by the very name of the Cossacks,
and which trembled on the 27th, 28th, and 29th of March at the
idea of pillage and fire, recovered its composure when it heard the
cannon.   During the battle, the great boulevards wore their accustomed aspect, with this difference that most of the shops were closed
and that few carriages passed.   But the crowd was more numerous,
more animated, more bustling than usual.   It was the boulevard
such as it was wont to be at festivals and on days of a change in the

government : a stream of pedestrians moving backwards and forwards, stationary groups engaged in discussion, all the chairs occupied, all the cafés full. The weather was cloudy and agreeable. At Tortoni's, the exquisites ate ices and drank punch as they watched the work-girls pattering by, and some prisoners marching along the street escorted by gendarmes, and crowds of wounded carried on stretchers and in small ammunition waggons and in cabs that had been requisitioned. The crowd appeared in no way dismayed. In some there was uneasiness, in others curiosity ; in the greater number tranquillity and even indifference was dominant. With the help of the national self-respect—or perhaps speaking more correctly, the Parisian vanity—they regarded the combat taking place at Romainville as a matter of no importance, the result of which moreover, was not in doubt. If it was observed that the noise of the cannon was drawing nearer, a fact which seemed to point to the enemy's advance, there were never lacking persons who replied with a knowing air : ' It is a manœuvre, the Russians are making the best use of their time.' The general quiet was, however, disturbed between two and three o'clock. A drunken lancer went down the Faubourg Saint-Martin at full gallop, shouting : ' Fly, every man for himself ! ' A panic was produced. Every one fled at a run. The movement of the crowd extended as far as the Pont-Neuf and the Champs-Élyseés. But this false alarm was transient, the boulevards filled anew."

According to the judgment of experts, Napoleon's two military masterpieces are the campaigns of 1796 and 1814. These two campaigns, very dissimilar as to their definite results, present this analogy, that Napoleon, disposing of very restricted military forces, had to fight an enemy four or five times his superior in numbers, and in both cases he employed the same tactics.

M. Henry Houssaye has established, it is true, that in several battles in the French campaign the disproportion of the forces has been exaggerated. It none the less remains true that the emperor operated with a small army. Military writers have found ground for debate about certain campaigns, those of 1812 and 1813, for instance. They have

had reason to dispute the good management of the
battles of Eylau, of Moskova, of Leipzig, but nobody,
no foreigner at least, has dared to disparage the
campaign of 1814. It is remarkable that the fewer
men Napoleon has to lead, the more strategical
resources he finds. His genius loves small armies.
In the French campaign he never had more than
thirty thousand men concentrated beneath his hand.
But by his divination of the enemy's plans and by the
crushing rapidity of his marches, he often succeeded
in reaching and fighting the enemy on almost
equal terms. Moreover, great captains seem to
have preferred small armies to large ones. Turenne
and Frederick were never such excellent artists as
when they had few men in hand, and we must
remember the famous saying of Marshal de Saxe:
" Beyond forty thousand men I am out of my
element." Modern war may have other require-
ments ; still this saying of Marshal de Saxe's gives
food for thought.

At the beginning of the campaign of 1814, Napoleon,
who had not yet concentrated all his forces, was
compelled to fight against the two united armies at
La Rothière. He retreated on Troyes, afterwards
on Nogent. The Allies then believed that they had
nothing more to do but to march on Paris. To facili-
tate their march, they divided themselves into two
great columns, one of which followed the course of
the Marne, the other of the Aube, and afterwards
the Seine. In order to further the blunder they
were about to commit, Napoleon kept quiet for four
days, then, when the separation had taken place, he
advanced with his small army between the two
hostile columns, burst upon Blücher, surprised the
four corps in echelons on the Marne, and destroyed

them in four battles in four days. Then he turned upon the left column, that of Schwarzenberg, inflicted three successive defeats upon it, and forced it to retreat.

All that genius could do, Napoleon did. But genius has in this world an opponent of its own stature—chance. Chance, fatality, placed itself in several decisive circumstances on the side of the Allies. At least the great captain hoped up to the end, and neglected nothing to summon fortune back.

The third part of the campaign, the great movement on Lorraine, was of an unprecedented audacity. Napoleon, boldly uncovering Paris, threw himself on the rear of the allied armies ; he summoned back to him the French garrisons of the Rhine, then, with his army thus doubled, he cut off the enemy from their base. For a moment the headquarter staffs of the Allies believed themselves lost.

At the council of war at Pougy on the 23rd of March, a retreat was under consideration. " The general movement of Napoleon on Saint-Dizier," M. Henry Houssaye very well says, " admirable in its conception, is justified in practice by this single fact that for an instant it inspired the Allies with the idea of retreating on the Rhine." That admirable manœuvre was on the point of succeeding, victory, safety was in sight, when the Allies learned through couriers who had fallen into their hands and through Talleyrand's emissaries that treason was waiting them, that it was summoning them to Paris. They marched there. But with what fears ! Since their entrance on the territory of France they had not ceased to tremble, and their fear increased with their progress on the soil that Napoleon and the peasants defended.   On the 3rd of April, when the Emperor, at Fontainebleau, had no longer more than a fragment of a sword and a handful of men, they still trembled: "That terrible Napoleon," said the emigrant Faugeron in his "Memoirs," from which M. Houssaye quotes, "we thought we saw him everywhere.   He had beaten us all one after another.   We were always afraid of the audacity of his enterprises, the rapidity of his marches, and his masterly combinations."

We saw the Germans again in France eighteen years ago, we saw our fortified posts surrender, and starving Paris open her gates to the victorious enemy.   This time we did not find a Napoleon We did not see, rising on the blood-stained tracks at the call of a great captain, those mortally wounded victories of which the eloquent Lacordaire speaks. But if a great captain was wanting to France, France was not wanting to herself.   Thanks be to God, the shame of 1814 was spared to the France of 1870.   We did not see Frenchmen in the ranks of the enemy.   Patriotism, born with democracy, is to-day purer, prouder, more delicate, more exquisite than ever; it is in the full flower of its feeling.

Compare the entry of the Allies to Paris in 1814 with the entry of the Prussians in 1871.   In 1814 the crowd of curious persons flocked to the passage of the conquerors.   The boulevards took on a festival air.   The entire city gave itself up to the spectacle of the Cossacks, acclaimed by a handful of royalists.   In 1814, as M. Henry Houssaye says, "Paris did not understand the dignity of deserted streets and closed windows."

TO-MORROW

 HAVE received the following letter :

" SIR,

" For a book which I am preparing, and which will appear in the autumn through the firm of Perrin, I am eagerly desirous of having an answer to the following questions :

" What do you think the literature of to-morrow will be, that which is still in embryo in the attempts of young writers of from twenty to thirty years of age ? What direction will it take under the contrary influences that divide it (idealism—positivism, æsthetic and philosophic patriotism—foreign letters and learning, objectivism—subjectivism, the doctrine of the exception—the triumph of democracy, &c.) ? Is the want of grouping that characterises it a good or an evil ? Is there not a profound schism between the traditions on which literature has hitherto lived and the new symptoms which we feel everywhere and which we cannot define ? Do you see a good or a bad sign in this dominance of all the arts, that of writing included, by modern criticism ? What is the future to be ?

" Accept, sir, &c.,
" CHARLES MORICE."

Such a letter is of a nature to flatter me and, above all, to embarrass me. But, to tell the truth, every reader of " Life and Letters " has a right to ask me the questions M. Charles Morice asks me. That is why I am going to answer as well as I can, and publicly :

To M. Charles Morice.

" Sir,

"You are an æsthete and you are ready to believe that I am one. That is flattering me. I shall confess to you, and my readers know it, that I have little fondness for discussing the nature of the beautiful. I have but a moderate confidence in metaphysical formulæ. I believe that we shall never know exactly why a thing is beautiful.

"And I console myself for that. I prefer to feel rather than to understand. Perhaps in this there is some laziness on my part. But laziness leads to contemplation, contemplation conducts to beatitude, and beatitude is the reward of the elect. I have not the talent for dissecting masterpieces in the way that our lamented colleague, M. Maxime Gaucher, did so excellently in these pages. I make this confession to you, sir, so that you may not be disagreeably surprised if my answers are entirely lacking in the systematic spirit. You ask me my opinion of the younger literature. I should like to answer you in smiling and auspicious words. I should like to turn aside the presages of misfortune. I cannot, and I am constrained to confess that I expect nothing good from the immediate future.

"This confession costs me something. For nothing is so pleasant as to be in love with youth and to be loved by it. It is the supreme recompense and consolation. Young people extol so sincerely those who praise them! They admire and they love as one ought to admire and love— to excess. There is no one like them for generously distributing bays. Oh! how I should like to be in communion with the new literature, in sympathy with future works. I should like to be able to

acclaim the verses and the ' proses' of the decadents. I should like to join myself with the boldest
impressionists, to fight with them and for them. But
it would be fighting in the darkness, for I utterly fail
to comprehend those verses and those ' proses,'
and you know that Ajax himself, the bravest of the
Greeks who were before Troy, asked Zeus that he
might fight and perish in the light.

$$\text{Ἐν δὲ φάει καὶ ὄλεσσον . . .}$$

" I am pained by it, but I feel myself attached
by no bond to the young decadents. If they were
Senegalese or Laplanders they would not seem
stranger to me.

" That is literally the case. Look you : there has
been offered for sale for a halfpenny, along the
boulevards, an account of the Hottentots in the
Jardin d'Acclimatation. I did not fail to buy it,
because I am, by nature, a lounger and a muser.
Similarly, in the time of the League, another
Parisian for whom I have a great deal of fellow-
feeling, Pierre de l'Estoile, bought all the lampoons
that were cried under his window in the old Rue
Saint-André-des-Arcs. I have read that notice
with some pleasure, and I found in it a song to the
moon, which a poet, Namaqua or Korana, composed
ten or a thousand years ago, I don't know which, and
which is sung, so they say, in the kraals, under the
bark huts, to the sound of savage guitars.

" This is the song :

" ' Be welcome, dear moon ! We regretted thy
beautiful light. Thou art a faithful friend. For
thee is this tender lamb and this excellent tobacco.
But if thou dost not receive our offerings we will eat
and we will smoke for thee, dear moon.'

" That is not a very poetical song. The Hottentots have neither god nor poetry ; or at least they
think that God does not occupy himself in human
affairs ; in which, I say it in passing, they think
like several of our great philosophers. The Hottentots
have no ideal. And yet their little song to the moon
touches me. I understand it when it is translated
for me. But MM. José-Maria de Heredia and
Catulle Mendès, in emulation with one another,
vainly translate for me the sonnets of the new
school ; they convey absolutely no meaning to my
mind. I repeat it, I find myself nearer to a poor
savage than to a decadent. I cannot conceive
what impressionism is. Symbolism astonishes me.
You will tell me, sir, that it is intended for that very
purpose. I believe it is not, and that it is a disease.
I even believe that people die of it. For I no longer
hear much talk about the sonnets of M. Ghil. Two
years ago I used to receive decadent newspapers and
symbolist reviews ; the good and faithful publisher of
the new ' Pléiade,' M. Léon Vannier, used to send me
strange little books which amused me infinitely in
my hours of perversity ; he even came to see me.
He pleased me greatly. He is a gentle and joyous
man. On his door-step in the evening he gazes at
the great outlines of the shadow of the towers of
Notre-Dame, and dreams that he is cradling the
childhood of a new Hugo. Nowadays, however,
nothing arrives from him, and I fear that the race
of symbolists is three parts extinct. Destiny, as
the poet says, has barely shown them to the
earth.

" They were extraordinary, those young poets
and those young prose-writers ! Nothing like them
had been seen in France, and it would be curious

to investigate the causes that produced and shaped
them. I do not wish to go too deep into this
investigation. I shall not trace them back as far
as the primitive nebula. That would be going too
far and not going far enough ; for, indeed, there
was something before the primitive nebula. I shall
only go back to naturalism, which began to invade
literature in the middle of the Second Empire. It
began with brilliance, and at the very start it produced a masterpiece: ‘Madame Bovary.’ And
let us make no mistake about it, naturalism was
excellent in many respects. It marked a return to
nature which romanticism had foolishly despised.
It was the revenge of reason. Ill luck brought it
about that naturalism soon came under the dominion
of a vigorous talent, but a talent narrow, brutal,
coarse, tasteless, and regardless of that moderation which is the whole of art. I believe I have
described closely enough the new candidate for the
French Academy, he who recently said with equal
elegance and exactness: ‘I have divided my visits
into three groups.’

“With him naturalism immediately fell into the
ignoble. Having descended to the last degree of
platitude, of vulgarity, destitute of all intellectual
and plastic beauty, ugly and stupid, it disgusted
delicate minds. You are aware that reactions know
no half measures. The most necessary are, perhaps,
the fiercest. The school of Médan raised up symbolism. Similarly, in the Roman Empire, if we
can compare little things with great, a coarse
sensualism produced asceticism.

“Rightly taken, our young poets are mystics.
I recently came across this phrase in the life of one
of the Fathers of the Thebaid: ‘He read the

scriptures in order to find allegories in them.' The
disciples of M. Mallarmé must have allegories and
all the esotericism of the ancient theurgies. No
poetry without a hidden meaning. It is even said
that the master requires that a book to be excellent
should present three superimposed meanings. The
first meaning, quite literal and crude, will be understood by the idle man who, stopping under the
galleries of the Odéon or outside the book-sellers'
shops, glances through the books without cutting
their leaves. The second and more spiritual meaning
will appear to the reader who uses a paper-knife.
The third meaning, infinitely subtle and yet
voluptuous, will be the reward of the initiated who
knows how to read the lines in a learned and secret
order. What is this order ? Perhaps 3, 6, 5, which
corresponds to the nocturnal eye of Osiris. But
that is only a conjecture. I am afraid that the third
sense will for ever escape me.

" I do not know exactly what a contemporary of
Ptolemy Philadelphus would have made of the
poem of Lycophron. But it seems to me that
certain subtle Alexandrians must have had their
brains fashioned a little like those of M. Mallarmé
and his disciples.

"I see beside them a swarm of young novelists, very
reasonable and not in the least symbolist. They are
those who model themselves on M. Emile Zola. You
know, sir, that M. Zola's novels can be easily imitated.
In them the method of procedure is always visible,
the effect always exaggerated, the philosophy always
puerile. The extreme simplicity of the construction renders them as easy to copy as Byzantine
virgins ; I ought, perhaps to have said, as the pictures
manufactured at Epinal. Others, as young and also

more original, express their own ideal. Unhappily
they are for the most part very rigid and very strained;
they aim too much at effect and are too anxious to
show their powers. There again is one of the blots
on contemporary art. It is brutal. It is afraid
neither of shocking nor of displeasing. People
believe they have done everything when they have
insulted morals and shocked the decencies. That is
a great mistake. It is excusable and almost touching
in young people, because in their case it is mingled
with an infinite candour. They do not know that
in a polished society the voluptuary is as interested
as the virtuous in the preservation of morality and
respect for the decencies. They do not know, in
short, that all instincts find their advantage in the
long run in a high standard of public morals. But one
would like the feeling of respect to be less alien from
the hearts of our young novelists.

" What is thoroughly praiseworthy in them is
the knowledge they have of the craftsmanship of
their art. If they construct their books badly, it is
less from ignorance than from disdain : for you
know that a well-constructed book is, according
to the reigning prejudice, by that very fact, a contemptible book. It is enough for M. Octave
Feuillet to be a master of construction for him to be
discredited. The prize is for our young people,
and they carry it off with remarkable address.
There are excellent workers who have their trade at
their fingers' ends. I know some, very well informed,
even learned, and well equipped for writing, who
inspire genuine hope.

" And when one thinks that a very young man
experiences great difficulties in showing himself to
advantage in a form which, like the novel, demands

a certain experience of life and the world, one does not despair of the future of that literary form which France has so happily renovated so many times since the fifteenth century.

"However, I confess to you, sir, it is with some mistrust and a little sadness that I see these piles of yellow books heaped up on my table. Two or three novels a day are now published. How many, out of the number, are destined to survive ? The eighteenth century has not bequeathed us ten, and it was one of the finest centuries for prose fiction. We have too many and too bulky novels. Big books ought to be left to the scholars. Are not the loveliest stories short ? What are always read are 'Daphnis et Chloé,' 'La Princesse de Clèves,' 'Candide,' 'Manon Lescaut,' each of which is only as thick as your little finger. It is necessary to be light in order to fly across the ages. The true French genius is swift and concise. It was incomparable in the primitive novel—*la nouvelle*. I would wish that the beautiful French *nouvelle* might still be written ; I should wish it to be elegant and easy, and to move swiftly. Therein, do you not agree with me, lies the supreme elegance of a writer ?

"A great deal can be said in a small number of pages. A novel ought to be read at a sitting. I wonder at the fact that those written to-day invariably consist of three hundred and fifty pages. It suits the publisher. But it does not always suit the subject.

"Permit me, sir, to leave for a moment unnoticed the details of the classification of 'recent literature,' as you, yourself, have laid it down. An examination of the tendencies of our intellectual youth would take us much too far. You testify to the fact that those tendencies are very divergent.

In fact it is more and more difficult to distinguish clearly defined groups. There are no longer schools, no longer traditions, no longer disciples. It was doubtless necessary to arrive at this excess of individualism. You ask me whether it is a good or an ill to have reached it. I shall answer you that excess is always an ill. Look how literatures are born and how they die. In their beginning they produce only collective works. There is not the shadow of an individual tendency in the ' Iliad ' and in the ' Odyssey '; several hands laboured at those great monuments without leaving a distinct impress upon them. To collective works succeed individual works ; at first the author seems still to be afraid of showing himself too much. He is a Sophocles ; but little by little personality displays itself more. It is irritated, it is tormented, it is exasperated. Already Euripides cannot refrain from figuring by the side of the gods and heroes. He wants us to know what he thinks about women and what his philosophy is. Such as he is, in spite of his indiscretion, perhaps even on account of his indiscretion, he interests me infinitely. However, he marks the decadence, the irreparable and rapid decadence. The fine epochs of art have been epochs of harmony and tradition. They have been organic. In them everything was not left to the individual. A man is a small thing, even a great man, when he is all alone. We do not pay enough heed to the fact that a writer, even if he is very original, borrows more than he invents. The language he speaks does not belong to him ; the form into which he pours his thought, ode, comedy, story, has not been created by him ; he does not own either his syntax or his prosody. His very

G 2

thought is inspired into him from all sides. He has received the colours, he only brings the shades, though these are, I know, sometimes infinitely precious. Let us be sensible enough to recognise it : our works are far from being all ours. They grow in us, but their roots are everywhere in the nourishing soil. Let us admit then that we owe a good deal to everybody and that the public is our collaborator.

" Let us not struggle to break the bonds that attach us to that public ; on the contrary, let us multiply them.   Let us not become too rare or too singular.   Let us be natural, let us be true.   Let us efface ourselves so that there may be seen in us not a man, but humanity.   Let us not torture ourselves : beautiful things are born easily.   Let us forget ourselves : our only enemy is ourselves.   Let us be modest.   It is pride that precipitates the decadence of letters.   Claudian died better pleased with himself than Virgil.   Lastly, let us be simple.   Let us say what we mean in such a way as to be understood ; let us think that we shall be truly great and good only if we address ourselves, I do not say to all, but to many.

" There, sir, is the advice that I would venture to give to our young people.   But I am afraid that long experience is necessary to discover its profound import.   Luckily it is useless to those who are born with great genius.   These are our masters from their cradles, and criticism, far from teaching them anything, ought to learn everything from them.

" You ask me, sir, ' if I see a good or a bad sign in the dominance of all the arts, that of writing included, by criticism.'   I have already said a few words on the excellence of criticism, when writing of

a book by M. Jules Lemaître. I think that criticism,
or rather the literary essay, is an exquisite form of
history. I say more : it is the true history, that of
the human mind. It demands, for adequate treat-
ment, rare faculties and a learned culture. It
presupposes an intellectual refinement that only
long ages of art have succeeded in producing. That
is why it only shows itself in societies that are already
old, and at the exquisite hour of their first decline.
It will survive all the other forms of art if, as a
scholium of Virgil, which I have seen quoted somewhere by M. Littré, says, ' we weary of everything
except comprehending.' But I believe rather that
men will never weary of loving, and that they will
always need poets to give them serenades.

"' What is the future to be ? ' you ask, sir, as you
end your letter.

" The future is in the present, it is in the past.
It is we who make it ; if it is bad it will be our
fault. But I do not despair of it.

" I perceive that I have not said the hundredth
part of what I wanted to say. I wanted, for
example, to try and indicate the new conditions
that democracy and industry will bring to the art
of to-morrow. I imagine that those conditions
will be decidedly tolerable. That will be the
subject of a letter shortly.

"Accept, &c."

M. CHARLES MORICE

 CHARLES MORICE has done me the honour of replying publicly to my answer, in the form of a pamphlet published by the "Librairie Académique." *

M. Charles Morice is very young, he himself belongs to the literature of to-morrow. He is a poet full of promise, of a talent already erudite and rare. He is also a man of meditative mind, skilful in intellectual speculations. How could he despair of a future on which he labours ardently ? Why should he not offer up his prayers for the triumph of an art that is his own ? He is in a hurry to see new writings. Those of to-day no longer have anything to say to him.

His perfect courtesy does not allow it to be seen, but I divine that he thinks we are lasting too long. I have some reason for not sharing his impatience. It is prudent to be always ready to depart, and I flatter myself that I am prudent. However, if by prolonging our peaceable intercourse my friends and I can attain to the last elms that border the way of life, I shall give thanks to the divine or natural providence that orders all things. I do not believe that the generation to which I belong has done

* " Réponse à M. Anatole France."

badly. It seems to me that it has been lacking neither in art, nor in reason, nor in feeling.

It seems to me that from the first poems of M. Sully-Prudhomme, from M. François Coppée's "Les Intimités," to the "Essais psychologiques" of M. Paul Bourget and the Vicomte Eugène Melchior de Vogüé's "Voyages intellectuels," twenty smiling years of poetry and study have flowed by. For my own part, I have lived those twenty years with delight. I have valued several of my contemporaries, I have loved and admired some of them; I can call myself happy. Let us advance our claims: we have cultivated art and studied nature. We have approached as close to truth as we could; we have discovered a little portion of beauty which still slept without form and without colour in the greedy earth. We have never declaimed, we have been conscientious artists and true poets. We have wished to learn a great deal without hoping to know a great deal. We have maintained our veneration for the masters; we have doubtless failed in great inspiration, in audacity, and in adventurous genius; but we have possessed, I believe, the sense of the exquisite and the sense of finish. I say it very proudly: O you, my contemporaries, my companions in labour, you have deserved well of letters, and the books you have published during the past nineteen years count for something among the consolations and the just grounds of our country's pride!

There is one work, among others, for which I am infinitely grateful to my contemporaries. It is for having displayed that happy intelligence which pardons and reconciles. They have put an end to the literary quarrels which romanticism had furiously

kindled.   Thanks to our masters, Sainte-Beuve and
Taine, thanks to us also, it is to-day permissible to
admire all forms of beauty.   The old scholastic
prejudices exist no longer.   We can at the same time
love Racine and Shakespeare.   I have travelled over
the field of letters with men of good will who sought
to comprehend everything.   The road has seemed
to me short and pleasant.   Let us be thanked at
least for having consolidated the liberty of sentiment
and the literary truce that is enjoyed at the present
hour.   It is possible that public indifference may
have helped us in our task.   All reconciliations
result from weariness of strife.   Finally, wrongly
or rightly, people are tired of quarrels about words.
Literary fanaticism will awaken no more echoes.
The revolutions which may be made by the younger
school will pass almost unperceived.   For my own
part I will not blame the public for its scepticism
in regard to new forms of art.   " A whole people
is never guilty," said old King Louis Philippe at
Claremont.   That is a wise saying.   It is imprudent
and vain to lay the blame on everybody.   And then
I do not believe in premeditated novelties.   The
best manner of being an innovator is to be one in
spite of oneself and to be as little of one as possible.
The conditions of art have changed little since
Homer.   I cannot imagine that they will change
much from now until the Universal Exhibition.
Humanity itself is very slowly modified.   Whatever
be the impatience of the young poets to give new
sensations to man, they must wait until man has
acquired new senses.   Now, such acquisitions are
made with infinite slowness.   M. Jules Soury
thinks, following Doctor Magnus, that the Greeks
of Homer did not perceive colours ; that for them

the sky was not blue, the trees were not green, the
roses were not rose-coloured, and that the universe
was reflected in their barbarous eyes as an immense
grey background. Mr. Gladstone thinks so too.
But neither Mr. Gladstone, nor M. Jules Soury,
nor Doctor Magnus are very sure of it; and if I
were sure of anything it would be precisely of the
contrary.

It is very probable that the first Hellenes saw
nature almost as we see it to-day, and that thousands
of centuries will pass before the human eye is
perfected to the point of seeing new tints. As much
must be said of hearing and even of smell. The
artists of to-morrow seem to believe that a short
time hence we shall distinguish ultra-violet. It is
ultra-violet which they persist in showing us.
And when we say we cannot see it, they answer
that it is because of our disinclination.

They flatter us when they suppose that we have
exquisite senses; our senses are almost as gross
as those of our fathers. Such as they are, they
procure us many joys and many pains. But they
are not adequate to enable us to perceive the
delicacies of the new art. I do not forgive the
symbolists for their profound obscurity. " You
speak in enigmas," is a reproach that the warriors
and the kings frequently make to one another in
the tragedies of Sophocles. The Greeks were
subtle, yet they wished people to express themselves
clearly. I think they were right. I have passed
the happy age in which one admires what one does
not understand. I love the light. M. Charles
Morice does not promise me enough of it for my
liking. I want to understand at once, and that is a
demand which seems to him insupportable.

" You are in a very great hurry ! " he seems to
say. " Can you be one of those frivolous beings
who cannot endure anything serious ? Why do you
not meditate upon the writings of the young school ?
Why do you not delve into them ? Why do you
not plumb them ? " And he adds in characteristic
terms : " The artist may be allowed the licence of
demanding from the well-disposed reader a serious, a
patient attention." I answer with perfect frankness
that, unless I am mistaken, this is a grievous maxim, a
dangerous precept which would be enough to make
me fall out with the whole new poetic theory and
take away from me the desire of seeing the fulfilment of M. Charles Morice's literary prophecies.

The more I see, the more I feel that nothing
except what is easy is beautiful.

I have got over the taste for obscurities. In my
opinion, the poet or the story-teller who would
be entirely without reproach will avoid causing
the least trouble or creating the least difficulty
for his reader. If he is wise he will not exact attention ; he will surprise it. He will fear to practise
on the patience of lettered people, and will think
he is not readable unless he can be easily read.

Science has the right of requiring application and
attentive thought from us. Art has not that
right. It is, by its nature, useless and charming.
Its function is to please ; it has no other. It must be
attractive without any conditions. I know well that
in these times everything has been jumbled up, and
that some persons have desired to apply the rules of
scientific work to literary production. M. Zola,
who does not fear ridicule, has somewhere said :
" We, men of science " ! There is, however,
some difference between a song and a treatise on

descriptive geometry. The pleasures that art procure ought never to cost the least fatigue.

M. Charles Morice, it is true, lets us understand that the new art is obscure and painful in spite of itself, against its will, and only because of the extreme difficulty it finds in realising its ideal. It proposes to itself, this new art, very difficult things, whilst the old art kept to very easy things. I hear this with some surprise. I did not think that all that had hitherto been done in letters had been so easy to do. But let us know what function the art of the future has allotted itself. It wants to take hold, not only of the mind, like the classics, or of matter, like the naturalists (it is not I who say this), but of the entire human being. It wants to make a synthesis of literatures ; it wants, according to M. Charles Morice's formula, " to suggest all that is man by all that is art."

That is a novelty. And, like all novelties, it is as old as the world. Art has in all times wished to represent man, and man in his entirety. This has not been always avowed, because at first there were ages of simplicity in which there were no disputes about the nature of the beautiful ; but in all times it has been thought, for it is the most natural thing in the world. Scholars claim that " Hop o' my Thumb " is older than the " Iliad " ; this is not impossible. Well, the old women who used to tell the history of " Hop o' my Thumb " to the children of Sapta Sindhou also had the idea of representing in their own way " all that is man by all that is art," as M. Charles Morice says. It was the same thing, do not doubt it, that was aimed at by the village poet who made this song, which was well known to La Fontaine :

"Adieu cruelle Jeanne.
Puisque tu n'aimes pas,
Je remonte mon âne
Pour galoper au trépas
—Vous y perdrez vos pas,
Nicolas ! " *

There, without any obscurity, body and soul, is all man and all woman. It is a long time since the laurels have been cut in the woods of Parnassus. They shoot up again, but always from the same stumps. Without troubling ourselves about so many systems, let us recognise this candidly : ancients and moderns, classics, romantics, naturalists, have represented, each in his own fashion, man and all man.

What is newer in M. Charles Morice's formula is the word " suggest." That I confess is terribly modern and even modernist. I feel its full value. Suggestion is something new, something still mysterious and ill-defined. The poet, to-day, ought to be suggestive. He suggests. What ? That which cannot be expressed. He is the Bernheim of the unheard, the Charcot of the un-utterable. No longer to express, but to suggest ! At bottom, that is the whole new poetic theory. It forbids ideas from being represented as was formerly done ; it commands sensations to be awakened.

They were barbarous and Gothic times when words had a meaning ; then writers expressed thoughts. Henceforth, for the young school, words have no longer a special significance, nor is there any necessary relation between them. They have been

* " Adieu cruel Joan. Since you do not love, I am mounting my ass again to gallop to death."—" You will have your pains for your trouble, Nicolas ! "

emptied of their meaning and freed from their syntax. They exist, however, in the state of sonorous and graphic phenomena ; their new function is to suggest images according to the chance form of letters and sound of syllables. In the poetry of the future their part is exactly that of the little bottles which Doctor Luys slips into young Esther's neck, and which provoke the subject to rapture, laughter, or tears, but which, to spectators uncontrolled by hypnotic influence, seem, what in fact they are, empty phials. That single word, *suggest*, has told me a great deal about M. Charles Morice's tendencies.

Would you like an example of the suggestive style ? Here is a sonnet on Edgar Poe :

" Tel qu'en lui-même enfin l'éternité le change
Le poète suscite avec un glaive nu
Son siècle épouvanté de n'avoir pas connu
Que la mort triomphait dans cette voix étrange

Eux comme un vil sursaut d'hydre oyant jadis l'ange
Donner un sens plus pur aux mots de la tribu
Proclamèrent très haut le sortilège bu
Dans le flot sans honneur de quelque noir mélange.

Du sol et de la nue hostiles ô grief
Si notre idée avec ne sculpte un bas relief.
Dont la tombe de Poe éblouissante s'orne

Calme bloc ici-bas chu d'un désastre obscur
Que ce granit du moins montre à jamais sa borne
Aux noirs vols du Blasphème épars dans le futur."

There is, in these fourteen unpunctuated lines by the master of the school, an abundant spring of sensations ; this sonnet is suggestive in the highest degree ; it affects sensitive subjects delightfully.

But it has no more effect on readers who are awake than Doctor Luys' empty phials. It is the new art. The misfortune is that all of us cannot read in our sleep.

M. Charles Morice recognises that poetry, in the paths which it is entering, will not fail to turn its back upon the crowd. He regards this separation as necessary, and thinks that each of them ought to take its own way. " The public," he says, " and the poets hardly follow the same way. The deviation between them and us is incessantly being accentuated; and, do not fail to note it, our very language, if we keep it pure, removes them from us, for little by little they have perverted that marvellous instrument, and now hardly enjoy anything except wrong terms and badly constructed metaphors, things without a name."

If I were in M. Charles Morice's place I should not be reconciled to this so easily. It is not good for a poet to live alone. Poets are vain and tender; they need to be admired and loved. Their pride is exasperated by solitude, and, when people do not listen to them, they sing out of tune. Disdain is very becoming to philosophers and scholars; with artists it is but a grimace. And why should not the poet take pleasure in being listened to by many ? He speaks to the feeling, and feeling is more wide-spread than intelligence.

I know well that there are no exquisite feelings without a certain intellectual culture. To enjoy poetry a moral preparation is necessary. But souls thus prepared are more numerous than people think; they form the poets' public. When one is a poet, one ought not to despise them.

M. Charles Morice will answer us that it is the

general public that he despises, the crowd, the profane vulgar. He is certain that it does not count in art. It ignores us and we ignore it. It has its own authors who work for it to perfection. It asks nothing from us. It does no harm, since it does not think. Is it true that it " perverts that marvellous instrument " ? I am sure that in fact it does wear out the language, for it makes use of it. But, after all, it has a right to do so : the language is made for it as well as for us. I will even add that it is made by it. Yes, " the marvellous instrument " is the work of the ignorant crowd. Lettered people have worked at a small part of it, and that part is not the best. That is the great point. The language is not the personal property of the lettered people. It is not a property which they can dispose of as they like. The language is everybody's. The most skilful artist is bound to keep its national and popular character ; he ought to speak the public language. If he wants to carve for himself a special idiom out of the idiom of his fellow-citizens ; if he thinks he can at his fancy change the meaning and relations of words, he will be punished for his pride and his impiety : like the workmen of Babel, that bad artisan of the mother tongue will be understood by nobody, and only an unintelligible murmur will issue from his lips.

Let us take care not to write too well. It is the worst manner of writing that there is. Languages are spontaneous creations ; they are the work of the peoples. They should not be employed with too great refinement. They have in them a robust savour of the soil : we gain nothing by perfuming them.

It is bad also to employ old terms too much, and

to affect archaism. Two years ago I saw M. Jean
Moréas constructing a lexicon for his own use out of
terms that have fallen into disuse since the time of
Queen Claude and Duchess Marguerite. That is
to choose writing in a dead language when there is
so much joy in speaking our very living, delightful
French tongue. It is so pleasant and so fresh, so
happy, so lively ! it is so kind when one does not
do violence to it ! I shall never believe in the
success of a literary school which expresses difficult
thoughts in obscure language.

Let us not torment either phrases or thoughts.
Let us not imagine that the time has come when the
old literatures are about to crumble into dust at
the sound of angelic trumpets, and that new
fascinations are necessary for the restless universe.
The artistic shapes that are manufactured out of
many pieces in the schools are generally complicated
and useless machines. Above all, let us not proclaim too loudly the excellence of our methods.
There is no true art save that which hides itself.

THE GREAT ST. ANTONY *

HENRI RIVIÈRE has just pub-
lished a collection of the water-
colours illustrating that " Tentation de Saint Antoine," of which
he gave a performance with so
much success at the Chat-Noir
this winter. The Chat-Noir has
an art of its own. That art is at once mystic and
impious, ironical and sad, simple and profound,
but never reverential. It is epic and mocking
in the hands of the precise Caran d'Ache ; it has
a bland and melancholy viciousness in Willette,
who is as it were the Fra Angelico of the cabarets.
It is symbolic and naturalist in the very capable
Henri Rivière. The forty scenes of the " Tentation " amaze me. They exhibit lively colouring,
daring fancy, impressive beauty, and forcible meaning. I put them far above the imps depicted by
the austere Callot. M. Henri Rivière has portrayed
St. Antony assailed by temptations which were
prophetic as regards the saint but contemporary
as regards ourselves. Following here the example
of the old masters, he has done wisely, for by this
means the good hermit interests us more deeply ;
we understand better the grandeur of his virtue.
In this respect at least M. Henri Rivière's album is a

* " La Tentation de Saint Antoine." By Henri Rivière.

work of the highest edification. To modernise
the merits of the father of the anchorites was certainly no easy task, but the artist of the Chat-Noir
has performed it with successful audacity. He has
conceived the devil in a black coat, showing the
holy man round our nocturnal Paris and carrying
him to the Halles, which are full to bursting of
fowls stuffed with truffles, galantines, melons,
Fontainebleau grapes, and Montreuil peaches! But
that is only the first assault of the Evil One. He
transforms himself into a croupier and urges Antony
into a gaming-house where a supernatural game is
played with living cards: he changes himself into
a Jewish banker and drags Antony to the Bourse
before the statue of the Golden Calf. I should
never end were I to describe all the modern snares
which the enemy of the human race lays for the
servant of God. He takes as his tools the most
staggering appliances of steam and electricity, even
the spectacle of the heavens themselves, which,
since Galileo, have no longer a Christian air, as M.
Sully-Prudhomme observes. Among his other
temptations are the Queen of Sheba—who appa-
rently represents the dangers of the imagination—a
ballet, and comparative mythology. In one of
these last temptations the ascetic is brought face
to face with the Buddha. It would be curious to
hear their conversation. For both of them, the
son of the King of Capilavistu and the poor Egyptian
monk, lived, willingly and from choice, the same
life of renunciation, misery, and poverty. But if
they acted in the same manner, it was for different
and even contrary ends. The one wished to gain
eternal life, the other absolute annihilation. I am very
sorry that their conversation has not been preserved.

Hagiography and legend have immortalised St. Antony. It is interesting to discover who this famous personage really was, and whether in any wise he deserves his fame. If you like, we will set about doing so now. The true St. Antony is not entirely unknown. His biography was written by St. Athanasius, who lived close to his time. Unfortunately, this work of the great doctor bestows more on edification than it does on curiosity. But Antony's personality is so strange, so peculiar, and on certain sides, so great, that it takes form of itself. I shall endeavour to show it as it was, though without flattering myself that I can reach anything more than probability. If I do even that it will still be very fine.

St. Antony retired to the desert about the year 271, in the reign of Aurelian, on the eve of the great crisis which preceded the definite triumph of the Christian religion. He was then in his twenty-first year, having been born in 251, near Heracleum in Egypt, in a village called Coman. This date is given as certain. But it may not be the right one, and, considering everything, it would be extraordinary if it were. His parents were well-to-do peasants living on the benefactions of the Nile. They cannot have been very different from those labourers who sowed the same fields four thousand years earlier, whom we see represented half naked, with thick, black hair, bodies as red as bricks, broad shoulders, and of small stature, on the hypogeums of the ancient empire. They were honest, ignorant, and faithful people. The Gospel bore abundant fruit among these simple and resigned souls, for the gentle Egyptian passed insensibly from the worship of Ammon, one god in three persons, to the religion

of Jesus Christ. Doubtless Greek culture had
penetrated into the neighbouring towns of Arsinoë,
Aphrodite, and Heracleum, but the richer peasants,
village elders like Antony's parents, showed themselves rebellious to the Hellenic spirit. The Church
in which, under the name of Jesus, they found
again the old god of their fathers, completely
satisfied their need for an ideal. Antony, like the
good little Copt he was, had no wish to learn the
humanities in the schools. Contemplative and
unsociable, he willingly remained shut up in the
house. We can imagine that house reflected in
the waters of the Nile, like a small white block, alongside a thin bunch of palm-trees. The interior of
the dwelling is bare, fresh, and dark. There, every
day, little Antony squatted on his mat.

What did he think of ? Of God whom he
represented to himself in a most naïve fashion.
Already he must have seen visions, but these visions
were very simple, very arid. There was not at the
time a sufficiently thick garland of Christian legends
to give them colour. Antony's imagination, although
exalted by solitude, was destined always to keep the
aridity of the desert. Except agriculture and
some texts of Scripture, he knew nothing. The whole
universe was summed up for him in a few tales of
robbers and caves, such as had been current in
Egypt for thousands of years, and doubtless were
very similar to those which Herodotus has taken such
pleasure in narrating.

He was not twenty years old when his parents
died and left him their fields, fructified by the tears
of that old Isis whom the Holy Virgin had driven
away. But Antony did not love the soil ; he had
not the tastes of a peasant. He was, from his

youth upwards, inclined to religion; he had the gift of divine things; he was marked with the sign of the seers; his temperament destined him for sainthood. Among these Orientals, certain physical faculties, either natural or acquired, mark out for public veneration the divine man. Antony possessed these faculties in the highest degree. He could remain for a long time motionless and fasting. That was the great point. He had also much intelligence, and, in his ignorance, a great subtlety, an indomitable energy, an irresistible power over souls.

There is a story that six months after he lost his parents he entered a church just at the moment when the deacon read the verse of the Gospel, " If thou wilt be perfect, go, sell that thou hast, and give to the poor, and come, follow me." These words made a profound impression on him, or rather they expressed what he inwardly felt. They were the voice of his heart. He obeyed them the more easily as it was obeying himself. He sold his fields to his neighbours and distributed the money in alms, only keeping what was needed for himself and for his young sister. But on another occasion, hearing this saying of Jesus, " Take no thought for the morrow," he got rid of the little he had left and put his sister in a convent of virgins. So religious a sacrifice doubtless cost little to this soul exempt from every attachment. However, he had afterwards some uneasiness about the fate of the poor child, for he heard voices reproaching him for having abandoned her. It was his conscience that spoke in this way, but he persuaded himself that it was a devil, and he ceased tormenting himself.

There were already hermits in the Thebaid.   In
all times the burning sand of the desert has ripened
fakirs, dervishes, and marabouts.   Paul was then the
most celebrated of the fakirs.   He, with several
others, possessed the great secret of fasting and
immobility, and on the banks of the Nile he renewed
the prodigies of the gymnosophists of the Ganges.
He was the model whom Antony determined to
follow.   Like a true Copt he invented nothing.
He withdrew to the desert quite close to Heracleum,
and led the life of a holy man.

His food was only bread and salt with a little
water.   He ate but once a day, after sunset, and
sometimes remained two or three days without
taking any nourishment.   He often spent the night
without sleep, and if he took any rest it was on the
bare earth, or on rushes, or on a hair shirt.   Then
he began to be tempted.   The Queen of Sheba
did not come with a numerous retinue to visit him.
He imagined nothing of that sort, for his temptations were naturally proportioned to his intelligence.   The demons who tempt young peasants
themselves bear the impress of rustic youth.   We
know nothing precise about the women whom
Antony saw in the desert, but it is extremely probable that, like the Fellaheen girls, they wore long
blue dresses open at the breast, and carried pitchers
on their heads.   These women threw him into a great
trouble.   All that is told us of the temptations of
the holy man is childishly simple.   The demons
accosted him at night with a great light.   " We
come to enlighten you," said they, and they made a
commotion in the hermit's cell.   Then they took
flight but returned suddenly, clapping their hands,
hissing and leaping.

In order to tempt him, one of them offered him gold, another a piece of bread. At the name of Jesus Christ these evil spirits were seized with madness and attacked each other. One of them, like the djinn who appeared to the fisherman in the " Arabian Nights," assumed the form of a giant whose head reached up to the sky. But Antony spat in his face, and the giant vanished. These hallucinations fatigued him greatly; he redoubled his abstinence in order to combat them, not suspecting that it was his prolonged fasts that were their only cause. Moreover, he could not have been greatly surprised nor even very angry that he was called upon to live amidst this sort of devilry. That was the necessary condition of fakirism as it was conconceived at the time.

So as to attain a higher degree of perfection, he went and hid himself in a sepulchre. There is nothing in the choice of such a dwelling that need surprise us much. Whilst he lived in the desert, Antony must have noticed a structure shaped like a truncated cone and recognised it to be one of those hypogeums where the ancient Egyptians placed their illustrious dead. This tomb had doubtless been violated by some of those nomad brigands against whom for centuries pious Egypt had such difficulty in protecting her mummies. The door had been broken, and the good Antony could enter without difficulty into the mortuary chapel. Perhaps it was spacious and magnificently decorated like the one which Mirri the scribe had erected for King Ousirtesen I. Mirri himself has described it in a text preserved at the Louvre which has been translated by M. G. Maspero. " My master," says the scribe, " sent me on a mission to prepare a great eternal dwelling for him. The passages of the inner chamber were of stone work, and recalled the marvellous buildings erected by the gods. There were in it sculptured columns, beautiful as the skies, a hollowed basin which communicated with the Nile, and a facade made of the white stone of Roou. So Osiris, Lord of Amenti, rejoiced at the monuments of my lord, and I myself was transported with gladness when I saw the result of my labours."

It is extremely probable that the tomb where Antony lived consisted, like others, of a chapel such as we have mentioned, a shaft, and a vault in which the corpse reposed. We are not told whether Antony descended through the shaft down to the vault itself and disturbed the slumber of an old embalmed Egyptian. It is more probable that he installed himself in the chapel, and it is not impossible that in it he saw paintings representing scenes of travel and rustic life. There he established himself at little expense, having first dislodged a brood of jackals. There also the devils pursued him, and he was even more tormented by them than he was before. His youth was far from having passed, and this was an advantage which the devils too seized upon. If we had Antony's diary of the time he lived in the hypogeum, a pupil of M. Charcot would have no difficulty in proving that the holy man experienced a logical succession of nervous disorders. But the documents that have been transmitted to us are of the vaguest sort. We see only that to chronic hallucination there was sometimes added a cataleptic state. One morning the man who brought him food found him motionless, and giving no sign of life. He dragged him to the church of the nearest village. There Antony, little by little, recovered his senses, and being restored, he related that the devils had beaten him all the night through, and he asked to be brought back at once to his sepulchre.

He remained in it up to the age of twenty-five, after which he withdrew to the mountains that enclose, on its eastern side, the narrow valley of the Nile. Having found a ruined castle which the Egyptians had formerly built to defend themselves against the incursions of the nomads, he established himself there in such solitude that he would not even endure the sight of those who brought him food. He required what he ate to be thrown over the roof. One readily believes that the devils followed him into this citadel. They persisted in behaving like boors, thinking they could astonish him by their hustlings and vociferations.

Once, indeed, they made a sensible enough remark to him. "This castle," said they to him, "is not yours." But Antony paid no heed to the remonstrance. He despised the things of this world too much to have any exact feeling of property.

The demons also appeared to him in the forms of lions, tigers, and frightful beasts who threatened to devour him. He did not fear them. However, he often suffered cruel wounds which he honestly attributed to the teeth and claws of these demons. We can suppose without improbability that he gave himself these injuries by falling down when overcome by the paroxysms of that terrible malady which the doctors of the old empire of Memphis called the divine malady, and which to-day we call epilepsy. But he was well compensated for his miseries and his terrors.

He had ecstasies; suddenly the roof of the building would open and a celestial clearness would surround the holy man. "In this light," says his biographer, "he recognised the presence of his Saviour." Then he uttered with exquisite tenderness the words of simple familiarity and gentle reproach that come to the lips of mystics who speak to their God: "Where wert Thou, my good Jesus? Where wert Thou? Why did'st Thou not come sooner to heal my wounds?"

Under the aspects which I have just indicated, Antony is not very markedly distinguished from other hermits of the Thebaid who, like him, were vegetarians and visionaries. Christian fakirism was destined some years later to perform far more amazing feats. What are the practices of Antony compared with those of St. Simeon Stylites, who passed the greater portion of his life on a pillar, and who equalled in his immobility the contemplative saints of India?

St. Antony was not a pure contemplative. He worked and prayed in turn, making mats of palm leaves. His austerities were temperate. When he was old, his disciples obtained from him permission to bring him every month olives, beans, and oil.

What makes the originality and grandeur of his life is that we find in it an extraordinary mixture of ecstasy and activity; a contrast which is found again thirteen centuries later in St. Teresa. The inert old hermit, the visionary, alien from this world, is at the same time the most active, the most practical, the most enterprising of men. He leads the double life of the mystic and the man of business. He is a great organiser and an excellent administrator. He founds and directs innumerable monas-

teries, and displays the prompt and clear-sighted
genius of a great ruler of men.   This same old man
whom we think of as solely occupied in fighting
with   stupid   imps,   founds   vast   establishments
throughout the whole of the Thebaid, and peoples
the desert.   At Pispir on the right bank of the Nile,
he establishes five thousand monks.   And that is the
smallest of the convents which he founded.   Those at
Memphis, its elder brethren, held more than twenty
thousand monks.   This single man commands an
innumerable army, obedient, ignorant, and fierce,
invincible in a three-fold way.   His glance takes
in vast outlines and penetrates into the smallest
details.   This ecstatic knows the value of time as
well as a good Roman functionary did.   He gives
audience to everybody, but he takes care to be
informed beforehand about the business of his
suitors.   His disciples are ranged like clerks, and
help him to dismiss intruders.   They tell him,
" This visitor is an Egyptian," he is dealt with
briskly ; " This other is from Jerusalem," great
attention is paid to him.   " Jerusalem " was the
password.   Our hermit is a politician.   In the depths
of his retreat he holds the threads of all great ecclesiastical affairs, corresponds with bishops and doctors
of the Church, receives letters from the Emperor
Constantine and his sons, conducts everything, regu-
lates everything throughout Catholicism.

He is the Mahdi of the Christians.   His activity
is amazing ;   twice he swoops like an eagle on
Alexandria to support the persecuted faithful and
to withstand the Arian heresy.   During his lifetime, he is already the great St. Antony.   And he
deserves the name.   It is in his character that he
is great.   Steadfastness of heart replaces in him

H

both learning and talent. He is iron, but his energy is wrapped in sweetness and gentleness. All who approach him admire his serenity, his grace, his patience. In extreme old age, he still has the gaiety of a little child. He is joyous, and recommends cheerfulness as a virtue. " The bow breaks that is too far bent," he says. Such is the real St. Antony : one of the most extraordinary men that the world has ever seen. " He gave back his soul to God," says his pious biographer, " on the seventeenth of January in the year of our Lord 356 and the one hundred and fifth of his age."

ANTHOLOGY *

I F, adopting the words of the courtly Meleager, we make appeal in our turn: " Beloved Muse, tell us who has woven this chaplet of verse ? " the Muse will answer: " It is M. Alphonse Lemerre and his friends who have entwined it."
Only the publisher of the "Passage Choiseul" could have formed so rich a garland of contemporary rhymes. Do we not know that the plants, some of whose flowers he offers us, have been cultivated in great part by the Digger who took for his motto *Fac et Spera ?* † Do we not remember the sheaves of the " Parnasse " ? Wee modest flowers of the singers of inward things, strange orchid blooms of the singers of chiselled verse and the calm sequestered choir, 'tis twenty years since I saw your petals unfold. " The Anthology of the Poets of the Nineteenth Century " opens with a poet of the eighteenth, André Chénier. M. André Lemoyne, in the first of the notices that precede the extracts, has undertaken to explain why this son of a Greek lady is set in the forefront of a collection reserved for the works of an age he did not live to see. The

---

* " Anthologie des poètes français du XIXᵉ siècle." " Poésies d'André Chénier." With fifteen illustrations by Bida.
† An allusion to M. Lemerre's device and motto.

first reason is a chronological one. The works of André Chénier, says M. André Lemoyne, are posthumous, and were published in our century. As a matter of fact, Latouche issued the original edition in 1819. This reason may seem a good one. Only, we ask ourselves if, on the same grounds, we should not levy toll in this new collection on certain poems of Parny, of Ducis, of the Abbé Delille, of the Chevalier de Boufflers, &c., published subsequently to the year 1801. At the very least, a fragment of " La Pitié " might have been admitted, the passage relative to the captivity of the little Louis XVII in the Temple for instance. Besides the fact that the extract does not lack interest, we should have discovered in its perusal one of the sources whence the young Victor-Marie Hugo was drawing inspiration when he composed his first odes. But I do not insist. It is enough that nothing essential has been omitted.

M. Lemoyne's second reason is æsthetic and demands more consideration. Here it is in its full force : " André Chénier is the true renovator of French poetry." First, let us do justice to M. Lemoyne. This maxim does not exclusively belong to him : it is current among the poets. As we reflect on it, we are surprised that so untenable a view could have become sanctioned even by artists alien from criticism and literary history. The truth is that, far from being an initiator, André Chénier is the last expression of an expiring art.

It is with him that the taste, the ideal, the thought of the eighteenth century end. He sums up the Louis XVI style and the encyclopædic spirit. He is the end of a world. That is precisely why he is exquisite, why he is perfect. Certainly he is a finished artist. He perfects one art and attempts no other. He completes a cycle. He has sown nothing ; he has reaped everything. It was for him that the Abbé Barthélemy endeared Greece to the powdered marchionesses, and inspired the Opera girls with a desire to imitate Lais and Phryne by banding their hair with woollen fillets. It was for him that Madame de Pompadour insisted on having the ceilings of her boudoirs supported by Corinthian columns, that the bedrooms looked like temples, that the backs of chairs were shaped like lyres, and that funeral urns were erected upon the mantelpieces. It was for him that M. de Caylus, with his coat off and his shirt open, a chisel and pincers in his hands, red with joy and fatigue, unpacked antique bronzes, Greek marbles, and vases which he believed to be Etruscan. It was for him that M. de Choiseul-Gouffier excavated the hippodrome of Olympia. It was for him that the painter David painted Leonidas and the death of Socrates. It was for him that the architect Ledoux decorated the barriers of Paris with friezes of maidens bearing escutcheons. It was for him that princes and cantatrices erected in their parks sham ruins, empty tombs, and altars to Friendship. It was for him that the Abbé Raynal wrote rapturously the "Philosophical History of the American Savages." It was for him that olive-skinned men, simple as children, and young girls, clothed in flowers, were introduced by Cook and Bougainville to a very civilised world whose over-refinement made it enamoured of nature. It was for him that tender women dreamed in English gardens of Pamela, of Clarissa, and of Julie. It was for him that great lords were anglomaniacs, philanthropists, and voluptuaries. It was for him that Buffon, d'Alembert,

Diderot, and the encyclopædists thought, observed, and laboured ; for him that Voltaire exalted tolerance, Rousseau nature, d'Holbach atheism, and Mirabeau liberty. He was everything that his time was—Neo-Greek, didactic, encyclopædist, erotic, romantic, tender, sentimental, tolerant, atheist, constitutionalist. It was in English gardens that he observed nature ; his taste for the antique was in reality only the Louis XVI taste. I praise him for it, after all, and admire him for it. He would have been an imitator had he not written in the Louis XVI style. He loves, he understands, he embraces the eighteenth century.

He does not divine, he does not anticipate, anything of ours. An innovator ! nobody has been less of one. He is aloof from all that the future is preparing. Nothing that is going to blossom is in germ in him. He is a true contemporary of Suard and of Morellet. He suspected neither René's anti-materialism nor his melancholy, nor Obermann's weariness, nor Corinne's romantic ardours. He foresaw neither the metaphysical curiosity nor the literary restlessness which drew Madame de Staël and Benjamin Constant towards Germany. He saw Shakespeare played in London and understood him less than Voltaire, Letourneur, and Ducis had done. The fire that runs in his veins is not the subtle flame that devoured Werther. He did not bear within him the great vagueness, the infinite discomfort of the new era. He is not enamoured of that madness of fame and love which is about to seize upon the children of the Revolution. He has none of the aspirations of the modern mind. Verses by Lemierre, by Millevoye, by Fontanes, by Chênedollé, could easily be quoted, which touch us more closely than his in tone, accent, and feeling. He is the least romantic of poets. Lamartine recognised this thoroughly despite his slight equipment as a student and a critic. In this victim of the Terror, he detected, with the certainty of instinct, the adept, the blind partisan of that abhorred enemy, the eighteenth century. That, without any doubt, is the secret and profound cause of an antipathy which is expressed with a blind injustice in the "Familiar Course of Literature." Suppose for a moment that André, having escaped the executioner, had lived under the Consulate. There is no doubt that he would have frequented the society of Suard and Morellet. He would have belonged to the group of philosophers, espousing the passions and the prejudices of his friends ; he would have had a difficulty in understanding the spiritual state which harmonised with the Concordat in politics and the "Genius of Christianity" in letters. Do you see him publishing his "Hermes," working in the didactic vein, treating "Atala" as a melancholy preachment, scoffing at the new barbarians who were stupidly enamoured of the architecture of the Goths, and deploring the return of fanaticism. All that youth then loved, all that reviving art exalted, would have horrified him, the sound of bells, the cathedrals, the cemeteries, the battles, and the Te Deums. Of all that then stirred men's imaginations, I see hardly anything except Ossian and Malvina with which he could have been pleased ; in everything else he would have been thoroughly out of his element, alien, and unhappy.

But I think I see one of my friends of the "Parnasse" coming to me, say one of the most famous of them, M. Catulle Mendès or M. Armand

Silvestre; I feel him pulling me by the sleeve, and I hear him saying:

" When speaking of a poet, you talk to me about religions, philosophies, public manners, tastes, and feelings. What has that to do with poetry? It matters little that André Chénier had the ideas of his contemporaries, or even that he had any ideas at all. That does not count. What counts is pure form, it is modulation, rhythm, a certain undulation in the verse. And in this, in certain cæsuras, Chénier is modern. He is the initiator, he is the master."

For my own part, I have an infinite regard for well-constructed verses. I do not believe that there is poetry without art nor art without craftsmanship. But I maintain that, even in the form of his verse, André Chénier is a pure classic of the eighteenth century. Doubtless he has a delightful turn which is peculiarly his own. His verse, at once strong and flexible, is of an audacious and charming harmony; he is by far the first of the verse-makers as he is the first of the poets of his time. But his art is not essentially different from theirs. His running on of lines, his modulations, were not without precedent when he employed them. Examples would be found in Bertin, in Parny, above all in Delille's " Georgiques," if people still read Delille and Bertin, who, in truth, are unreadable, and Parny, who is exquisite.

Nevertheless, the idea that Chénier opened new sources to poetry, while in reality he only exhausted the old ones, is accepted indiscriminatingly by the poets. André's lamented editor, the learned and fastidious Becq de Fouquières, thought like them on this point. A new edition of André Chénier's poems has just appeared from the house of Charpentier, a sumptuous and magnificent edition, a monument of typography and art, ornamented with fifteen illustrations by Bida. This fine quarto contains a new preface by the best of editors, in which I find this phrase: " Upon the smallest attentive study of our contemporary poetry we shall be struck with the permeating influence that André Chénier's art has not yet ceased to exercise upon it." We see that M. Becq de Fouquières clearly affirms the influence of the works of his poet upon the modern school. But when it is a question of proving it, he is distinctly embarrassed. He feels strongly that he cannot verify this influence either in Victor Hugo or in Musset; still less in Lamartine. He was too clever a man to seek it in the " Poèmes Antiques " of Alfred de Vigny. Indeed, if one might at first sight believe that three or four pieces in this collection, such as " Symetha " and " La Dryade " were derived from André's elegies and eclogues, the fact remains that " Symetha " was composed in 1817 and " La Dryade " in 1815, two years and four years respectively before the first edition of Chénier's works appeared. In the last analysis it is in M. Leconte de Lisle's " Poèmes Antiques " and M. José-Maria de Heredia's sonnets that, according to M. Becq de Fouquières, Chénier's influence on modern poetry is embodied. For my own part I discover no resemblance between the Hispano-Latin Muse of M. de Heredia and the nymphs of Luciennes whom Fanny's lover evoked. As for M. Leconte de Lisle, we know that several of his early poems are studies from the antique. He steeped himself in the sources; it was in Homer, in Hesiod, in Theocritus, and

H 2

not in André Chénier, that he sought forms and images.

I will say, more generally, that André Chénier's influence is not perceptible in any of the poets of this century, and it is a pure whim for the editors of the new "Anthology" to have placed "L'Aveugle" and "La Jeune Captive" in the front of the collection, like a Louis XVI portico at the entrance of a modern building.

And yet the divine André is none the less deserving of immortal honours. He has nothing to fear from rational criticism, founded on history. On the contrary, the more one studies him, the better one admires him. Restored to his own time, replaced in his own environment, put back into his true frame, he no longer appears as only a delightful maker of little pictures and pseudo-Greek and Neo-Roman statuettes, a sort of painter on wax, or a potter gay with the memories of Pompeii; he is an ardent and virtuous soul, a virile genius inspired with the spirit of a century. And what a century! the boldest, the most attractive, the greatest! Behold him then, our André, as he was in full life, in the midst of things! Behold him, mingling with the people and the heroes of 1789, sharing their powerful ideal and their noble illusions! Look at this man with the large brow, filled with thoughts and images, and the athlete's neck, this little choleric man, who, with kindling eyes, has thrown himself into the conflict of parties, and will consecrate to liberty his heart, his genius, his life; it is he, it is the generous André. He joins to the wisdom of a politician the candour of a hero. He is quite willing to be a dupe, if he is deceived in the company of the virtuous. He is not merely a skilful artist, he is a good citizen, he is a man, he is a great man. Courageous, eloquent, loyal, prudent yet energetic, pure in the midst of crimes, alien from violence because he knows not fear, he has a right to say :

"And thou, O Virtue ! mourn me if I die."

His life was short, but it was a full one. No, he was not a thoughtless singer whom the proscribers cut down by chance. André Chénier was marked out for the executioner by his courage, by his love of liberty, by his respect for the laws. He truly deserved his death. He was worthy of political martyrdom. He was a great victim to whom we owe an expiatory monument.

THE WISDOM OF GYP
I. "LES SÉDUCTEURS"*

PRONOUNCE Gyp to be a great
philosopher. And if you ask me in
what sense I mean it, I answer " In
the right sense." I should be very
sorry if this had the air of a paradox.
I take good care not to risk any
paradoxes ; to sustain them requires
a wit I do not possess. Simplicity suits me better.
And it is in all innocence that I declare Gyp to be a
great philosopher. But let us distinguish. There
are philosophers and philosophers. He is called a
philosopher, who seeks out principles and causes.
That is not precisely Gyp's manner. In regard to
causes, Gyp is acquainted with hardly more than
one ; it is true that that one is a host in itself ; it is
what is politely called love. The philosophers who
seek out principles and causes have been said to
resemble elephants, who, when they walk, never put
a second foot on the ground until the first is very
firmly planted. How different is Gyp's way of
walking ! But the name of philosopher is also given
to one who applies himself to the study of man and
society. La Bruyère said : " The philosopher con-
sumes his life in observing men, and wears out his

* " Les Séducteurs." " Loulou."

218

mind in analysing their vices and absurdities." On these grounds, although I do not picture Gyp to myself as wasted and outworn by meditation, there is no philosopher who has philosophised more than Gyp, and one cannot doubt that Gyp's little books are great manuals of philosophy. "Autour du Mariage," "Le Petit Bob," "Dans l'train," "Pour ne pas l'être," "Plume et Poil," "Les plus heureux de tous," and "Les Séducteurs" ought to be ranged among the moral collections where wisdom flowers.

Not to reveal an open secret is, doubtless, exquisitely discreet. But there would also perhaps be some affectation in not saying, in the wake of so may others, that the pseudonym of Gyp conceals a graceful woman, the great-grand-daughter of Mirabeau-Tonneau, whose alert, indomitable, and mordant spirit she recalls. I can even say that at this moment the portrait of that lady may be seen at the exhibition of the Thirty-Three in the Rue de Sèze. The eye is keen, the mouth mocking, the countenance charming. One divines, merely by looking at the portrait, that the owner of that pretty face houses an ironical soul in her little person.

And it is true that she is a terrible scoffer. In an infinite number of witty dialogues, she fits with phrases a whole world of men-about-town and idlers, and from this mass of frivolous chatter the conviction emerges that man, in the civilised state, is a vain, coarse, and ridiculous animal. It is this profoundly sincere idea that makes Gyp a philosopher and a moralist. It has been fashionable for some time to charge with immorality the pretty fantasies that our author scatters with a negligent hand in the "Vie Parisenne." For my own part, I have never understood this severity. I have never discovered in

Gyp's dialogues the least incitement to vice. It has
seemed to me, on the contrary, that in them
pleasure was represented as a very complex, very
fatiguing, and perfectly sterile labour. For my own
part, every time Gyp has shown me the rich and the
happy making holiday, as they say, I have felt in
myself a redoubled desire to live in the magnificent
humility of science, *in angello cum libello*. Yes, I
have never been able to see Paulette's friends making
soap-bubbles and pouring champagne into the piano
in order to amuse themselves, without thinking that
the humble scholar who is patiently writing a
treatise on Greek metres in the suburb of some little
town, has not, upon the whole, chosen the worst
part of the things of life. Sometimes even, as I
count the empty hours that Gérard has painfully
killed at his club or at Blanche d'Ivry's or Madame
de Fryleuse's, I have suddenly surprised myself
thinking—excuse the strangeness of my reverie—of
the simple and full life of some good man, of an old
priest, for instance, occupied in study, and waking
up in the April nights with the thought that it is
freezing and his apple-trees are in blossom. The
example is taken from Rollin. That good man
entertained no other uneasiness in his soul, which
was as pure as that of a child. I tell you in truth
that Gyp has taught me to esteem the worthy
Rollin. She teaches us that the happy in this world
are not to be envied, that they are miserable in their
joys and ridiculous in their elegances. I had sur-
mised as much. But everybody does not know it.
Gyp seems to say to us : " It is neither in the beauty
of equipages nor in the luxury of women that the
sovereign good resides, and one can pass all one's
spring mornings in the Allée des Poteaux without

discovering gladness of heart. I imagine that if Saint Antony had read Gyp in the desert, he would have recovered a little tranquillity in the thought that the world is not worth regretting. He would have said to himself that his death's head and his wooden bowl were well worth all little de Tremble's soap-bubbles and all Joyeuse's bumpers of champagne. And then he would not have been able to prevent himself from laughing, and a saint who laughs is nigh to becoming a sage ; he is saved. The more I think of it, the more I am tempted to recommend the works of Gyp to persons who profess asceticism.

Gyp has philosophically fathomed the vanity of clothes cut in the English style. I, on my side, suspect that there is some vanity in the study of Greek prosody and Byzantine mosaics. But, if we must choose among the vanities, we will prefer those which make us forget, which console, which give peace and dignity to existence. That is what Gyp smilingly teaches. It is why I regard her as one of the most moral of writers. If I were M. Camille Doucet I should have no rest until " Dans l'train " and "Les Séducteurs" had received a Montyon Prize from the French Academy.

I know well that Gyp's women are enchanting, and that they have as much wit as their adorers have little. I know that Paulette is exquisite, I know that Madame de Flirt and Madame d'Houbly are of a sort to cause us some uneasiness. But what would you have ? Philosophy must come to terms with the charm of women. There is no wisdom equal to the task of suppressing living beauty, and if there were it would be a repellent wisdom. It is a fact that there are pretty women on the earth. If books

did not say so, it would be seen all the same. Gyp
is not afraid of showing us enchanting creatures;
but at the same time she makes us understand that
to love them at too close quarters is arduous and
disillusioning, and it is exactly here that she shows
herself to be a consummate moralist.

I shall let you judge for yourself, and shall take
my example from my author's latest book. It is
called " Les Séducteurs "! and it is dedicated to
M. Jules Lemaître. A book with such a title can
offend none of the Muses, the thing is so light and
agreeable. I shall fearlessly choose the most intimate dialogue in the whole book, because, when
understood properly, it is also the most philosophic.
The scene takes place in a little ground-floor flat in
the Avenue Marceau. The closed room is wrapped
in a pleasant obscurity:

" MADAME D'HOUBLY. What time is it ?
" FRYLEUSE. I don't know. . . . Don't bother about the time. . . .
What does it matter ?
" MADAME D'HOUBLY (*aside*). He speaks familiarly to me already.
" FRYLEUSE. You don't know how happy I am !
" MADAME D'HOUBLY. Yes. . . . I can imagine.

It must be very late.
" FRYLEUSE, *looking at the clock.* Scarcely half-past five.
" MADAME D'HOUBLY, *springing up.* Heavens ! Then we have
been two hours shut in here !
" FRYLEUSE, *in a melancholy tone.* The time has then seemed very
long to you.
" MADAME D'HOUBLY. No. . . . but. . . .
" FRYLEUSE. Yes it has. . . . I see it plainly, go ! You regret
having given me . . . these two hours.
" MADAME D'HOUBLY. No. . . . In the first place, I never
regret. . . . It is useless to regret !

" FRYLEUSE. I see plainly that something is wrong.
" MADAME D'HOUBLY. Not at all. . . . *A pause.* I cannot

fasten this boot without a button-hook ! . . . Will you give me a button-hook ?

"FRYLEUSE. A button-hook ? Good Heavens ! I haven't one ! I didn't think, I didn't look forward. . . .

"MADAME D'HOUBLY. Didn't look forward. . . .   Well, indeed ! . . . If I had known that you didn't look forward, I . . . well, I shouldn't want a button-hook !

"FRYLEUSE, *disconsolate.* Oh !

"MADAME D'HOUBLY, *struggling with her button.* Ah, I can't ! There is no way ! . . . .

"FRYLEUSE, *timorously.* If you will allow me. . . .

"MADAME D'HOUBLY. Oh, I ask nothing better ! . . . I have had enough of it. . . .

"FRYLEUSE, *taking Madame d'Houbly's foot in his hand and looking at it admiringly.* What a foot. . . . It's a marvel !

"MADAME D'HOUBLY, *irritated.* Oh ! if it's for this that. . .

"FRYLEUSE. No, pardon. (*He vainly tries to push the button through the button-hole.*)

.   .   .   .   .   .

Suppose you tried a hair-pin ?

"MADAME D'HOUBLY. A hair-pin ! I don't wear such beastly things !

"FRYLEUSE. But your hair is fastened up.

"MADAME D'HOUBLY. Yes . . . with a comb . . . (*unnerved*). Do you want me to button my boots with a comb."

.   .   .   .   .

And Fryleuse's lucky day will have no successor. Gyp is not tender to the poor seducers. She scoffs at their prudence and their artifices ; she despises their toil ; she is pitiless to their sorrows and their miseries. To her the practised skill of M. d'Orange is as ridiculous as the youthful inexperience of Fryleuse. She victoriously opposes to little de Tremble's longings the fifty-two buttons on Madame de Flirt's dress, " fifty-two buttons, without counting the braids and the silver olives which cross on top. . . . It takes twenty minutes to do them up." In a word she is delighted to show that selfish sensuality joined to foolish self-love makes a sad

brute of man.   Gyp is right, all this is ridiculous.
Those men and those women are wretchedly petty.
Yet give them a single thing which they lack, and
they will become touching and beautiful.   Let
them have passion, let it be a true feeling, a deep
emotion, which throws them into one another's
arms, and they will immediately cease to appear
ridiculous and paltry ; on the contrary, they will
inspire us with a gentle sympathy, and we shall say
as we see them pass: "These are happy !   They
have brought down heaven to earth.   They are a
living ideal for each other.   They put infinity into
an hour, and they realise God in this world.   We
must envy them even their sorrows.   For they
contain more joys than the felicity of other men."

That is another inspiration which we owe to the
author of "Plume et Poil."   I affirm that there are
few writers who help as Gyp does towards the cultivation and improvement of the moral person.

II.   "LOULOU"

I am reading "Loulou" on the railway, in the
express train, to the accompaniment of the rumble
of the wheels on the rails, and the whistle of the
engines.   Loulou and steam, there are harmonies
for you !

Loulou is also "in the train" as Gyp says.   I even
think I met her just now, at the buffet, when dusty,
sleepy, preoccupied, and black as shadows, we enjoyed the comfort of hot soup and twenty minutes
of liberty around a table.   With their soft hats
crushed upon their heads, the men took their ease ;
but the women still fought against the brutalities of
the journey for some remnants of grace and elegance.

Among them a little person of fifteen years old was biting into the flesh of a peach with her beautiful teeth, and laughing with her large eyes at her embarrassed or pretentious neighbours. She had a lively, brazen, easy-going air. She was thoroughly badly brought up. It was Loulou, or some one who greatly resembled her.

Besides, where do we not meet Loulou? Loulou is the modern little girl; Loulou is the living novelty of the day. Loulou is the flower and fruit of our restlessness and our follies. Would you like to have her portrait? Gyp has drawn it with two or three strokes of her pocket pencil. "A thick, curled, mahogany-coloured mop of hair, brilliant complexion, green eyes spangled with gold, little teeth like a dog's, and too large a mouth." Not beautiful, scarcely pretty, but expressive and shrewd. She is to the taste of the day, and after her marriage will not fail to make a " sensation " in the world. She will be the modern woman, the new ideal. Her nose, her mouth, are precisely the nose and the mouth we were waiting for. She is " smart," as they say, and has no contour, nothing classic. May she be welcome!

The majestic women with the beauty of goddesses, whom the seventeenth century has celebrated, would greatly bore our fashionable men of to-day, who reckon the pleasure of admiring as nothing. Even maidens, as Greuze painted them, would seem a little insipid to us, in spite of their cream and roses. We must have something better than broken pitchers, something better than Aline's overturned milk-jug. We must have Loulou, with her insolent little nose and her mouth like a Paris street arab's, Loulou who has a vague resemblance to Gavroche.

She is crude wine, made to whet jaded and burnt palates for a moment. And, as that crude wine is drunk out of fine crystal, its savour becomes stronger and more piquant by the contrast.

Let us make no mistake : Gyp is a great ironist, an ironist without anger and without bitterness, with a naturalness that sometimes goes as far as unconsciousness. The great world, which is mirrored in Gyp's delicate portraits, whilst it smiles at finding in them so much elegance, does not suspect, I am sure, the more or less deliberate raillery there is in the choice the artist makes of the attitudes, expressions, and movements of her figures. Most certainly, I should not like, for anything in the world, to sow distrust in the minds of simple readers of these dialogues, written by a later Lucian, less affected and more natural than the earlier one ; but, without wishing to discover what charming perfidy the mind that created Bob, Paulette, and Loulou is capable of, I ask myself, not without disquiet, if when ill-disposed posterity wants to represent our society to itself, it will not be tempted to borrow some touches from the light sketches of the story-writers of the "Vie Parisienne." We give ourselves fu l freedom to track down in Restif de la Bretonne,—who, however, had neither subtlety nor grace,—some of the secrets of our great-great-grandparents.

Those who judge of our daughters by Loulou will say that these children lacked neither wit nor sense nor a sort of amiable ease ; that they were not wicked, but that they were as badly brought up as it is possible to be.

They will not be entirely mistaken. Education in France has lost its force and its firmness. Formerly it flourished vigorously in this ancient home

of high breeding. Here it produced the finest
society in the world. Now the middle-class family
has ceased to be the excellent educator which
formerly shaped from their childhood men capable
of any employment, any trust. It was by those
domestic labours that the middle-class elevated its
sons above the nobles, and took possession of the
government. Alas! we have not kept the secret of
what our fathers called "strong diets." We no
longer bring up our children very well. We shall
be less surprised than distressed, if we reflect that
education is made up in great part of constraint,
that it requires firmness, and that this is above all
things what we have lost. We are gentle, affectionate, tolerant, but we are no longer able either
to impose or to render obedience.

We have thrown over all the yokes. The word
discipline, which was formerly applied to the direction of the whole life, has now no longer any
application in civil life. In this state of moral
independence, it is impossible that the development
of our children's faculties should be directed so as
to attain the desired end.

When one studies (as M. Gréard has done in a
book full of wisdom and experience) the education
of girls under the old régime, one recognises that
the gentlest governesses of former days were not
satisfied with making themselves loved, that they
also wished to be respected and sometimes even
feared. Parents then endeavoured to hide their
tenderness. They would have been afraid of making
their children effeminate by caressing them. Education, according to their sentiments, was an iron
corset, which one laced prudently, but firmly. In
the houses of those poor noblemen who proudly

said that they had given everything to the King,
the domestic virtues were still military virtues.
They brought up their daughters like soldiers, for
the service of God or of the family. The convent,
or an honourable and profitable alliance, such was
the future. Nothing, or almost nothing, was left
to the child's feeling:

> " A daughter's duty in obedience lies."

Those men of the sword had simple, narrow, and
strong ideas. They bent everything to them.

To-day, we are more intelligent and better instructed, we have more tenderness and kindness.
We understand, love, and doubt more. What is
lacking to us above all is tradition and habit. By
losing the ancient faith, we have become unaccus-
tomed to that long backward look which is called
respect. Now, there is no education without
respect.

Our convictions are sometimes obstinate, but at
the same time they are uncertain and new. In
morality, in religion, in politics, everything is dis-
putable, since everything is disputed. We have
destroyed many prejudices, and, we must recognise
it, prejudices—I mean noble and universal prejudices—are the sole bases of education. We only
agree about prejudices; everything that is not
admitted without examination can be rejected.

Loulou's parents do not know how to bring up
their daughter, because they do not know why they
are bringing her up. And how should they know ?
Everything around them is changing and uncertain.
They belong to those directing classes who no longer
direct, and whom their own incapacity and selfish-
ness have struck with decadence. They form part

of an aristocracy which rises and falls according as it gains or loses the money which is the sole cause of its existence. They have no ideas on anything. They are themselves derelict and forsaken. Loulou grows up like a wild plant.

Is this tantamount to saying that we should regret the old disciplines and the old houses, the Saint-Cyr establishment for young ladies, the convents in which Loulou would have learnt the politeness and respect of which she will always be ignorant ? Certainly not. The strong and narrow education of the old régime would be of no value to modern society. Our aspirations have widened with our horizons. Democracy and science draw us towards new destinies which we vaguely foresee.

Loulou is instructed and well instructed. She learns a good deal of history, chronology, and geography. She passes all her examinations. It is the prejudice of our time to set great store on instruction. In the eighteenth century, girls were hardly instructed in anything save ignorance and religion. To-day, we wish to teach them everything, and perhaps in this too fervent zeal there is an obscure instinct for the new conditions of life. In truth, if aristocracies can live for a long time on precepts, maxims, and usages, democracies exist only by useful knowledge, the practice of the arts, and the application of the sciences. All that is wanted is to know what true science is, and not to teach Loulou mere useless nomenclature.

Let us be chary of words. People die of them. Let us be scholarly, and let us make Loulou scholarly ; but let us attach ourselves to the spirit and not to the letter. Let our teaching be full of ideas. Hitherto it has been stuffed only with facts. The teachers of former days rightly wished the memory of children to be gently treated. One of them said : "In so small and so precious a reservoir one ought only to pour exquisite things." Far removed from this prudence, we are not afraid of heaping up paving stones in it. It is not only at the buffet eating peaches that I have seen Loulou. I have also seen her bent over her desk, pale, short-sighted, and hump-backed, crushed under those proper names which are the vanity of vanities.

Loulou grumblingly undergoes this incomprehensible fatality. Take comfort, Loulou. This new barbarism is transient. It had to be thus at first. The greater part of our sciences are new, unfinished, enormous, like worlds in formation.

They are incessantly increasing and overflowing upon us. In spite of all our efforts we do not take them all in ; we cannot over-rule, reduce, abridge them. We have not yet mastered the guiding principle and philosophy of them. That is why we embody them in our curriculum in an obscure and cumbersome form. When we can free the spirit of the sciences from its encumbrances, we shall present its quintessence to our youth. In the meantime we discharge our dictionaries at them. That, Loulou, is why the chemistry that is taught to you is so tiresome.

ANTHOLOGY

THIS morning a generous sun is drinking up the dew of the meadows, gilding the vine-leaves on the hillocks, and penetrating with its subtle flames the already ripened grapes. Seated before my writing-table, which I have drawn to the window, as I lean forward a little I can see the barn where the workmen are threshing the corn. They are working hard, but the pleasant light of the day bathes and pervades them. Harnessed to the machinery that sets the threshing machine in motion, are two sturdy horses, tired and patient; with their heads in sacks, they go round and round unceasingly and make the wheels hum and the straps hiss. A child is cracking his whip to hurry them and to drive away the flies who are eager to drink their sweat. Men wearing that blue cap which came from the Pyrenees to the Gironde are bearing on their backs heavy sheaves which the women, in large straw hats with their bare feet on the grey canvas of the threshing-floor, feed by handfuls into the thresher, which keeps humming like a hive of bees. A thin, strong youth takes away the denuded and broken straw on the end of his fork, whilst the grains of corn as they are poured into a winnower that turns with a handle, give up the refuse of their light

garb to the wind.   Animals and men act in concert
with the slow persistency of the rustic nature.   But,
behind the sheaves, in the shade of the barn, some
little children, whose wide-open eyes and smudged
cheeks are alone visible, are laughing in the hay
waggons.   These women, these sunburnt men, with
their wan looks, heavy mouths, and weighed-down
bodies, are not without beauty.   The freedom of their
rustic costume displays exactly all the movements of
their bodies, and those movements, learnt from
their ancestors from time immemorial, are of a
solemn simplicity.   Their faces, which are marked
by no distinct thought, reflect only the soul of the
soil.   One would say that they had been born in a
furrow like the corn they sow and whose bread they
chew with respectful stolidity.   They have the
profound beauty that is born of harmony.   Their
tanned flesh beneath the dust that covers it, that
dust of the fields which does not make one dirty,
takes on in the light something tawny, ardent, and
opulent.   The gold of the sheaves encompasses
them, a light-coloured dust floats around them, as
if the glory of the antique Ceres were still scattered
in our fields and in our barns.

And thus, laying aside books, pen, and paper, I
look with envy at those threshers of corn, those
simple artisans of the work that is pre-eminent over
all others.   What is my task by the side of theirs ?
And how humble and petty I feel myself before
them !   What they do is necessary.   And we,
frivolous jugglers, vain flute-players, can we flatter
ourselves that we do anything which is, I do not say
useful, but merely innocent ?   Happy the man and
the ox who trace out their furrow straight !   All the
rest is madness, or, at least, uncertainty, a cause of

trouble and cares. The workmen that I see from my window will to-day thresh three hundred trusses of corn, then they will go to bed tired and satisfied, without doubting the goodness of their work. Oh ! the joy of performing an exact and regular task ! But I, shall I know this evening, when my ten pages are written, whether I have filled my day well and earned my sleep ? Shall I know whether I have carried the good grain into my barn ? Shall I know if my words are the bread that sustains life ? Let us at least know, whatever be our task, that we perform it with a simple heart, with good will. For two years already, I have been discoursing of the things of the mind to a select public, and I can bear witness on my own behalf that I have never concealed from it what I have honestly thought. You have often seen me uncertain, but always sincere. I have been truthful, and on that ground, at least, I have preserved the right of addressing myself to my kind. I make no other claim. To lie effectively requires a rhetorical skill the very alphabet of which I am unacquainted with. I am ignorant of the artifices of language, and know no other use for speech than to express my thoughts.

On this hillside, among the vines whose stalks writhe on the surface of a burning soil, no new book has arrived to invite my lazy criticism. I open again the " Anthology of the Poets of the Nineteenth Century." In 1820, when Lamartine was publishing the " Méditations " and opening up a new well of poetry, a young officer of the idle army of the Restoration, a poor nobleman, equally alien from the servile royalism of the sons of the emigrants and from the criminal violence of those affiliated to the Carbonari, was employing his leisure while in garrison by composing for himself some short, chaste, and elegant poems that showed a new feeling ; ancient scenes animated and vivified by a modern soul ; moving memories of the old France whose despised and tattered traditions poetry was soon to collect piously. It was still Millevoye, Millevoye whom, in spite of our pride, we must recognise at the hidden well-spring of romanticism, for he was celebrating with the hectic nymphs whose haunt it was, all those still indistinct figures of our national legends. But it was a larger and purer Millevoye, rid of the tatters of an antiquated Muse. Or rather it was no longer Millevoye, it was already Alfred de Vigny. His " Poèmes " were published in 1822. Less abundant, less largely inspired than Lamartine, from the beginning he surpassed the poet of the " Méditations " in sureness of language and in knowledge of versification. Later, he carried higher than any poet of his time the luminous audacity of thought. His destiny was a strange one. Only two collections of poems mark his fairly long life. The first is a youthful, the second a posthumous, volume. The intervening years of that studious existence are filled with works in fiction and drama, one at least of which, " Servitude et Grandeur Militaires," is a real masterpiece. Alfred de Vigny was a pioneer. He gave examples, before the *début* of Victor Hugo, who was five years his senior, of the type of full and sonorous verse that was to prevail. But his har-monious thought formed slowly, like crystal, its prisms of light. His entire existence distilled but a small number of verses.

Is it on that account that a poet so rare, and of the most intelligent genius, had, upon the whole, little influence on his contemporaries ? Without

doubt too long a silence made him forgotten by the
crowd ; renown must be given nourishment continually in order to make it robust. That is what
Victor Hugo, the most valiant of poet-workers did,
and it is what Alfred de Vigny did not do.

But was there not, in his very distinction, an
obstacle which withheld him from literary popu-
larity ? That ivory tower into which it was said he
retired, what was it, if not his talent itself, his lofty
and solitary mind ? Alfred de Vigny was early
aware of the call to solitude. He conceived of the
poet as a new Moses on the Sinai of souls. He was
calm and disdainful. He had not Lamartine's and
Hugo's good fortune ; he did not communicate
with the crowd, and did not live in sympathy with
public feeling. Romanticism, which sprang from
the Revolution pell-mell with Parliamentary eloquence, patriotic exaltation, and liberal ardours, was,
in its essence, a blind and violent reaction against
the spirit of the eighteenth century. It was a
religious rocket. The lyric poets of 1820 to 1830
all sang the canticle of an ethereal and picturesque
Christianity. Alfred de Vigny entered ill into the
concert : he had not the neo-Christian feeling. He
was not even a believer in the supernatural. At the
end of his life, he inclined towards a sort of stoical
atheism : we know the fine symbolic poem in which
he shows us Jesus sweating the bloody sweat on the
Mount of Olives, and calling in vain on his Heavenly
Father. The clouds remain deaf, and the poet
exclaims :

" S'il est vrai qu'au jardin sacré des Écritures
Le Fils de l'Homme ait dit ce qu'on voit rapporté,
Muet, aveugle et sourd au cri des créatures,
Si Dieu nous rejeta comme un monde avorté,

Le sage opposera le dédain à l'absence
Et ne répondra plus que par un froid silence
Au silence éternel de la divinité." *

You will not find these sombre verses from
" Destinées " in the new Anthology. You will
meet there, in compensation, with that " Maison
du berger " which, as a poet, M. André Lemoyne,
says, " is one of the finest love poems of all the ages."
It is also the expression of a sombre and pathetic
philosophy whose painful eloquence is unsurpassed :

· · · · ·

" Sur mon cœur déchiré viens poser ta main pure,
Ne me laisse jamais seul avec nature,
Car je la connais trop pour n'en pas avoir peur.
Elle me dit : . . .
Je roule avec dédain, sans voir et sans entendre,
A côté des fourmis les populations ;
Je ne distingue pas leur terrier de leur cendre,
J'ignore en les portant les noms des nations.
On me dit un mère et je suis une tombe.
Mon hiver prend vos morts comme son hécatombe,
Mon printemps n'entend pas vos adorations.

Avant vous j'étais belle et toujours parfumée,
J'abandonnais au vent mes cheveux tout entiers,
Je suivais dans les cieux ma route accoutumée,
Sur l'axe harmonieux des divins balanciers.
Après vous, traversant l'espace où tout s'élance,
J'irai seule et sereine, en un chaste silence ;
Je fendrai l'air du front et de mes seins altiers." †

---

* " If it is true that, in the sacred garden of the Scriptures, the
Son of Man said what is recorded, if God, silent, blind, and deaf
to the cry of His creatures, rejects us as an abortive world, the sage
will oppose contempt to withdrawal, and will no longer answer save
by a cold silence to the eternal silence of divinity."

· · · · · ·

† " On my torn heart come and place thy pure hand, never leave
me alone with nature, for I know her too well not to fear her.   She
says to me : . . . I whirl round contemptuously, unseeing and

This philosophical sadness is singular, and strikes a note not often heard in romanticism. For we must not compare it with Lamartine's " Désespoir." Lamartine blasphemed then, and blasphemy is only possible in a believer. Besides, " Désespoir " is succeeded in the " Méditations " by a formal apology for Providence. As for Victor Hugo, he was born and died a choir-boy. In all things he changed his ideas as ideas changed around him. His deism alone remained fixed in that perpetual transformation. At eighty, his beliefs were without a wrinkle ; his faith in God was that of a little child. One evening, having heard one of the guests in his house deny the existence of Providence, he began to weep.

The romanticism of 1820 was moral and religious ; that of 1830 was picturesque. The first was a sentiment, the second a taste. And what a taste ! Knights, pages, varlets, the lady of the castle, pale and melancholy, resting her head in her hands at the window, ribald men and ribald women, people hung, hell-fire taverns, an incredible multitude of inn-keepers, in a word, the whole Middle Ages, seen in the shadow, through a red and green Bengal fire ; then all the lovers of the German ballads, elves, goblins, gnomes, phantoms, skeletons, and death's

unhearing, the peoples of the earth side by side with the ants ; I do not distinguish their dwelling from their ashes, and as I carry them I am ignorant of the names of the nations. I am called a mother and I am a tomb. My winter takes your dead as its hecatomb, my spring does not hear your adorations. Before your day I was beautiful and always perfumed, I abandoned to the wind my whole hair, I followed my accustomed way in the heavens on the harmonious axis of the divine scales. After your departure, I shall go on alone and serene, traversing in a chaste silence the space through which all things move ; I shall cleave the air with my brow and my haughty breasts."

heads. Victor Hugo's "Ballades" are the most complete literary evidence of that puerile taste of which Boulanger's sketches and Nanteuil's lithographs offer us the plastic representation. The Anthology which serves me as a guide, has very discreetly preserved the traces of that fashion which was innocent even in its madness. Its forms and colours are found in a "ballad" by that Louis Bertrand who, like a good romantic, signed himself Aloïsius Bertrand.

> "O Dijon, la fille
> Des glorieux ducs,
> Qui portes béquille
> Dans tes ans caducs. . . .
>
> La grise bastille
> Aux gris tiercelets
> Troua ta mantille
> De trente boulets.
>
> Le reître, qui pille
> Nippes au bahut,
> Nonnes sous leur grille,
> Te cassa ton luth." *

Does not that seem *Middle Age* enough for you ? But the masterpiece of this taste is assuredly the prologue to "Madame Putiphar." There are in it three symbolic cavaliers, superbly coloured :

> " Le premier cavalier est jeune, frais, alerte ;
> Il porte élégamment un corselet d'acier,
> Scintillant à travers une résille verte
> Comme à travers des pins les cristaux d'un glacier.

---

* "O Dijon, daughter of glorious dukes, who bearest a crutch in thy decrepit years. . . . The grey fortress where the grey falcons shelter has rent thy cloak with thirty bullets. The brigand who plunders the clothes from the coffer, nuns behind their grill, have broken thy lute."

Son œil est amoureux ; sa belle tête blonde
A pour coiffure un casque, orné de lambrequins,
Dont le cimier touffu l'enveloppe l'inonde.
Comme fait le lampas autour des palanquins.

    .   .   .   .

Le second cavalier, ainsi qu'un reliquaire,
Est juché gravement sur le dos d'un mulet
Qui ferait le bonheur d'un gothique antiquaire ;
Car sur son râble osseux, anguleux chapelet,
Avec soin est jetée une housse fanée,
Housse ayant affublé quelque vieil escabeau,
Ou carapaçonne la blanche haquenée
Sur laquelle arriva de Bavière Isabeau
Il est gros, gras, poussif. . . ." *

This second cavalier, seems to me to mark the
time when the Hôtel de Cluny was furnished with
refuse from the Middle Ages and became a museum.
But it is the third cavalier who reveals a whole
ideal. Behold, I pray you, this third cavalier :

" Pour le tiers cavalier, c'est un homme de pierre,
Semblant le Commandeur, horrible et ténébreux ;
Un hyperboréen, un gnome sans paupière,
Sans prunelle et sans front, qui résonne le creux
Comme un tombeau vidé lorsqu'une arme le frappe.
Il porte à sa main gauche une faux dont l'acier
Pleure à grands flots le sang, puis une chausse-trape
En croupe où se faisande un pendu grimacier." †

---

* " The first cavalier is young, fresh, alert ; he jauntily wears a
corselet of steel sparkling through a green net like the crystals of a
glacier through pine-trees. His eye is amorous ; his beautiful
blond head is covered by a helmet decorated with fringes the tufted
summit of which envelopes and inundates him like the silk awnings
round a palanquin.

" The second cavalier is, like a reliquary, perched gravely upon the
back of a mule who would make the happiness of a Gothic antiquary ;
for, like an angular garland, a faded saddle-cloth is carefully placed
upon his bony back, a saddle-cloth that had been wrapped round
some old stool, or adorned the white hackney on which Isabel came
from Bavaria. He is large, fat, and scant of breath. . . ."

† " As for the third cavalier, he is a man of stone, resembling the
Commander, horrible and darksome ; a hyperborean, a gnome

I

That is the ghastly cavalry whose galloping the good Pétrus heard in his heart ! Ingenuous dream of those young lettered and sedentary people who, whilst leading the most peaceful of lives, gave the middle classes to believe that all night long they drank flaming punch out of their mistresses' skulls ! In those times a Young Frenchman did not go to the office where he was a clerk without exclaiming with a sarcastic laugh : " I am damned ! "

Not that everything is ridiculous in this second romantic movement of which Victor Hugo was the most dazzling expression. The Young Frenchmen who threw themselves with much frenzy and still more ignorance into what was exotic and archaic, followed, none the less, two lucky paths. Conquerors of that poetic Germany which Madame de Staël discovered, they brought back from it lieds and ballads and the precious cup of the King of Thule. They thus brought into French literature, which is naturally reasonable and reasoning, a little of the happy vagueness that makes the poetry of the Germanic races echo indefinitely in the soul. On the other hand, by studying the Middle Ages, of which, moreover, they formed so odd an idea, they awoke, after the fashion of the great Augustin Thierry, the ancient memories of our country, and discovered the true springs of inspiration from which a national poetry should drink and refresh itself. They did not understand much of this, being very

without an eyelid, without an eyeball, and without a brow, who sounds hollow like an empty tomb when an arm strikes it. He bears in his left hand a scythe whose steel weeps great clots of blood, then there is a caltrop on the crupper on which rots the grinning corpse of a victim of the gibbet."

little of philosophers ; but they had instinct : they
were artists.

One of the finest poems of that period, " Roland,"
is signed with the obscure name of Napol, the
Pyrenean. That is the pseudonym of M. Napoléon
Peyrat, who was born in 1809 at Mas-d'Azil, in the
Ariège, near the falls of the Arise, and who died a
short time ago, a pastor at Saint-Germain-en-Laye.
This " Roland," an ode in an epistle, is the jewel of
romanticism. You will find it complete on pages
258 to 263 of Lemerre's Anthology. I can only
quote two or three stanzas. I shall do so without
any preliminary analysis, and without commentary,
trusting to the belief that a fragment of a fine work
of art often causes the splendour of the whole to be
divined :

> " L'Arabie, en nos champs, des rochers espagnols
> S'abattit ; le printemps a moins de rossignols
> Et l'été moins d'épis de seigle.
> Blonds étaient les chevaux dont le vent soulevait
> La crinière argentée, et leur pied grêle avait
> Des poils comme des plumes d'aigle.
>
> Ces Mores mécréants, ces maudits Sarrasins
> Buvaient l'eau de nos puits et mangeaient nos raisins
> Et nos figues, et nos grenades,
> Suivaient dans les vallons les vierges à l'œil noir
> Et leur parlaient d'amour, à la lune, le soir,
> Et leur faisaient des sérénades.
>
> Pour eux, leurs grands yeux noirs, pour eux, leurs beaux
> seins bruns,
> Pour eux, leurs longs baisers, leur bouche aux doux parfums,
> Pour eux, leur belle joue ovale ;
> Et quand elles pleuraient, criant ' Fils des démons ! '
> Ils les mettaient en croupe, et par-dessus les monts
> Ils faisaient sauter leur cavale." *

---

* " Arabia, in our fields threw down her Spanish rocks ; spring has
fewer nightingales and summer fewer blades of rye. Fair were the

Further on there is a touch which Victor Hugo
has reproduced in his " Aymerillot " :

> " Les âmes chargaient l'air comme un nuage noir
> Et notre bon Roland, en riant chaque soir,
> S'allait laver dans les cascades." *

Singular sport of fate ! Napol, the Pyrenean, is
the least known of the poets of 1830. Their obscure
companion, and disappearing before his time, he yet
leaves the finest and most complete masterpiece of
his period.

Whilst I am blackening paper with images of
romanticism, the sun is sinking and slipping towards
the purple horizon.

Here is evening coming. The threshing machine
no longer makes its monotonous humming heard.
The tired workmen pass under my window dragging
along their clogs. I see their slow and peaceful
shadows gliding by, shadows which the setting sun
immeasurably lengthens. Their even step reveals
the peace of heart which only assiduous labour
assures. They have threshed the three hundred
sheaves of corn. They have earned their bread.
Can I, like them, say that I have done my day's
work ?

horses whose silvered manes were tossed by the wind, and their
slender legs had hairs like an eagle's feathers. These unbelieving
Moors, these cursed Saracens, drank the water of our wells and ate our
grapes, and our figs, and our pomegranates, followed the black-eyed
maidens in the valleys, and spoke to them of love in the evenings by
moonlight, and serenaded them. For them their large eyes were dark,
for them their brown bosoms were fair, for them their kisses were long,
the odour of their mouths was sweet, for them their fair cheeks were
rounded ; and when they wept, crying : ' Sons of demons ! ' they put
them on their cruppers and galloped across the mountains."

* " Souls filled the air like a black cloud, and our good Roland
went laughing each evening to wash in the cascades."

M. GASTON PARIS AND THE
FRENCH LITERATURE OF
THE MIDDLE AGES *

HAVE received here among the vines a book which has been to me like the visit of a learned friend. It is the " Manual of French Literature in the Middle Ages." which M. Gaston Paris edited at first for the pupils of the School of Higher Studies and afterwards had printed for the use of those rare spirits who are animated by a methodical curiosity. As the morning was warm and calm, I carried the welcome book to a little oak wood, and I read it under a tree to the song of the birds. A reading done in this way is a happy reading. One does not think of taking notes on the grass. One reads from pleasure, from amusement, and without ulterior motives. One is very disinterested, for there is nothing like the living air of the woods for rendering us indifferent to ourselves and causing our souls to melt into their surroundings. The moving shadow that trembles on the page, and the humming of the insect that passes between the eye and the book blend

* " La Littérature française au moyen âge, XIᵉ et XIVᵉ siècles." By Gaston Paris.

with the author's thought into a delicious impression of nature and life.

With what docility I followed, in my wood, the teaching of M. Gaston Paris! How willingly I entered with him into the soul of our ancestors, into their robust and simple faith, into their art, sometimes gross, sometimes subtle, almost always symmetrical and regular as the treeless gardens of the old miniatures! The pity is that in a few hours I devoured a book formed for long study, one in which the ideas are very condensed. That is why I feel a sort of trouble, an hallucination, as it were. It seems to me that this old France which I have traversed so quickly, this beloved land with its forests, its fields, its white churches, its castles, and its towns, was as small as the meadow which I saw down there through the branches ; it seems to me that those ages of great sword-strokes, of prayers, and of long songs, passed away in a few hours. Knights, burgesses, peasants, clerics, minstrels, jugglers, appeared to me like those insects who people the grass at our feet. It is a miniature of which my eyes have kept the impression, a miniature so delicate that one could discover the slightest details by looking at it with a magnifying-glass. The fairy-tales speak of a cloth woven with such artifice that it was held in a nut-shell, and on this cloth all the kingdoms of the earth were represented, with their kings, their chivalry, their towns, and their countries. It was the work of a fairy. M. Gaston Paris' book bears a marvellous resemblance to that marvellous cloth, as I picture it to myself, beneath my oak. My hands scarcely feel its weight, and I see in it the faces of all those who, in pleasant France in the ages of chivalry, spoke

of combats, of love, and of wisdom. What I admire
is the clearness of the picture. I distinctly see the
land, clothed, as the chronicler Raoul Glaber says,
with the white robe of the churches. On it move
simple men who believe in God and are assured of
the intercession of Our Lady. Some are clerics,
and their life, ruled like the pages of an antiphonary,
is breathed forth with the harmonious monotony of
plain-song. When they fall into sin, which is the
result of Adam's curse, they still remain faithful
to God, and do not despair. They have no families,
they write in Latin, and they dispute subtly. They
are the shepherds of the flock of souls. Others go away
to the wars ; it sometimes happens that they pillage
convents and do evil to the nuns, who are the brides
of Jesus Christ. But they will be saved by virtue
of the divine blood that flowed on the Cross. They
have slain many Saracens and fasted punctually
on Fridays, and these good works will be credited to
them. The villeins, who labour for them, are men,
for they have been baptized. They can endure
great ills upon earth, for they will share in the
eternal felicity. The parish priest, who every
Sunday promises them Paradise, is in his ingenuous
way a marvellous economist. To those who have
no land here below, he shows the flowery lands of
Heaven. Heaven, where God the Father sits,
dressed like an emperor, is quite near : you could
go up to it on a ladder if only Saint Peter were
willing, and Saint Peter is a good man ; a poor man
and of humble birth, he is friendly to the villeins,
and, perhaps, a little deferential to the nobles.
Moreover, the Holy Virgin, the angels, and the
saints of both sexes, are descending at all moments
to the earth. There is nothing strange about the

blessed, they are worthy men and ladies who, just
like little genii and fairies, favour those who are
devoted to them. The goings and comings from
the church militant to the church triumphant
are perpetual ; the spires of the cathedrals mark
the undefined limit between heaven and earth.
As for hell, it is in the earth itself, and sometimes
shepherds see, in the depths of the caverns, its
infected mouths. Hell frightens, as François Villon
says. But in whatever way you live, you count
on avoiding it ; you can, you ought to hope : hope
is a virtue. Shall I speak of purgatory ? It is
hardly distinct from this earth to which the souls
in torment return every night to ask for prayers.
That is the world of the Middle Ages ; it could be
represented, fairly well, by an old, rather complicated
clock, like that of Strasburg. Three stages of
marionettes, which the wheels would move, would be
enough. I know well that in speaking thus I am
still dreaming. For, indeed, the men who lived
between the eleventh century and the fifteenth,
were subject, like all of us, to the infinitely complex
laws of life ; the immense nature which envelopes
us bathed them as it does us in the ocean of illusions ;
they were men. But they had neither our fears
nor our hopes, and their world was quite small
compared with ours. If we compare it with the
universe of Galileo, Laplace, and Father Secchi,
it was in truth but an ingenious picture-clock.

The simplicity of their imagination is a thing to
enjoy. It is painted in delightful touches in the
" Miracles of the Virgin " and in the " Lives of
the Saints." M. Gaston Paris' learned criticism
is quite softened by it. Is not, in truth, the account
of the nun who from weakness of the flesh left her

convent that she might give herself up to sin, an engaging story? She returns after long years, having lost her innocence but not her faith, for in the time of her misdeeds she had not ceased to address a prayer every day to Our Lady. Having gone back to her convent, she heard the sisters speaking to her as if she had never left them. The Holy Virgin had assumed the appearance and costume of her who loved her even in sin, and had performed the sacristan's duties for her, so that no one had perceived the absence of the disloyal nun. But M. Gaston Paris knows another and more touching miracle.

There was once a monk of an extreme simplicity of mind, and so ignorant that he did not know how to recite anything except the " Hail Mary ! " He was despised by the other monks, but, when he died, five roses sprang forth from his mouth in honour of the five letters of the name of Mary (Marie). And those who had so mocked at his ignorance honoured his memory as that of a saint. Finally, here is a still more ingenuous miracle, that of " The Tumbler of Our Lady." He was a poor juggler who, after having performed feats of strength in the public places to gain his living, thought of eternity and retired to a convent. There he saw the monks honouring the Virgin, like the good clerks they were, by learned prayers. But he was no clerk and could not imitate them. At last he thought of shutting himself up in the chapel and, before the Virgin, alone and in secret, doing the somersaults that had brought him the most applause in the time when he had been a juggler. Some of the monks, anxious because of his long retreats, set themselves to spy on him, and surprised him at his pious exercises. They saw the Mother of God herself after each somersault descend and wipe the brow of her " tumbler."

It is in these popular imaginings, it is in the legends that came from the East, in the stories of Saint Catherine and Saint Margaret, that we must seek, it seems to me, for the obscure feelings which, after three or four centuries of existence, ended in the vocation of Joan of Arc, and in the hour of danger rendered possible the most charming of marvels, the deliverance of a whole people by a shepherd girl. I am explaining myself badly on this point, and I could not do better without completely leaving my subject. I shall do nothing of the kind. One can dream under a tree ; still some connection is necessary, even in a dream. That figure of feudal France which we have just sketched after the manner of the fourteenth and fifteenth century illuminators, with strokes that are too light and colours that are too vivid, is the art, is the epic, lyric, and sacred literature of those times, as M. Gaston Paris, who suggested to us the idea of it, presents it to us.

M. Paris is not a mere scholar. He unites the philosophic sense with literary taste, and his " Manual of Old French," of which I am speaking to you here, has so much interest only because in it one continually sees general ideas arising out of the assembly of facts. The author first shows us the fatality which will not cease to weigh upon the whole literature of the Middle Ages, and which will finally determine its character. The clerics, who almost alone read and wrote, kept up the use of Latin. They regarded that language as the only instrument worthy of expressing a serious thought.

"That," says M. Paris, "is an event of great importance, a capital fact, which destroyed all harmony in the literary production of the epoch : it divided the nation into two, and was doubly fatal by withdrawing from the cultivation of literature the most distinguished and instructed minds, and by imprisoning them in a dead language, alien from the modern genius, where an immense and consecrated literature imposed on them its ideas and its forms, and where it was almost impossible for them to develop any originality."

Despised by instructed people, the writings in the vulgar tongue were scarcely addressed to anybody but the ignorant. At first they could be only tales and songs. And since these songs were composed for the pleasure of the nobles and burgesses who did not read, it was necessary to read them aloud to them, or better, to sing them. Thus the " Chanson de Roland," and, in general, all the old heroic poems were sung by the wandering minstrels. Hence the essentially popular character of the French literature of the Middle Ages.

This literature, abundant and simple, brutal and yet clever, like the people of whom it was the ideal, was above all modelled by hands the most skilful in moulding souls, the hands of the Church. The Church carved it like an image. It gave it its principal characteristics : an ingenuous faith, an air of a tender and cruel child, a familiar and rustic fondness for the marvellous, an unbecoming fear of the beauty of the flesh (which did not prevent it from being obscene when it took the fancy), perfect serenity, the absolute certainty of possessing immutable truth. This latter feature, the essential feature, has been admirably noted by M. Gaston Paris.

" The name," says that scholar, " which we have
given to the Middle Ages, indicates how really
transitory the period was, and yet what characterises
it most profoundly is its idea of the immutability of
things. Antiquity, above all in its last centuries,
is dominated by belief in a continuous decadence ;
modern times have since their dawn been animated
by faith in an indefinite progress. The Middle
Ages did not know either that discouragement or
that hope. For the men of that time, the world
had always been such as they saw it (it is on that
account that their paintings of antiquity seem
grotesque to us), and the judgment day would
find it no different. . . . The material world
appeared to the imagination as stable as it was
limited, with its revolving star-bedecked vault of
heaven, its motionless earth, and its hell ; it is
the same with its moral world : the relations of
men to one another are regulated by fixed pre-
scriptions on the legitimacy of which there is
no doubt, save to observe them more or less
exactly. Nobody thinks of protesting against the
society in which he is, or dreams of a better-con-
structed one ; but all would like it to be more
completely what it ought to be. These conditions
took away from the poetry of the Middle Ages
much that makes the charm and depth of that of
other epochs : man's anxiety about his destiny,
the painful examination of great moral problems,
doubt about the very bases of happiness and virtue,
tragic conflicts between individual aspiration and
the social order." (Page 34.)

What then is the interest, what are the merits
of this literature, condemned from its birth to an
irremediable humility, ignorant of the beauty of

forms, of the pleasure of things, of the universal
Venus, and still more aloof from those noble curiosities, that anxiousness of thought, that sublime
evil, that divine monster, which we caress whilst
it devours us ? By what charms can the immense
library of the Middle Ages, long forgotten beneath
the dust, and only discovered yesterday, still
attract and please us ?

The scholar whom we are consulting will answer
us. That forgotten literature, he will tell us,
remains interesting because it is " the simple, and
above all, the powerful expression of the ardent
passions of feudal society." It will interest also
by its picture of " the new relations between the
sexes, as they were formed under the influence of
Christianity," and it will please us by the note,
until then unheard, of *courtesy*. Lastly, we shall
enjoy in the common works of the twelfth century, " the good sense, the wit, the malice, the
shrewd good-nature, and the airy grace," that
are the qualities of the race, the gifts that the
fairies of our woods and our fountains granted
to Jacques Bonhomme to console him for all his
ills.

And M. Gaston Paris concludes with these fine
words :

" On the whole, the great interest of this literature, the thing that renders its study especially
attractive and fruitful, is that it reveals to us better
than all historical documents our ancestors' state
of manners, ideas, and feelings during a period that
was not without splendour nor without profit for
our country, and in which, for the first time and
not for the last, France had, in regard to the neighbouring nations, a part to play which was accepted

everywhere as one of intellectual, literary, and social initiative and direction." (Page 32.)

And the old oak under which I am sitting speaks in its turn, and says to me:

Read, read under my shade the Gothic songs whose refrains I formerly heard mingling with the rustling of my leaves. The soul of your ancestors is in these songs, older than myself. Know these ancestors, share their joys and their past griefs. It is thus, ephemeral creature, that you will live through long centuries in a few years. Be pious, venerate the soil of your country. Never take a handful of it into your hand without thinking that it is sacred. Love all those old relatives whose dust has mingled with that soil which has nourished me for centuries, and whose spirit has passed into you, their Benjamin, the child of better days. Reproach not these ancestors for their ignorance, nor for the weakness of their thought, nor even for the illusions of fear which sometimes made them cruel. It would be equivalent to reproaching yourself for having been a child. Know that they have laboured, suffered, hoped for you, and that you owe them everything !

DICTIONARY *

THE cold and quiet rain, which is slowly falling from the grey sky, strikes little blows on my window as if to call me; it makes but a faint noise and yet each drop resounds sadly in my heart. While sitting at the fire-place with my feet resting on the andirons, as I dry by a fire of vine-twigs the healthy mud of road and furrow, the monotonous rain chains my thoughts in a melancholy reverie, and I reflect. I must go away. The autumn is casting its humid veils upon the woods. To-night the sonorous trees shuddered at the first beatings of its wings in the perturbed sky, and here is a peaceful sadness come from the West with the rain and fog. Everything is mute. The yellow leaves fall noiselessly in the lanes; the animals are resigned and silent; one hears only the rain; and this great silence weighs upon my lips and upon my thought. I would like to say nothing. I have only one idea, that I must go away. Oh! it is not the gloom, the rain, and the cold that are driving me off. The country pleases me even when it has no longer any smiles. I do not like it for its joy only. I like it because I like it. Are those whom we love less dear in their sadness?

* " Dictionnaire Classique." By M. Gazier.

No, I am leaving these woods and these vines with sorrow. In vain do I tell myself that I shall find again in Paris the pleasant warmth of friendly homes, the cultured conversation of master minds, and all the presentations of the arts by which life is adorned. I regret the elm-tree hedge by which I used to walk as I read verses, the little wood which sang in the least wind, the great oak in the meadow where the cows pastured, the hollow willows by the border of a stream, the path through the vines at the end of which the moon rose ; I regret that eternal mantle of foliage and sky in which one puts all ills so well to sleep.

Besides, I have always felt to excess the bitterness of departure. I feel too deeply that to go away is to die to something. What is life but a succession of partial deaths ? We must lose everything, not all at once, but hourly ; we must leave everything on the way. At each step we break one of those invisible bonds that attach us to beings and to things. Is not that to die continually ? Alas ! this condition is hard ; but it is the human condition. Am I going to distress myself at this ? Am I going to parade my futile regrets ? Shall I remain here, before the fire, listening to the rain fall, watching the rapid tongues of flame lick up the vine-twigs, and bemoaning myself without reason ? No ! I will throw off the vapours of autumn. I will perform my daily task with application. I will speak to you of books ; I will converse with you about good literature which sweetens and ennobles life. The schoolboys have gone back a week ago already. They are doing themes, exercises, dissertations. I, an old schoolboy, will, like them, do my page of writing. I will no longer listen to the rain counselling me to idleness and sleep. This very moment I find, thrown down on my table, a little book whose honest and modest appearance inspires ideas of work and duty. Severely clad in black cloth and buff paper, it wears the traditional livery of school-books. It is in truth a school-book, a dictionary, the " New Illustrated School Dictionary," by M. A. Gazier, lecturer of the Faculty of Letters of Paris. Forgotten by some schoolboy a week ago, I have several times found myself handling it, and I have turned over its pages with a good deal of interest.

It is a new book, hardly six months old. The first edition bears the date of 1888. But I do not speak of it on the ground of this vain and transitory novelty, which is often accompanied by an irremediable decay. So many works are born old ! There are many compilers in the University as well as elsewhere, many little Trublets who copy from one another. Originality is perhaps rarer and more difficult in matters of teaching than in anything else. M. Gazier's work is new in plan, in structure, and in spirit. It is conceived and executed in an original fashion. It is therefore well worth while saying a word about it. Besides it is a dictionary, and I have a mania for such books.

Baudelaire relates that when he was young and unknown, having begged for an interview with Théophile Gautier, the master, as he welcomed him, asked him this question :

" Do you read the dictionaries ? "

Baudelaire answered that he read them eagerly. He took the right course, for Gautier, who had devoured innumerable vocabularies of arts and crafts, regarded a poet or a prose-writer as unworthy

to live if he did not take pleasure in reading lexicons
and glossaries. He loved words and he knew many
of them. If he complimented Baudelaire, what
praises would he not have awarded to our friend,
M. José-Maria de Heredia, who roundly declares
that in his opinion the perusal of Jean Nicot's
dictionary imparts more amusement, pleasure, and
emotion than reading " The Three Musketeers " !
There's an artist's imagination for you ! According
to M. José-Maria de Heredia's taste, the alphabetical table of precious stones or the catalogue of
the artillery museum is the most moving of romances
of adventure. For myself, who put the matter
less subtly and do not ordinarily find more meanings
for words than ordinary usage gives them, I have
often been surprised into playing truant in some
great dictionary, leafy as a forest, Furetière, for
example, or Le Trévoux, or even the worthy
Littré, so confused, but so rich in illustrative
quotations. Ah ! words are pictures, a dictionary
is the universe in alphabetical order. On a fair
estimate, the dictionary is the book above all books.
All the other books are in it: it is only a matter of
taking them out. Also, what was Adam's first
occupation when he left God's hands ? Genesis
tells us that he first named the animals by their
names. Before everything, he made a dictionary of
natural history. He did not write it because the
arts were not then born. They were only born
with sin. Adam is none the less the father of
lexicography as well as of humanity. It is strange
that in ancient and mediæval times so few dictionaries were made. Lexicography, in the rigorous
sense of the word, hardly dates further back than
the seventeenth century. But since then what

progress it has made and what services it has
rendered! All the dead or living languages, all
the established sciences, all the arts have now their
vocabulary. There are in them magnificent inven-
tories which do honour to modern times. I have
told you that I love dictionaries. I love them not only
for their great utility, but also for their inherent beauty
and magnificence. Yes, beauty! magnificence! Here
is a French dictionary, that of M. Gazier or any
other, think that the entire soul of our country
is within it. Think that in these thousand or twelve
hundred pages of little signs, there is the genius and
the nature of France, the ideas, the joys, the labours,
and the sorrows of our ancestors and of ourselves,
the monuments of the public and domestic life of
all those who have breathed the sacred air, the
pleasant air which we in our turn are breathing;
think that to each word in the dictionary there
corresponds an idea or a feeling which was the idea,
the feeling, of an innumerable multitude of beings;
think that all these united words are the work
of the flesh, the blood, and the soul of the country
and of humanity.

An old heroic poem relates that the Countess de
Roussillon, the daughter of the King of France,
watched from the summit of her tower a great
combat which was being waged for her dowry,
between her father and her husband. The combat
was bloody and lasted all day. When night fell,
the Countess came down alone from her tower, and
went to gaze on the dead, " her beautiful dear dead,
lying in the grass and the dew." And the poem
adds: " She wanted to kiss them all." Well, I
also feel a deep tenderness rising in my heart
before all the words of the French tongue, before

this army of lofty or lowly terms. I love them all, or at least they interest me, and I press with a fondling sympathetic touch the little book that contains them all. That is why I especially love French dictionaries.

I told you that M. Gazier's is new in plan and execution. It combines with the French vocabulary some of the elements of a general encyclopædia. It includes the scientific terminology, which has become considerably extended within the past few years. Lastly, and this is its greatest originality, it contains maps and illustrations. I see with pleasure that the University is beginning to admit teaching by means of pictures. In my time, I mean at the time when I was at college, and that is not yet so very long since, the professors regarded all engravings without distinction as objects of dissipation. The teacher of the fourth class, among others, held the most rapid glance at a portrait or engraving to be a frivolity unworthy of a youthful student of the humanities. I remember, not without a certain resentment, that one day he surprised in my hands an old edition of the " Garden of Greek Roots," of which this copy, bound in mottled calf and half worn out by some pupil of M. Lancelot, M. Lemaître, or M. Hamon, should have been held sacred by everybody. The pedant seized it, opened it roughly, then tore out the frontispiece which represented a child, clad in the antique fashion, opening a manorial gate of the Louis Quatorze style, and penetrating into a kitchen-garden laid out in the taste of Le Nôtre, the garden

" Of those nourishing roots
That make the spirit learned."

Yet it was an innocent picture, a naïve allegory. The design was both well conceived and well engraved. The solitaries of Port-Royal had not been afraid to enliven a book intended for the pupils of the Junior Schools with it. A little art did not alarm their austerity. But this profane ornament which the saints of the new Thebaid had tolerated, offended my ignorant pedagogue. I see him still tearing the pretty engraving with his clumsy and dirty fingers, and it is with a sort of avenging joy that after twenty-five years, I deliver up his stupid crime to the indignation of people of taste.

The proscription of pictures was especially vexatious in the history classes. One forms an idea of a people only by the sight of the monuments it has left. Illustrated history exercises a powerful charm on the imagination. But we were taught the life of peoples as it would be taught to moles. M. Victor Drury's books appeared about that time. One found here and there in them costumes and buildings. They created a revolution. I see with pleasure that great progress has been made in this direction. Last year I glanced through a Greek history, the illustration of which appeared to me as rich as the moderate price and small size of the book permitted. The text of that history is by M. Louis Ménard.

To apply illustration to lexicography is a very happy idea upon which M. A. Gazier is to be congratulated. He has put into his dictionary a thousand little engravings, and these, at need, complete the definitions which are necessarily a trifle too summary and too vague. These little engravings amuse and instruct me. I think they will amuse and instruct children, if indeed they are not more

serious or more learned than I am. But what seems
to me perfectly ingenious in these illustrations are
the pictures of things as a whole. One finds at the
words SHIP, CHURCH, ARMOUR, CASTLE, SKELETON,
DIGESTIVE (APPARATUS), LOCOMOTIVE, RAILWAY, &c.,
representations of those different totalities, together
with the names of the parts that compose them.
Thus we see at the word CHURCH, the respective
positions of the nave, of the transept, of the sanctuary, of the buttresses, of the flying-buttresses, of
the gables, of the steeple with its bell-turrets, its
louvre-windows, &c. The schoolboys of to-day are
lucky to have books so handy and so attractive.

M. ZOLA'S PURITY *

ROM the outset a little official announcement, inserted in several newspapers, has made us aware that M. Zola's new novel was chaste, and written expressly to " be put into the hands of all women and even of young girls." Its exceptional and distinctive modesty was extolled. This time, said the puff preliminary, this time " the novelist has determined on a purely idealistic flight, a soaring towards what is most poetically gracious and affecting." And the announcement did not err. M. Zola resolved on the flight and the soaring, and the poetry and the touching grace, and if, in order to be poetic, graceful, and touching, it were enough to resolve, M. Zola would certainly be, at the present moment, the most touching, the most graceful, the most poetic, the most winged, and the most uplifted among novelists.

Assuredly, we can but praise him for his new profession. He espouses chastity and thus affords us the most edifying example. One can only regret that he celebrates this mystic alliance with too much noise and uproar.

Could he not be modest without publishing it in the newspapers ? Must Saint Joseph's lily become

* " Le Rêve."

in his hands an instrument for advertisement ?
But doubtless he wished to be reticent, and has not
succeeded.

In truth, fame is sometimes importunate. M. Zola
is in the same case with that husband in the fable
who confessed one morning that he had laid an egg,
and who, in the evening, according to the gossips,
had laid a hundred. The author of " Le Rêve "
confided one day to his shadow his desire to be
quit of our mire and to soar into the empyrean,
and next day all Paris knew that he had grown wings.
They were described, they were measured; they
were white and like the wings of doves. People
cried out that it was a miracle. Journalists, ordinarily
not tender-hearted, were moved by this touching
marvel. " See," said they, " how easily this soul
which has long wallowed in the dung-heap soars into
the azure. Henceforth, the author of ' Le Rêve '
surpasses in purity Saint Catherine of Siena, Saint
Theresa, and Saint Aloysius Gonzaga. We must
open wide for him the doors of the literary salons
and of the French Academy. For God has lifted
him up as an example to the people of the world."

For my part, I should prefer a less noisy chastity.
Otherwise, I confess that M. Zola's purity seems to
me very meritorious. It costs him dear : he has
paid for it with all his talent. One does not find a
trace of this talent in the three hundred pages of
" Le Rêve." Confronted with the impalpable
heroine of this nebulous recital, I am forced to agree
that Mouquette had her good points. And, if it is
absolutely necessary to choose, I prefer M. Zola on
all fours to M. Zola winged. The natural, you see,
has an inimitable charm, and one cannot please if
one is no longer oneself. When he does not force

his talent, M. Zola is excellent. He is without a rival in painting washerwomen and zinc-workers. I confide it to you in a whisper : " l'Assommoir " delighted me. I have read ten times and with unmixed joy the marriage of Coupeau, the feast on the goose, and Nana's first communion. They are admirable pictures, full of colour, movement, and life. But one man is not qualified to paint every thing. The most skilful artist can comprehend, seize, and express only what he has in common with his models; or, to put it more clearly, he never paints anything but himself. Some, in truth, such as Shakespeare, have represented the universe. That is because they had an all-embracing soul. Without offence to M. Zola, his soul is not of that sort. However vast it is, zinc factories and flat-irons occupy too much space in it. He is a good painter when he copies what he sees. His mistake is to wish to paint everything. He wearies and exhausts himself in a disproportionate enterprise. He had been already warned that he was falling into what was false and chimerical. The warning was thrown away! He thinks himself infallible. He has long ceased to study from the model. He composes his imaginative pictures from some badly taken notes. His ignorance of the world is prodigious, and, as he has no philosophy, he falls each instant into the monstrous and the absurd. This chief of the naturalist school affronts nature every moment.

This time the error is complete, and one cannot imagine a more irrational novel than " Le Rêve." It is the story of a foundling, brought up in the shadow of a cathedral by some chasuble makers, pious and unaspiring, who occupy an old family mansion adjoining the church. The child is called

Angélique and has been found by the good chasuble makers one snowy morning in the porch of Saint Agnes.

She becomes a mystical embroiderer and rediscovers the secrets of the old master-embroiderers. On one occasion a young glass-maker appears to her, as beautiful as Saint George in a stained glass window. She immediately recognises him for whom she has been waiting, her dream. She loves him, she is loved by him. She knows beforehand that he is a prince. Her dream had not deceived her : in fact, this glass-maker is Félicien VII of Hautecœur, the archbishop's son. Angélique and Félicien are betrothed to one another. But his lordship refuses his consent. The good chasuble makers, in order to break off an attachment that frightens them, tell Félicien that Angélique no longer loves him, and tell Angélique that Félicien is marrying a noble maiden. Angélique dies of it. His lordship himself comes to give her extreme unction. Then he kisses her on the mouth and pronounces these words, which are the device of his family : " If God wills, I will." Then Angélique raises herself up on her bed and receives Félicien into her arms. She revives, and in the cathedral she marries the young heir of the ancient Hautecœurs. After the ceremony, having joined her lips to Félicien's, she dies as she kisses him, and his lordship, who had officiated at the altar, returns, says the author, " to the divine nothingness."

M. Zola ends this little fable with a profound thought : " All is but a dream," he says. And that, I believe, is the only philosophical reflection which he has ever made. I do not want to contradict it. I believe, in truth, that eternal illusion lulls us and

envelopes us, and that life is but a dream. But I
have a difficulty in picturing to myself the author of
" Pot-Bouille " anxiously interrogating the smile of
Maya, and casting his plummet into the ocean of
appearances. I do not represent him to myself as,
like Porphyry, celebrating the silent orgies of metaphysics. When he says that all is but a dream, I
fear he is only thinking of his book, which is in fact
one long reverie.

A great deal is said in it about Saint Agnes and
the Golden Legend. It is beneath the porch of
Saint Agnes that Angélique is found, and it is the
image of Saint Agnes, clad in the golden robe of her
own hair, that Angélique embroiders on his lordship's
mitre before she dies. I have some devotion to
Saint Agnes, and I like the legend of that virgin so
much that, if you are willing, I will repeat it to you
from memory, as it was set down by Voragine :

" Agnes, a virgin of great wisdom, suffered death
in her thirteenth year, and thus found life. If one
only reckoned her years, she was still a child ; but
for prudence and judgment she had the ripeness of
age. Beautiful in face, more beautiful in faith, as
she was coming back from school, the proconsul's
son became enamoured of her and promised her
precious stones and riches without number if she
would consent to become his wife. Agnes answered
him : ' Depart from me, shepherd of death, decoy
of sin, and nutriment of felony. For there is
another that I love.' And then she began to praise
her lover and divine spouse. . . ." I would relate
all the rest to you, if you asked me ever so little, and
above all how the governor having had her stripped
naked, her hair miraculously grew long, and made a
golden robe for her. That is a charming story, and

the legends of the virgin martyrs, which flourished
in the thirteenth century, are so many jewels the
dazzling richness and barbarous simplicity of which
should be enjoyed together. They are masterpieces of a childlike yet marvellous jewellery.
The good people remained dazzled by them for a
long time, and down to the sixteenth century they
were the poetry of the poor. But M. Zola is
greatly mistaken if he thinks that the religion of
to-day has retained the slightest memory of them.
These Gothic legends, having become suspect
among theologians, are now known only to the
archæologist. In setting his Angélique in that
restricted poetic world which filled with joy and
fantasy the heads of the peasant women of the
time of Joan of Arc, he has committed a strange
anachronism. It is true that he supposes his
heroine has herself discovered all this Christian
fairyland in an old sixteenth-century book. But
even that is very improbable.

In reality what is learned by a little girl, brought
up like Angélique in piety, amid the odour of
incense, is not the Golden Legend, but prayers, the
ordinary of the mass, and the catechism ; she con-
fesses, she goes to communion. That is her whole
life. It is inconceivable that M. Zola has forgotten
these practices. There is not a single prayer,
morning or evening, not a confession, not a communion, not a low mass in this narrative of a pious
childhood and mystic youth.

Thus his book is but an idle story on which it is
neither permissible to reflect nor possible to reason.
And this idle story is very long and very clumsily
written. I know another, which I prefer, and which
I am going to tell you. It is the same, after all, and

it is also called a " Dream." It is by a very simple
and engagingly natural poet, M. Gabriel Vicaire.
Yes, the same story, with this difference that it is a
young boy and not a young girl who dreams, and
that the apparition is not a bishop's son in the shape
of a Saint George, but a king's daughter with her
distaff:

> " Vous me demandez qui je vois en rêve ?
> Et gai, c'est vraiment la fille du roi ;
> Elle ne veut pas d'autre ami que moi
> Partons, joli cœur, la lune se lève.
>
> Sa robe, qui traîne, est en satin blanc,
> Son peigne est d'argent et de pierreries ;
> La lune se lève au ras des prairies.
> Partons, joli cœur, je suis ton galant.
>
> Un grand manteau d'or couvre ses épaules,
> Et moi dont la veste est de vieux coutil !
> Partons joli cœur, pour le Bois-Gentil.
> La lune se lève au-dessus des saules.
>
> Comme un enfant joue avec un oiseau,
> Elle tient ma vie entre ses mains blanches.
> La lune se lève au milieu des branches,
> Partons joli cœur, et prends ton fuseau.
>
> Dieu merci, la chose est assez prouvée :
> Rien ne vaut l'amour pour être content.
> Ma mie est si belle, et je l'aime tant !
> Partons, joli cœur, la lune est levée." *

---

* " You ask me what I see in a dream ? It is indeed the King's
daughter ; she wants none other than me. Come away, dear heart,
the moon is rising. Her trailing robe is made of white satin, her
brooch is of silver and precious stones ; the moon is rising to the level
of the meadows. Come away, dear heart, I am your lover. A great
mantle of gold covers her shoulders, and I, my coat is made of old
matting ! Come away, dear heart, to the Pleasant Wood. The moon
is rising above the willows. As a child plays with a bird, she holds
my life in her white hands. The moon is rising among the branches,

There is the beat of the wing, there is the flight, there is poetry, there is the true dream! As for that of M. Zola, it is very extravagant and at the same time very dull. I even wonder that it should be so clumsy while it is so dull.

come away, dear heart, and take your distaff. Thank God it has been well proved that nothing is as good as love for bringing contentment. My dear is fair, and I love her so much! Come away, dear heart, the moon has risen."

"THE TEMPEST"

 HENRI SIGNORET'S marionettes have just acted Shakespeare's "Tempest." It is hardly an hour since the curtain of the little theatre fell on the harmonious group of Ferdinand and Miranda. I am still under the charm, as Prospero says, I " do yet taste some subtilties of the isle." What a delightful play ! And how true it is that exquisite things are doubly exquisite when they are unaffected ! M. Signoret proposes to produce with his little actors the masterpieces, I will call them the holy works, of all dramatic literature. Yesterday Aristophanes, to-day Shakespeare, to-morrow Kalidasa. His little actors are made of wood like the gods whom Polyeucte hated. But Polyeucte was a fanatic ; he understood nothing of art, and he did not know how much that is divine and adorable a wooden god can contain.

As for me, I feel a sort of piety mingled with a species of tenderness for the little beings made of wood and pasteboard, and clad in wool or in satin, who have recently passed before my eyes, making gestures pre-ordained by the Muses. My friendship for marionettes is an old one. I expressed it last year when I said that wooden actors have, in my opinion, many advantages over other actors. I am

flattered to see that M. Paul Margueritte, who has
fine taste, a love for what is rare, and a feeling for
what is precious, is also a strong partisan of these
artificial and tiny actors. Discussing the Little
Theatre, he delivered a brilliant eulogy of marionettes.

" They are," he says, " never tired, always ready.
And whilst the too familiar name and appearance of
a flesh and blood actor inflicts an obsession on the
public which renders illusion either impossible or
very difficult, these impersonal puppets, these beings
of wood and pasteboard, possess a droll mysterious
life. Their truthful bearing surprises, even disquiets us. In their essential gestures there is the
complete expression of human feelings. We had it
proved at the representations of Aristophanes.
Real actors would not have produced this effect. In
them the foreshortening aided the illusion. Their
masks in the style of ancient comedy, their few and
simple movements, their statuesque poses, gave a
singular • grace to the spectacle." I could not
have said that so well, but I have felt it. I
add that it is very difficult for living actresses, and
even more difficult for living actors, to be poetic.
Marionettes are poetic naturally : they have at once
style and artlessness. Are they not the sisters of
dolls and statues ? Look at the marionettes of the
" Tempest." The hand that carved them im-
printed on them the features of the ideal, whether
it be tragic or comic.

M. Belloc, a pupil of Mercié, has modelled for the
Little Theatre heads which are either powerfully
grotesque or of a charming purity. His Miranda
has the subtle grace of a figure of the early Italian
Renaissance and the virginal fragrance of that

fortunate fifteenth century which made beauty bloom a second time in the world. His Ariel, in his gauze tunic spangled with silver, reminds one of a miniature Tanagra figure, doubtless because aerial elegance of form is a particular attribute of Hellenic art in its decline.

These two pretty puppets spoke with the clear voices of Mesdemoiselles Paule Verne and Cécile Dorelle. As for the more masculine actors in the drama, Prospero, Caliban, Stephano, poets such as MM. Maurice Bouchor, Raoul Ponchon, Amédée Pigeon, Félix Rabbe spoke for them. Not to mention Coquelin *cadet*, who did not disdain to repeat the prologue as well as the amusing part of Trinculo, the clown.

The decorations certainly had also their poetry. M. Lucien Doucet represented Prospero's cave with that cunning grace which is one of the characteristics of his talent. The blue which struck a note in that charming tableau added an additional harmony to Shakespeare's verse.

The translation of "The Tempest" which we have just listened to is by M. Maurice Bouchor. It pleased me greatly, and I am anxious to read it at my leisure. It is in prose, but in a rhythmical and imaged prose. I can this evening give only a momentary impression of it. Moreover, there is some reason why this translation should be good. M. Bouchor is a poet, he is a poet who loves poetry, and that is something rarer with poets than people think. He is, also, half an Englishman, and full of Shakespeare. He is, like Shakespeare, very careless of fame, and he is, I am told, greatly attracted by the honest pleasures of the table, in which he is again like Shakespeare. It needed a M. Bouchor to

K

give us some idea of that Shakespearean style which
Carlyle so well called a festive style.

It is generally believed that " The Tempest " is
the last in date of the works of this great Will, and
that he presented it as his farewell to the theatre
before retiring to his native town of Stratford-on-
Avon. He was approaching his fiftieth year,
thought that he had done enough for the public,
and eagerly desired to lead the life of a gentleman
farmer. He had no literary ambitions. Some have
discerned in the scene where Prospero dismisses the
delicate Ariel the symbol of Shakespeare renouncing
the enchantments of his art and his genius.

I do not know. But it seems to me that Shake-
peare cared very little about his genius, and thought
more of planting a mulberry-tree in his garden.
Moreover, people have seen everything and found
everything in " The Tempest." This prodigious
work contains everything in it. It is, if you like, a
geographical play of the same sort as M. Victorien
Sardou's " Crocodile," a Robinson Crusoe put on
the stage before Robinson Crusoe's day, to please a
public greatly interested in travels and navigation.
And, in fact, " The Tempest " treats of the customs
of savages such as they were known in the times of
Elizabeth.

It is also a fairy tale, and the most beautiful of
fairy tales ; it is also a treatise of magic or a moral
symbol. Lastly, it is a political play, a social study
which, as regards the justice, extent, and profundity
of its views, leaves far behind those State tragedies
that were so highly esteemed in the seventeenth
century in France.

I confess that from this point of view the personage
of Caliban both interests and disquiets me very

much. M. Ernest Renan clearly saw that the future is Caliban's. Ariel, between you and me, is done with, he no longer aspires to anything but rest and liberty. Heaven preserve me from slandering so charming a spirit. He is an accomplished minister. He performs his sovereign's orders most skilfully. He brings about arrests with dexterity. He seizes people without annoying them. He separates or puts to sleep the enemies of the constitution. All ministers cannot do as much. He is very dictatorial, but in most winning ways. His external appearance is enticing, and he can, when he pleases, transform himself into an Oread. He can, in addition, plunge into the bowels of the earth even when it is hardened by frost. By this trait we recognise him to be a mining engineer prompt to descend a shaft and anxious not to spare himself. He must have been Minister of Public Works before he became Minister of the Interior and he has succeeded in performing admirably the most diverse functions. His mind is supple, quick, nimble, and mobile ; he transforms himself incessantly like the clouds ; he is a true genius of the air.

But, in the end, we do not know whether he directs or is directed. He continually escapes from Prospero, who thinks him exquisite but who nevertheless ends by giving him his liberty and definitely relieving him from his duties. In a word Ariel has belonged for too long to what we call the directing classes.

As for Caliban, he is a brute, and his stupidity is his strength. This "moon-calf," as Stephano calls him, is the people and the people in its entirety. In opposition he is priceless. He has astonishing aptitude for destruction. He understands nothing ;

but he feels, for he suffers. He knows not whither he goes, yet his gait is slow and sure ; and as he crawls along he insensibly raises himself up. What renders him formidable is that he has instincts and but little intelligence. He has great needs whilst the exquisite Ariel has none. He is an animal, he is hideous, but he is robust. He wanted to marry the prince's daughter, the fair Miranda, but he went to work a little too quickly and she was not given to him. But he is patient, he is obstinate ; he will one day obtain another Miranda, and he will have children not quite so ugly as himself. He creates many difficulties for those who govern him. He groans, he threatens, he murmurs ceaselessly. He loves to change masters but he always serves. Prospero himself admits it.

> " We cannot miss him : he does make our fire,
> Fetch in our wood ; and serves in offices
> That profit us."

That is an admission we should bear in mind, and when, afterwards, he calls him " abhorréd slave," " being capable of all ill," " a thing most brutish," " vile race," " hag-seed," we shall recognise that it is not the language of justice. If, in the continual conflict between the master and the slave, the noble Duke of Milan thus loses his composure, can we demand from the poor brute perfect moderation and sense of proportion ? We must however do Prospero this much justice that he has endeavoured to enlighten the unhappy Caliban's understanding. He spared nothing to make the brute into a man and even an educated man. Perhaps he has performed this task with an excess of zeal and ardour. Prospero is himself a scholar. At Milan, whilst he was studying the art of governing in old books, conspirators carried him off from his duchy and left him on a desert island where he began his experiments anew. He lives in books, and loudly declares that a certain volume in his library is more precious than his duchy. He is as persuaded as any of our republican statesmen of the advantages of instruction, and in this he is preparing for himself the same sort of deception as they are beginning to experience. He sends Caliban to school. But Caliban, who is not formed to taste the pure joys of the understanding, wants to be rich as soon as he knows how to read. To Prospero, who is extolling the benefits of education, he answers briefly :

> " You taught me language ; and my profit on't
> Is, I know how to curse : the red plague rid you
> For learning me your language."

Originally, the relations between Prospero, the ruler, and Caliban, the ruled, were not so strained. There was even a period of good understanding and sympathy between them.

> ' This island's mine (he says to the Duke of Milan) by Sycorax my
>   mother,
> Which thou tak'st from me. When thou camest first,
> Thou strok'st me, and mad'st much of me ; would'st give me
> Water with berries in't ; and teach me how
> To name the bigger light, and how the less,
> That burn by day and night : and then I loved thee,
> And shew'd thee all the qualities o' the isle,
> The fresh springs, brine-pits, barren place, and fertile ;
> Cursed be I that did so !—All the charms
> Of Sycorax, toads, beetles, bats, light on you !
> For I am all the subjects that you have,
> Which first was mine own king : and here you sty me
> In this hard rock, whiles you do keep from me
> The rest of the island."

We see that the government of this island has
entered into an era of difficulties, and that the social
crisis is very acute. Caliban asks Prospero for all
the goods of this world, and Prospero, who has
perhaps promised them, is very embarrassed when
it comes to giving them. Besides, the son of
Sycorax is hard to please ; he wants everything
and does not know what he wants, and when
he is given what he has asked for, he does not
recognise it.

Still, Prospero and Caliban would sometimes come
to an understanding were it not for the religious
question that is always dividing them. They have
not the same gods, and that is a great cause of dis-
cord. Prospero, who is a scholar and a philosopher,
conceives a purely rational image of the universe.
He does not interpret cosmic phenomena by
imagination and feeling. Observation, experiment,
deduction, are his only guides. He believes only in
science ; while Caliban has another faith. Sycorax,
his mother, was a witch. And that is what Ariel
and Prospero will not take into consideration. She
worshipped the god Setebos whose body was painted
in divers colours, as Eden tells us in his " History of
Travel." With the help of this god, Sycorax was
powerful. She commanded the moon, she made
the ebb and flow of the tides, she composed
efficacious charms out of toads, beetles and bats.
It is very natural that Caliban should worship
Setebos. He is a god carved out by strokes of an
axe, and he speaks to the gross senses and simple
imagination of the cave-dweller. Then, I do not
fear to say it, there is in the unenlightened soul of
Caliban a secret need of poetry and idealism which
Setebos abundantly satisfies.

Consider that Setebos is picturesque, and that, planted like a stake and all besmeared with blue and vermilion, he is a striking object.

Finally, is Prospero absolutely sure that Setebos is not the true god?

THE BLOND TRESS *

HAVE a friend who lives in solitude, among the apple orchards of the Perche. Florentin Loriot is his name. He has an exquisite and retiring soul. He reads little and meditates much, and all the ideas that enter into his head take a mystical turn. A painter and a poet, he discovers symbols under all the presentments of nature. He is at once the simplest and the most ingenious of men. He believes everything he wants to believe, and never believes anything that he hears. Innocent, candid, prodigiously self-willed, he would go to the stake for an idea, and if at this hour he is not a martyr, the fault is solely due to the gentleness of contemporary manners.

When he comes to Paris, where he makes only too rare and too short visits, he brings to his friends, along with his smile, treasures of fancy and thought. He always arrives at the moment when one least expects him, and he is always welcome. It is a joy to see him come in with his case of water-colours under his arm, his pockets stuffed with ragged old books and illegible manuscripts, kindly, oblivious of everything, beaming, and with a far-away look in his eyes.

" Sit down, Florentin Loriot, and give us some

* " La Tresse Blonde." By Gilbert-Augustin Thierry.

fresh news of Providence. How goes the Absolute, and how is the Infinite keeping ? ”

And he sets to work unfolding his metaphysics ! Oh ! his metaphysics, they are a note-book full of pictures with legends in verse. But Florentin Loriot is acute and argues with skill.

The last time I had the pleasure of seeing him, he expounded to me his ideas on the novel.

“ My friend,” said he to me, “ write a novel of adventure ; nothing is so fine as that.”

He had just discovered “ The Three Musketeers,” and this discovery had been followed for him by some others still more marvellous. He communicated them to me with a grace of which I cannot display even the shadow. But what he said came on the whole to this.

Old Dumas composed stories, and he was right. For pleasure and instruction, there is nothing like stories. Homer composed them also. We have changed that, and there lies our mistake. The novelists of to-day content themselves with observing attitudes or analysing characters. But attitudes have by themselves no significance and consequently no interest. As for characters, they remain obscure to those who persist in studying them from within. Action alone reveals them. Action is the whole man. “ I live, therefore I must act,” cries Homunculus as soon as he comes out of the retort where Wagner concocted him. There is no real interest, there is even no true truth, in showing me the interior man who is incomprehensible. Put him back in the world, in the bosom of the material and spiritual universe. Show him at grips with his destiny ; show us God everywhere (my friend Florentin Loriot is a believer in the supernatural

K 2

and a Christian); act, act, act, throw us into the midst of important affairs, no longer with the rather childish materialism of the good Dumas, but in accordance with the transcendent views of the philosopher and the moralist, and then you will have created the true, the great novel of adventure.

That is what my friend Florentin Loriot has decided under his apple-trees. He wants " Musketeers," but mystic " Musketeers." He loves adventures, but spiritual adventures.

Still it remains to be known whether the greatest of human adventures is not thought. M. Stéphane Mallarmé has, it is said, taken for the hero of a cape-and-sword drama a fakir who has not made a single movement for fifty years, but whose brain is the theatre of continual vicissitudes. I would not answer for it that, if it were absolutely necessary to choose a hero, my friend Florentin Loriot would not prefer M. Stéphane Mallarmé's fakir to Alexandre Dumas's Porthos. Upon the whole, and without more quibbling, what Florentin Loriot wants is that the novel should cease to be naturalist, for to be naturalist is to be nothing. What he asks is that the novel should be moral, that it should proceed from a systematic conception of the world, and be the concrete expression of a philosophy.

That is why I intend sending him M. Gilbert-Augustin Thierry's new novel, " la Tresse blonde." In truth, that novel, forcibly conceived and nobly written, was inspired, if I am to believe its preface, by an ideal that is not without analogy with the ideal of my friend, the philosopher of the Perche.

" Henceforth," says M. Gilbert-Augustin Thierry, " the student of man (in the novel) should pursue his search far higher than man, towards those regions of the infinite of which we are atoms endowed with passions, but atoms in a state of impotent restlessness. Raising itself towards the occult, boldly uplifting itself towards the great unknown, the new novel should endeavour to penetrate the abysses that are regarded as impenetrable, to pierce the darkness in which the Absolute enwraps its being : its continuous logic, its immanent justice, its implacable morality—the very laws of its eternity. Toward the *Unknown God !* . . . a difficult pursuit, but a necessary exploration since the deity we seek, a living and personal Whole, envelopes and enfolds us—we who live in Him, we who only exist through Him."

If these things are obscure in themselves and in their nature, M. Gilbert-Augustin Thierry's idea does not the less disengage itself with sufficient clearness. According to the author of " la Tresse blonde," the action of a novel ought to have fatality as its motive. To show men in a novel is little : men are nothing ; it is necessary to make one feel in it the unknown forces that forge and hammer out our destinies. It is necessary to create not only beings, but also fates. That is the moral novel, that is the philosophical novel, that is, in a word, the novel as my friend from the land of apple-trees understood it, with this difference that he thought like a Christian and that M. Thierry inclines towards a sort of mystical determinism. I mention these theories because they are of a nature to raise an interesting discussion at the moment when there is a general recognition of the inanity of a naturalism which is, on the whole, but the negation of intelligence, reason, and feeling.

Naturalism forbids the writer any intellectual act,

any moral manifestation ; it leads straight to sheer imbecility. It is thus that it has produced the literature called decadent and symbolist. Its unpardonable crime is that it kills thought. It has fallen from nonsense to nonsense into the most lamentable absurdities. Its claim was that it arose from science and proceeded according to the experimental method. But who does not see that the experimental method is absolutely inapplicable to literature ? It consists in calling forth at will a phenomenon in predetermined conditions. Now it is clear that such a method is outside of our resources.

But, if you wish, let us take the word experiment in a metaphorical sense, and let us admit that there is, in art, a sort of ideally experimental method. Every experiment presupposes an anterior hypothesis which this experiment has as its aim to verify. Now naturalism, forbidding any hypothesis, has no experiment to make. The chief of this literary school, who speaks so much about experiments, recalls in this respect a mad physiologist, known in the history of the sciences, the worthy Magendie, who experimented a great deal without any profit. He feared hypotheses as causes of error. Bichat, he used to say, had genius, and it led him astray. Magendie did not want genius for fear of being led astray also. Now, he had no genius and he never was led astray. Every day he cut open dogs and rabbits, but without any preconceived idea, and he discovered nothing, for the reason that he sought nothing. That is naturalism in the scientific world. Claude Bernard, who succeeded Magendie, gave its due to hypothesis. He had great imagination and an exact mind. He supposed things and verified them afterwards, and he made vast discoveries. If hypothesis is necessary in the scientific world, we will not believe that it is fatal in the literary world, and we will permit M. Gabriel-Augustin Thierry to consider, with preconceived ideas, the fatalities of atavism, the struggle for prey, and even the conflict between suggestion and responsibility.

AN HONEST GIRL*

WO years ago last August, I was with three or four friends, crossing the Bay of Somme, at low tide, barefooted. We were leaving behind us those high ramparts of Saint-Valery whose old sandstone the spray has covered with golden rust. But it had not been without turning back several times to see the marvellous church which uprears above the ramparts its five sharp, pierced, fifteenth-century gables, with great pointed windows, its slated roof shaped like an inverted keel, and the cock on its steeple. Before us the light-coloured sand of the bay stretched to the bluish cape of Le Hourdel, where the land ends, and to the low lines of that Crotoy which received Joan of Arc as the prisoner of the English. In the offing, from whence a north wind was blowing, we perceived a Norwegian schooner, doubtless laden with pine-wood planks and pig-iron. The sun blazed on the edges of the great, dark clouds. The wild and exhilarating infinite enveloped us, and turned our thoughts to very simple things. Then, following the natural inclination of my mind, I came to think of nothing at all. We were advancing slowly, fording the little streams which the crabs and shrimps inhabited, and sometimes feeling the edges

* "Brave Fille." By M. Fernand Calmettes.

of broken shells beneath our feet. Around us the water was unsmiling and the wind held no caress; but healthful gusts poured a peaceful joy and forgetfulness of life into our breasts. Suddenly I heard my name borne on the wind like an affectionate summons. I was greatly astonished. It seemed to me inconceivable that any one should remember my name at a time when I myself had forgotten it. I no longer felt myself to be distinct from nature, and that simple call made me shudder. I must tell you that I have never been very sure that I exist; if, at certain times, I incline to believe that I do, I experience a sort of amazement at it, and I ask myself how it is possible.

Now, at that moment, I really did not exist, since I did not think. I had at the most but a virtual existence. The voice that called me drew near, and, when I turned to the side whence the sound came, I saw a sort of sailor, wearing a blue cap and wrapped in a knitted woollen vest, who was rushing towards me with great strides, his trousers pulled up above his knees, with a pair of hob-nailed shoes slung over his shoulder and dancing upon his back. His face was as bronzed as that of an old pilot. He stretched out to me a massive hand, but too soft to have taken in many reefs or hauled for long at the ropes.

" Don't you recognise me ? " said he to me.

Indeed I did, I recognised my excellent friend Fernand Calmettes, witness of those years of youth the experience of which was so often bitter, and the fragrance of which remains so sweet in the memory! How happy we were then! We had nothing and we expected everything. Yes, I recognised him, my old comrade in arms! Yes, comrade in arms, for

in 1870 we had gone to the war together, Fernand
Calmettes and I, as private soldiers in a regiment
of the mobilised national guard, under the orders
of brave Captain Chalamel. Side by side, wearing
the cap with red piping and the brass-buttoned
pilot jacket, we defended Paris as well as we could,
but I must admit that we were soldiers of a special
sort. I remember that, during the battle of
December 2nd, having been placed in reserve
under the fort of La Faisanderie, we read Virgil's
" Silenus," amid the noise of shells falling into the
Marne. Whilst the Prussian batteries sent white
clouds of smoke afloat upon the hills on the horizon
of the grey and bare country, we two, seated on the
river bank, near the piled rifles, our heads leaning
over a copy of Bliss's little " Virgil," which I have
yet and which is dear to me, were making comments upon that cosmogony, which the poet, by
a delightful caprice, enshrined in an idyll. " He
sings how, through the great void, the seeds of
earth, and air, and sea, and of liquid fire withal,
were gathered together ; how from these germs
sprang the beginning of all things, and the
sphere of the nascent universe waxed and took
form, &c., &c." Fernand Calmettes was then
leaving the École des Chartes, where he had
publicly delivered his thesis on the manuscripts of
Tacitus.

The defence of this thesis had been marked by a
rather sharp altercation between M. Quicherat,
who presided at the sitting, and the candidate
archivist, on the subject of the transcription of
Latin proper names into French. The pupil held
out for a fixed method ; like M. Leconte de Lisle,
he wanted all names to be transcribed letter for

letter, respecting the foreign termination, *Roma*, *Tacitus*, *Tiberis*.

The master defended oral transmission, founded on the laws of accentuation, *Rome*, *Tacite*, *Tibre*. The pupil than asked M. Quicherat if, in order to observe these same laws, he should say *Quinte Fabie Favre* instead of *Quintus Fabius Faber*. M. Quicherat alleged customary usage, and got red and angry. Fernand Calmettes learned that day that it is sometimes dangerous to be in the right. But he did not profit by the lesson ; his is a logical mind which will never learn the charming art of being wrong at the right moment and when necessary. Yet that is an irresistible gift. The world decides only in favour of those who are sometimes wrong. When I first knew him, in 1868, Fernand Calmettes was occupied with the study of inscriptions and numismatics, and used to copy documents on the fine summer nights. He was a great archæologist for his twenty years ; but a thoroughly singular archæologist, for he had undecided ideas and a marvellous abundance of philosophical methods. He has given me two or three of them which have been very useful to me.

I have never known a builder who erected so much scaffolding. That is not all. This archæologist did not like archæology, and did not long delay before he conceived a detestation for it. Yet he excelled in it, and if the works on inscriptions which he has written were signed with his name he would to-day be a member of the Institute. It is questionable whether that would please him, for he has a terrible love for the open air. His leanings are towards the rustic. In 1870, during our long watches under arms, he took a liking for painting, and set to work to draw with that patient ardour and that methodical imagination which are the basis of his nature. Since then he has become the painter that we know, and whose energetic, sincere, and thoughtful talent we value.

When he grasped my hand in that lovely Bay of Somme, I recognised him under the sunburn and the tan, my old friend Fernand Calmettes ! I learnt from him that he was staying quite near, in one of those villages of the coast into which wind drives so much sand that you walk in it in the streets up to your knees. He used to spend four or five months there every year, and from an instinct for harmony he had made himself like the sailors among whom he lived and whose grave simplicity and naïve grandeur he loved. He felt the sympathy of a painter and a poet for these simple persons who, in the combat of life, have no weapons but their nets, these great children who know the wiles of fishes and do not know those of men. He felt pleased to be among these honest people whom life wears out as time wears out stones, without touching the heart, and whom even old age does not render miserly.

M. Fernand Calmettes brought back from the Bay of Somme and the grey strands of the Vimeu studies, notes, recollections, from which he has since developed some fine pictures and a book, a novel which I received yesterday, and which has made me think of all I have just told you, a novel about the fisher folk, a story told for young girls with simple earnestness. This book is illustrated: I have no need to tell you that the drawings are by M. Calmettes himself. They please by their simple and massive style. The text also has true grandeur and beautiful simplicity.

Among the fragments attributed to the poetess,
Sappho, there is a funeral epigram in the style of the
most ancient poems of that class which the " Anthology " has preserved for us.   It is a vigorous elegy
in two lines, of which this is the sense, rendered as
exactly as possible :
"Here is the tomb of Pelagon, the fisherman.
There are graven on it a net and an eel-pot, monuments of a hard life."
These two lines should be traced on the frontispiece of M. Fernand Calmettes' book.   That book,
entitled " Brave Fille," is the story of a young
orphan girl, Élise, in whom there live again the
hereditary virtues of the poor fisher folk who gain
their livelihood in peril of the sea.   She has a
courageous and pious heart.   She was born with the
love of that terrible Ocean which has taken her
father from her.   Like the old pilot, who speaks
so well in M. Jean Richepin's " Le Flibustier," she
despises the land and landholders, and thinks the
rivers are but pale, ungrateful, and insipid water,
since they pass and never come back.   Look at
her, the honest girl, on the road to Saint-Valery,
which dustily winds between two rows of trees
contorted by the wind from the west.

" Five leagues of that melancholy road ! They had rendered
Élise's spirits wearier than her legs. She took hardly any interest
in the country. Everything in it grew smaller and narrower. From
it you could see only corners of the sky, in it you could breathe only
a close breeze. Horizons that you could touch with your hand ;
a land so hard to deal with, so niggardly, that in order to tear its
wealth from it, you are reduced to divide it into little squares, and
your life is spent in tracing furrows hardly a cable's length in extent.
What is that compared with the great sea ? It opens your lungs
with its gusts that nothing stops, and in a voyage from North to
South you spend less time than it would require to plough a field no
bigger than a harbour.

"That is the large and generous life which reanimates all your senses at once and nourishes you with the virgin forces of nature. Élise was in haste to see it again, that sea, as beautiful in its rages as in its caresses, that sea which had made her courageous and strong."

Élise has a task which she is determined to accomplish. Before yielding to lawful love, she must win her father's body from the depths of the sea and bury it. Her father himself appeared to her to give her this order. You are, of course, free to believe that the poor fisherman's phantom has no more objective reality than Banquo's ghost, and that it is the product of a generous hallucination. When she saw her father returned from the depths of the sea in which he had lain for several months, Élise was not asleep.

"No, she was not asleep. By the gentle light of the moon she distinctly recognised, one after another, the familiar objects, exactly as she had found them on her return just before; the little box-bed under the garret staircase, the big sideboard on which her mother's wedding-bouquet, an enormous rose with golden leaves, shone beneath a glass shade; then, on each side, the two pewter candle-sticks, then the nets and fishing-tackle hung up everywhere, on the walls, and from the beams of the ceiling. All these companions of her former life, she had them there, under her eyes, in their exact material form, with their shapes and their colours.

"She was not asleep, and yet she could not turn towards the door without encountering a sad and gentle face, clear-eyed and wrinkled.

"'Father, what do you want me to do?'

"For the first time since she had lost him, Élise really saw her father again, as he had been in his lifetime, with his large fur cap, his red scarf, and his brown jersey. He scolded her gently for forsaking him, him her father, in the depths of the sands, for not having attempted the impossible with the maritime authorities and demanded, what was sometimes conceded, that the place should be dragged, and the body, which can know no repose while banished the beloved land, snatched from the abyss. . . .

"'Father, I swear to you I will take no rest until I have buried you by my mother's side'."

She succeeded in burying him by her mother's side. It was almost impossible. But what cannot love and courage do ? I have quoted two passages in this book so as to exempt myself from extolling an old friend. You will judge that these quotations bear their praise in themselves.

To represent these fisher folk to us, M. Fernand Calmettes has the eye of a painter and the soul of a poet, and thus he has expressed their forms and their souls. There is one quality of the sailors which is not exactly rendered in his book, the religious quality. We do not meet in it with Catholic worship under any precise form, and, a strange thing, the name of God is not even mentioned in it.

I have enquired the reasons for this peculiarity, and I have learned them ; they are too interesting not to be revealed here. It is the publisher of the book who has not allowed the name of God to appear once in the text, giving as his motive that he published books intended to be given as prizes in the schools.

The philosophical and religious ideas of this publishing house, which is in other respects very honourable, would be of little account, but it is patronised by certain politicians who would repudiate its books if they contained an allusion to any worship or any religious ideal whatsoever. That is what we have come to ! That is the breadth of ideas, the openness of mind, of our radicals ! That is how they understand tolerance, intellectual liberty, respect for conscience. These are the liberal inspirations of the Hôtel de Ville ! I am not suspect of too much faith, and those who do me the honour of reading me know that I am here defending only spiritual liberty and heart's ease.

But, in truth, this proscription of the ideal of so many respectable persons, this war on the God of women and children, on the consoling God of the afflicted is something extremely wicked and extremely clumsy. I deeply regret that M. Fernand Calmettes' book has undergone the insult of so stupid a censorship. I should regret it still more, if the author had not in some sort compensated by his superior idealism for the mutilations which it has had to suffer at the hands of the sectaries. A sort of naturalistic mysticism pervades his work and is ingeniously substituted for the more traditional cult that is in reality professed by the fisher folk of our coasts.

M. Fernand Calmettes raises the feeling of family, the piety of the heart, to the height of a religion. In his book, heaven is always visible; it inspires all the characters, illumines them with its radiant clearness, or envelopes them in its serene melancholy. That is excellent, but it is not thus that the fisher folk of Saint-Valery conceive of the divine ideal.*

* I learn with pleasure that, in a new edition, M. Fernand Calmettes is restoring the full text of his manuscript.

"THE HISTORY OF THE PEOPLE OF ISRAEL" *

UST I endeavour to give you the impression I experienced in reading this second volume of the " History of Israel " ? Must I show you the state of my soul as I reflected over its pages ? It is a class of criticism for which, as you know, I have only too great a leaning. Almost always, when I have said what I felt, I cannot think of anything else to say, and all my art consists in scribbling on the margins of books. A page which I turn over is like a torch that is brought to me, and around which immediately twenty butterflies escaped from my brain set themselves adancing. These butterflies are indiscreet, but what am I to do with them ? When I drive them away, others take their places. And there is quite a choir of little winged beings, fair and golden as the day, or blue and sombre as the night, light and frail but unwearied, who flit about vying with each other, and who seem to murmur in the beating of their wings: "We are little Psyches ; friend, do not drive us away with too harsh a gesture. An immortal spirit animates our ephemeral forms. See: we seek Eros, Eros, who is never found, Eros, the great secret of life

* " Histoire du peuple d'Israel." By M. Ernest Renan.

and death." And, in fact, it is always one of these tiny Psyches who makes my article for me. Heaven knows how she does it, but without her I should do it even worse still.

At this moment then, as I read in M. Renan's admirable volume about the reigns of David and Solomon, the schism of the tribes, the victory of the prophets, the agony and death of the Kingdom of Israel, as with linguistic and archæological science, with the memories of his travels in his mind, and above all with a divinatory sense of very ancient things, the historian recreates and shows me the nomad shepherd seeing Elohim in every mirage of the desert and wrestling for a whole night with one of those mysterious Beings; as he restores for me the Temple of Solomon, with its gateway in the Egyptian style, and its two columns of bronze with their capitals shaped like lotus sheaves, its golden cherubim as monstrous as the Sphinx of Memphis or the man-faced bulls of Khorsabad, and all around, erected on the hills or hidden in the groves, the impure idolatry of the Phœnician temples.

He traces for me across the ages the evolution of the religious feeling, changing among this singular people from the adoration of a fierce and jealous god to the worship of that divine providence whose ideal it has finally imposed upon the world—during all this engaging and spirited history which interests me by its learning and enchants me by its exquisite art, what do you think my little winged hovering creatures, my little anxious Psyches, are doing ? They are showing me my old Bible with its engravings, the Bible my mother gave me, the Bible which as a child I devoured even before I was able to read.

It was a good old Bible. It dated from the beginning of the seventeenth century; the illustrations were by a Dutch artist who had represented the Garden of Eden under the aspect of a landscape in the neighbourhood of Amsterdam. The animals one saw there—all domestic animals—gave the impression of a very well kept farm and poultry yard. There were oxen, sheep, rabbits, and also a fine Brabant horse, well clipt, well-groomed, ready to be harnessed to a burgomaster's carriage. I don't speak of Eve, who was a dazzling example of Flemish beauty. She was a treasure wasted on me.

Noah's ark interested me more. I still see its round and ample hull surmounted by a plank cabin. O marvel of tradition! I had among my playthings a Noah's ark exactly similar, painted red, with all the animals in couples, and Noah and his family all extremely well made. That was to me a great proof of the truth of the Scriptures. *Teste David cum Sibylla.* Dating from the time of the Tower of Babel, the personages of my Bible were richly dressed according to their condition, the warriors in the style of the Romans of Trajan's column, the princes with turbans, the women like Rubens' women, the shepherds like brigands, and the angels in the fashion of those of the Jesuits. The tents of the soldiers resembled the rich pavilions that are seen in tapestries; the palaces were imitated from those of the Renaissance, the artist not having imagined it possible to conceive anything older of that kind. There were nymphs in the style of Jean Goujon in the fountain where Bathsheba was bathing. That is why those pictures gave me the idea of a profound antiquity. I doubted whether my grandfather himself—although he had received a wound at Waterloo, in remembrance of which he always wore a bouquet of violets in his button-hole— could have known the Tower of Babel and the baths of Bathsheba. Oh, my old illustrated Bible! what joys I used to feel in turning over your pages in the evenings when my eyes already half swam in the delightful waves of childish slumber! How I used to see in you God with His white beard! And after all, perhaps that is the only fashion of seeing Him really. How I used to believe in Him!

I thought Him, between ourselves, a little strange, violent, and wrathful; but I did not ask Him for any explanation of His actions; I was accustomed to see all grown-up people act in an incomprehensible manner. And, besides, I had at that time a philosophy; I believed in the universal infallibility of men and things. I was persuaded that all was reasonable in the world and that so great an undertaking was carried on seriously. I have laid aside that piece of wisdom with my old Bible. But I regret it deeply. Just think. To be quite little yourself and to be able to reach the end of the world at the end of a good walk. To believe that you have the secret of the universe in an old book, under the lamp, in the evening when the room is warm. To be troubled by nothing and yet to dream! For at that time I used to dream as soon as I was in bed, and all the personages of my old Bible used to come and defile before me. Yes, kings bearing crown and sceptre, prophets with long beards, draped under eternal clouds, passed with mingled majesty and good-nature before me as I slept. After the procession, they used to go and settle down of their own accord in a box of Nuremberg toys. That is the first idea I formed of David and Isaiah.

We have all of us done something similar ; we have all, in times gone by, turned over the pages of an old illustrated Bible. We have all formed some simple, naïve, and childish idea of the origin of the world.

There is something that stirs one, I think, in comparing this childish idea with the reality as science shows it to us. In proportion as our understanding takes possession of itself and of the Universe, the past recoils indefinitely, and we recognise that we are prohibited from reaching back to the beginnings of man and of life. Yes, ere we attain to far-off times new perspectives and unexpected depths are continually opening up before us ; we feel that there is an abysm beyond. We see the dark chasm, and fear seizes on the boldest of us. That nomad shepherd, who is pointed out to us, surrounded in the night of the desert by shades of the Elohim,—he was the son of a humanity even then old and, so to speak, as distant as we are from our common cradle. Modern man too has torn up his old illustrated Bible. He too has left in their old Nuremberg box the ten or twelve patriarchs who, by joining their hands, formed a chain which went backwards to creation. It is not only in our days, indeed, that exegesis has discovered the true sense of the Hebrew Bible. The old tenets on which the faith of so many ages rested have, for a hundred years, for two hundred years, been subjected to the free examination of science. I am unable to indicate precisely M. Renan's place in Biblical criticism. But I am sure that he possesses the art by which to animate the distant past, to give us an understanding of the antique East whose soil and peoples he knows so well, a talent for painting landscapes and figures of which he has the acuteness of sight to discern what is probable and possible in the absence of certainties; in a word, the special gift of pleasing, charming, and bewitching. In his new work, if the style has not the abounding suavity which makes the " Origins of Christianity " such delightful reading, we find, in compensation, a simplicity and naturalness of which this great writer has as yet given no better example. Those who have had the happiness of listening to his voice, will believe, as they read this book, that they are listening to it still. It is himself, his accent, his gesture. As I close the book, I feel tempted to say like the pilgrims at Emmaus : " We have just seen Him. He was at this table." In this book, one thing among the rest is peculiarly individual to him and recalls his conversations—the pleasure he shows in historical comparisons. In one passage, for instance, so as to give a better comprehension of the spirit of an old nomad chief he will speak of Abd-el-Kader; in another, he will compare David to the Negus of Abyssinia. Sometimes the comparisons are more unexpected ; he tells us, for instance, that Notre Dame de Lorette will give a fairly good idea of Solomon's Temple.

There are also charming and familiar touches, as when speaking of Jahve, of the terrible Jahve, he calls him " a most narrow-minded creature." This is the whole passage :

" There is no moral feeling in Jahve, as David knows him and worships him. This capricious god is favouritism itself ; his fidelity is thoroughly material. He holds to his rights in a way that reaches the absurd. He is angry with people,

without their knowing why. Then they offer him
the smoke of a sacrifice to inhale and his anger is
appeased. When a man swears abominable things
by his name, he requires them to be executed to the
letter. He is a most narrow-minded creature ; he
takes pleasure in unmerited punishments. Although
the rite of human sacrifices was antipathetic to
Israel, Jahve took pleasure in these spectacles.
The execution of the sons of Saul at Gibeah was a
true human sacrifice of seven persons, performed
before Jahve, to appease him. The ' wars of Jahve '
all end with frightful massacres in honour of this
cruel god."

Where now is my old collection of sacred pictures
in which this very Jahve walked with such majesty
through a Dutch meadow in the midst of white
sheep, tiny guinea pigs, and Brabant horses ?

THE ELOQUENCE OF THE TRIBUNE *

THE SENATE

 CHALLEMEL-LACOUR yesterday delivered a speech which still echoes in every heart sensitive to eloquence. There are many such in France ; our hearts will always go out to those fortunate mortals from whose lips to our very ears the golden fetters of which the Gallic legends speak stretch their linked sweetness ; we shall always allow ourselves to be led by eloquence. Would it not be appropriate to consider, from the point of view of art, and of art alone, three or four of our political orators, taking them from the Senate, if you like, and beginning with M. Challemel-Lacour himself ? After the example of old Cormenin, we might attempt to sketch a portrait. The painter would have, to compensate for his weakness, the advantage of having studied his model.

The attitude is one of majestic stiffness. The gesture is sober ; the voice grave, sonorous within its moderate compass. The breath, a little short, is

* This was written on the occasion of a speech delivered by M. Challemel-Lacour in the Senate at the session of December 19, 1888.

so well economised that it suffices for the longest
periods. As for the phrasing, it is ample and
unfolds itself with severe magnificence. By the
quiet of his attitude, the art of his diction, and the
pure taste of his composition, this orator recalls all
that we imagine of ancient eloquence. He speaks,
and you see the bees of Hymettus flying around his
silver beard.

He has a meditative mind, and everything he
says bears the impress of wisdom. I need not say
that by wisdom I here mean the disposition of a
mind inclined to search out causes and to follow the
connection of ideas from fact to fact. M. Challemel-
Lacour is a philosopher. Hence a sort of grave
sadness is diffused over all his words. There is
no gay philosophy, and his is particularly sad.
He is impressed by the universal flux of things
and the instability which is the necessary condition
of life. The idea of universal evil never leaves
him, and he brings a sort of Stoical pessimism
into the parliamentary debates. One felt this on
Wednesday when he delivered that speech, so
finished in its art. One felt it still more when, in
1883, he spoke from the same place as Minister for
Foreign Affairs. His philosophy dominated his
politics ; he seemed more convinced of the malignity
of men and things than of the success of his own
negotiations. He is one of those who have
abandoned hope, and his speech retains a bitter
savour of this. It betrays a stoical pride which one
thought had died with Brutus. M. Challemel-Lacour
unceasingly shows us his reason standing upright
on the ruins of the world, and he seems to say :
" What matter though the universe crumble, if
I remain steadfast in my uprightness ! " No !

Philosophy is never gay. And we must also say: Faith is never sad.

Look at M. Chesnelong who sits in the Senate on the benches of the Extreme Right. He is not a philosopher. On the contrary, he is a believer. Everything in him bespeaks the most ardent faith. His eloquence has the transports of sacred eloquence. It retains, even in financial questions, the pious zeal of the apostolate. M. Chesnelong has hardly spoken in the Senate save to give utterance to complaints and lamentations. But there is gladness in his complaints, a serene joy is mingled with his lamentations. Look at him: he is weeping. But in spite of himself, hosannah bursts forth from his soul. He is joyous because he has faith. His broad face is lit up, in the tribune, with a peaceful smile. M. Challemel-Lacour never smiles.

And what vision could enliven him for a moment ? He is for ever alone, confronting his reason amid the universal nothingness. The Senate this week gave its applause to the last of the Stoics.

I do not know whether M. Buffet will speak this year in the debate on the Budget. M. Buffet is an excellent orator, and he ought to be mentioned side by side with the best. He sits, as you know, on the Right, and shows himself constantly mindful of the interests of the Catholics. But whatever be the strength of his religious opinions, his language does not receive from them the lightest impress of mysticism. He is a business orator. His upright eloquence desires no adornment save strength and precision ; it shines with a robust bareness. M. Buffet was not born to sacrifice to the lighter graces. He seems carved from the knotty heart of an oak. His angular and stooping person expresses

the dignity proper to an old Parliamentarian who
has grown grey in public debates. He has, in
the highest degree, what is called authority. You
listen to him even before he has begun to speak.
His face is severe, almost gloomy, with an expression
of perfect simplicity. With his powerful head
borne well forward, his bony, angular face, the
piercing pupils of his contracted eyes, his bent nose,
his sunken mouth, and projecting chin, he speaks
in a voice as heavy and intractable as if it came
from a mouth of iron. His gesture is that of a
woodman hewing down trees. M. Buffet himself
might be called the axe of his opponents. He
strikes with sure and regular blows. His very
faults, an awkward articulation and an over-
scrupulous persistence, add to the power of his
talent. He has that urgent and compact logic
which is the muscle of speech. He has a strong and
simple style, the accent of sincerity, and honest
stubbornness. It is he before any other who
should be proposed as a model for 'prentice
orators.

I say M. Buffet and not M. Jules Simon, because
the latter is inimitable. His is perfect art. When the
Gracchi spoke to the people, they caused themselves
to be accompanied, it is said, by a flute-player.
When M. Jules Simon speaks, a delightful flute
accompanies him ; but it is invisible and sings
upon his lips. M. Jules Simon is as much of
a philosopher as M. Challemel-Lacour, and even
more of one. He knows how to forget at the right
moment. He knows everything. By turns insinuat-
ing, ironical, tender, vehement, he has all the qualities
of the orator. When he mounts the tribune, he seems
to be overwhelmed. Leaning with both hands on

L

the little mahogany rail, he casts over the assembly
a languishing eye which in a moment will be charged
with lightnings ; he draws out the sounds of a
scarcely audible voice, which little by little becomes
animated, expands, and then softens to tears or
peals like melodious thunder. He is master of himself as well as of the audience. Easily moved but
ever on the alert, he pounces on interruptions and
sweeps them into the harmonious movement of
his thought, as a river carries away branches that
are thrown into it. Everything serves him ; he is
the great artist whose plastic genius easily transforms
all the materials his hand encounters, and he has
nothing but his own perfection itself to fear.

What a fine gallery one could make of the portraits of the principal orators of the upper Chamber !
What a diversity in the faces, what happy contrasts,
and how the figures would set off one another !

Here would be M. le Duc d'Audiffret-Pasquier,
at the back of the tribune, throwing himself against
the President's desk, collected and composed in his
strength and his energy, bitter, savage, proud,
showing his teeth, and multiplying the fiery stings
of his exasperated eloquence. His voice and his
eyes spit fire, and even in his anger he retains an
expression of nobility and kindness.

There, M. le Duc de Broglie (for it would be
permissible to place in this gallery the illustrious
men whom popular suffrage proscribes, those whose
absence is striking : " Præfulgebant eo quod non
visebantur ") would send forth in a feeble voice
those magnificently arranged speeches, rich and
supple in their style, woven with absolute purity,
the remembrance of which has never faded from
the minds of all who are judges of such matters.

There, M. Léon Say, an easy, charming, copious, and precise speaker, giving life to figures, expounding the most difficult questions with lucidity, telling delightful anecdotes, taking his speech as it were for long walks through the country, and giving greater effect to his familiar good humour by the sarcasm of his voice and the subtilty of his irony.

There, M. Bocher, in his pure and noble eloquence, passing his little handkerchief over his lips, and with unflagging memory, youthful voice, and pliant gesture, spreading grace and clarity over questions of finance, and showing in the discussion an imperious brevity, a cold politeness, a haughty courtesy.

There, also, M. de Freycinet, so slender, so thin, and so pale, raising clarity to the height of splendour, making his colourless and lucid phrasing flow in little singing and caressing waves, and building up, before an astounded audience, speeches which, in their frail elegance and rather arid grace, resemble marvellous suspension-bridges.

I should name many others also, all different, who interest me by their very diversity. Eloquence is at bottom only the powerful and sudden expression of an original temperament. That is why faults as well as good qualities co-operate to create it. To speak is to give oneself ; to speak well is to give oneself generously and fully.

ROMANCE AND MAGIC *

ET us admit it: in the bottom of our hearts all of us have a liking for the marvellous. The most thoughtful among us loves it without believing in it, and does not love it the less for that. Yes, we, the sages, we love the marvellous with a desperate love. We know that it does not exist. We are sure of this, and it is even the only thing of which we are sure, for if it existed it would no longer be marvellous, and it is so only on the condition of not existing. If the dead came back, it would be natural and not marvellous for them to come back. If men could be changed into animals, like the Lucius of the old story, that would be a natural metamorphosis, and we should be no more astonished at it than at the metamorphoses of insects. There is no going outside nature. And that idea is in itself absolutely disheartening. The possible is not enough for us, and we want the impossible, which is only the impossible on condition that it is never realised. Mérimée has told of the adventure of Don Juan, who as he was walking along the bank of the Tagus, rolling a cigarette, asked a light from a passer-by, engaged in smoking a cigar on the other bank.

* "Apulée romancier et magicien." By Paul Monceaux.

" Willingly," said the latter, and, with an arm
that stretched out long enough to cross the river,
he handed Don Juan his lighted cigar. Don Juan
was not astonished at this, for he made a profession
of being astonished at nothing. If he had been a
philosopher, he would not have been astonished
either. When, at Paris, we hear the voice of a friend
who bids us farewell over the telephone from Mar-
seilles, before he embarks on a voyage, we do not
think that marvellous, and in fact it was only
marvellous when it did not exist. We must admit
one of two things : either Don Juan's adventure is
not true, which is probable enough, or it is true,
in which case it is as natural as our communications
by telephone, although, I agree, a little rarer.
Mérimée lets us understand that this smoker was
the devil in person. I admit it. You see I grant
a great deal. But if the devil exists, he is within
nature, like you and me, for nature contains everything, and it is natural for him to reach his arm across
rivers. If our manuals of physiology do not say so,
it is because they are incomplete. It is certain that
all phenomena are not described in books. I sometimes walk, in the fine summer nights, along the
Paris quays, in the shadow of the colossal black
tracery of Notre-Dame, on the border of those
dark waters in which thousands of twinkling lights
are quivering. The moon rides in the clouds ;
you hear the gleaming and doleful tide moaning
under the arches, and think at once of all the
horrors of life and all the necromancy of death.
If the devil has fire not only for the great scorners
of God and of women's virtue, if he deigns also to
want to seduce a gentle philosopher, he will
perhaps have the politeness to stretch me his cigar

from one quay of the Seine to the other. Then,
faithful to my principles, I shall hold the fact
to be natural, and I shall make a communication
about it to the Academy of Sciences.

That is a resolution which testifies, I think,
to a steadfast enough intelligence and a reason
which desires in no way to be astonished. Yet there
are moments, I know, when the coldness of reason
freezes us. There are hours when one does not want
to be reasonable, and I confess that those hours are
not the worst. The absurd is one of the joys of life;
observe also that of all human books, those whose
fortune is most constant and most lasting are tales
and perfectly unreasonable tales—" The Goose
Girl," " Puss in Boots," " The Arabian Nights,"
and, why not say it? . . . . " The Odyssey "
which is also a child's tale. Ulysses' travels are full
of charming absurdities which we find again in
the " Voyages of Sindbad the Sailor."

The marvellous is a falsehood. We know it, and
we want to have lies told to us. That is becoming
more and more difficult. The good Homer and the
Arab story-tellers do not deceive us. It needs, to
seduce us to-day, imaginations fertile in wiles, very
skilled and very ingenious minds. Edgar Poe, for
example, and his " Tales of Mystery," or Gilbert
Augustin Thierry with " Larmor," " Marfa," and
that " Tresse blonde " of which we spoke recently.

Old Apuleius is no mediocre impostor, and he
also has given me, I admit, the delightful illusion
of the marvellous. I am going to tell you everything: Apuleius is my darling sin. I love him
without respecting him, and I love him greatly.
He lies so well! he turns nature upside down so
well for you, and that is a spectacle which fills.

us with joy in our hours of perversity. He shares
so fully, in order to gratify it, that depraved taste
for the absurd, that desire for the unreasonable
which each of us has in a corner of his heart ! When
the harmony of the world has wearied you by its
inexorable fixedness, when you find life monotonous
and nature tiresome, open the " Golden Ass "
and follow Apuleius, I mean Lucius, through his
extraordinary journeyings. From the very beginning
an atmosphere of insanity poisons you and maddens
you. You share the lunacy of that strange traveller :

> " Here I was then in the midst of that Thessaly, the classic land of
> enchantments, celebrated in this respect through the entire world. . .
> I did not know whither to direct my desires and my curiosity ; I
> regarded each object with a sort of uneasiness. Of all that I perceived
> in the town, nothing seemed to me to be such as my eyes showed it
> to me. It seemed to me that, by the infernal power of certain incan-
> tations, everything must have been metamorphosed. If I saw a stone,
> my imagination recognised it to be a petrified man ; if I heard birds,
> they were men covered with feathers ; the trees of the street were
> men loaded with leaves ; the fountains, as they played, escaped from
> some human body, I believed that the portraits and statues were
> on the point of walking, the walls of speaking, the oxen of foretelling
> the future."

After that are you astonished that he is changed
into an ass ? Saint Augustine more than half
believed in it.

" We also," he says, in the " City of God," " we
also, when we were in Italy, heard accounts of this
sort in regard to a certain part of the country.
It was related that inn-keepers, expert in these
sorceries, sometimes gave to travellers, in their
cheese, ingredients which immediately changed
them into beasts of burden. These wretches were
made to carry loads and, after painful servitude,
they resumed their natural forms. In the interval,

their soul had not become that of an animal, they had retained a man's reason. Apuleius, in the work which he has entitled ' The Golden Ass,' relates that this adventure happened to him ; by the power of a certain drug, he was changed into an ass, though keeping a man's mind. It is not known whether the author here records a real fact or one of his tales."

Undoubtedly, Apuleius tells a tale, a tale imitated from the Greek, and he has not even invented Lucius and his metamorphosis, but he has contributed the grain of hellebore.

He is an interesting man, this Lucius, as M. Paul Monceaux describes him to us in a very complete and, as it seems to me, very judicious study— assuredly a very agreeable one.

This African, a contemporary of the Antonines, of a light, facile, rapid, and brilliant mind, was not at bottom very original ; he improvised and compiled. If he was mad, we must agree that everybody was a little mad at that time. An unhealthy curiosity exercised all imaginations. The prodigies of Apollonius of Tyana had sent a shudder through the world. An anxious belief in enchantments troubled the best minds. Plutarch makes shades glide into the fields of history ; the steadfast soul of Tacitus is easily shaken by prodigies ; Pliny, the naturalist, shows himself as credulous as he is curious. Phlegon of Tralles writes a book of " Marvellous Doings " for an astrological Cæsar, and relates minutely the adventure of a dead woman who deserts her mortuary chamber for the bed of a young stranger.

It was the good fortune of Apuleius to be born, in this troubled environment, with an astonishing capacity for conceiving of the absurd and the impossible. He studied all the sciences and drew from them nothing but puerile superstitions. Physics, medicine, astronomy, natural history, everything with him was turned into magic. And as he had a vivid imagination and a bewitching style it was given to him to write the masterpiece of fantastic romances.

This clever, frivolous, and vain man left behind him the memory of a magician and a thaumaturgist. At the period of the great religious disputes, when Christians and pagans opposed miracles to miracles, the Fathers of the Church mentioned the author of the " Metamorphosis " with a hatred mingled with dread. Already in the middle of the third century, Lactantius exclaims that the miracles of Apuleius are massing themselves in crowds. St. Jerome places this magician with Apollonius of Tyana. St. Augustine, who, as we have seen, almost confuses him with the hero of the tale, deplores that such a man should be sometimes opposed and even preferred to the Christ. During this period the worshippers of the gods who were departing venerated the rhetorician of Madaura as one of their last sages. It was natural that they should be attached to the philosopher who had been enamoured of all the creeds and had been admitted to all the initiations. The statue of Apuleius was erected at Constantinople, in the Zeuxippus, and the " Anthology " designates in these terms him whose image it preserves : " Apuleius, with meditative look, celebrates the silent orgies of the Latin Muse, he whom the Ausonian Siren has filled, as one of her initiates, with ineffable wisdom." We have a difficulty in recognising in this distich the author of that little magical and very free romance which I accuse myself of enjoying in my hours of unreason. And M. Paul Monceaux satisfies us better when, praising him in a less exalted tone, he shows us this extraordinary Apuleius under the features of a clever rhetorician, handsome " with an insolent Southern beauty," even a little common, boastful, eloquent, clever in seizing hold of the public, deceiver and deceiving himself with supreme skill, making people believe in everything and believing everything.

Yet, there are here and there, it seems to me, in those of his works that remain to us, some pages bearing the impress of a truly philosophical gravity, in which one believes that one hears as it were a last echo of that Greek wisdom which nothing in the world has surpassed. It is a very long time since I have re-read the little treatise on " The Demon of Socrates." I have retained an agreeable remembrance of it. You know that Apuleius believed in demons. The demons, he said, inhabit the aerial regions up to the first circle of the moon, where the ether begins.

These are permissible reveries. Men would be very unhappy if they were prevented from dreaming of the unknowable. But what most touched me formerly, as I read that treatise on " The Demon of Socrates," is a definition of man which is to be found there, and which I have copied. I find it to my hand among my old papers, and that is a sort of miracle, for I have no properly arranged bundles of papers, and shall have none all my life, so much does paper that has been written on inspire me with horror and weariness. This is how Apuleius defines the condition of men :

" Men, acting by reason, powerful through
speech, have an immortal soul, perishable organs, a
light and restless mind, a coarse and infirm body, dissimilar manners, common errors, obstinate audacity,
persistent hope, vain labours, an inconstant fortune ;
mortals if taken singly, immortal through the repro-
duction of the race carried on in turn by succeeding
generations, their years are rapid, their wisdom
tardy, their death prompt. Throughout their
moaning life, they inhabit the earth."

Does not one feel in this a virile sadness that
recalls the first aphorism of Hippocrates ?

And then is not this little novel itself, whose
picturesque absurdity and expressive marvellousness
I was just now admiring, is it not philosophical in
its own fashion and even in its licence ?   Is not
Apuleius, in his " Metamorphosis," the ingenious
interpreter of the dogmas of reincarnation ;   does
he not expound in a light form, the doctrine of
trials and expiations through a series of successive
existences, and is not even the transformation of
Lucius the affecting expression of the labours of
human life, of those changes which incessantly
modify the complex elements of that *ego* which tends
incessantly to know rather than not to know ?   Is
there a hidden wisdom in this book which displays
such amusing folly ? How do I know ?

M. OCTAVE FEUILLET

JULIETTE'S DIVORCE *

ERE is a little volume which M. Octave Feuillet, recently plunged into a mourning which will never leave him, has allowed to be torn from him by his publisher. "Le Divorce de Juliette," a comedy in three acts and four scenes, gave a great deal of pleasure when it appeared in the "Revue des Deux Mondes." Would it succeed as well on the stage? Excellent judges have pronounced that it would. They know these things infinitely better than I do. I am not one to contradict them. But having a particular liking for looking at spectacles from my armchair, I am satisfied with the performance as I have seen it with my feet on the fender. I flatter myself that I have seen a Juliette who was pretty enough, though a little thin as becomes her youth: she is only twenty-two. Juliette wants to divorce her husband, and not without reason. If M. d'Epinoy married her, it was not because she is charming, but solely in order to carry on his intrigue with the beautiful Princesse de Chagres with more security. The Prince had

* "Le Divorce de Juliette—"Charybde et Scylla"—"Le Curé de Bouron."

some suspicions, and he was a man to kill M.
d'Épinoy as he had previously killed, at Florence,
that poor devil Borgo-Forte.   M. d'Épinoy married
in order to divert the Prince's suspicions.

It was the Princess who thought of this excellent
subterfuge.   Once M. d'Épinoy was married, the
Prince would no longer have any suspicions, and the
Princess could love M. d'Épinoy with perfect tranquillity.   But one does not take everything into
account.   The Princess has not foreseen that
M. d'Épinoy might fall in love with his wife ; yet
that is what happens, or almost happens, when
Juliette suddenly discovers her husband's intrigue
with Madame de Chagres and learns that she has
herself been married only to turn aside the suspicions
of the terrible Prince who, but for that diversion,
would infallibly have killed M. d'Épinoy like another
Borgo-Forte, which would have been serious, for
his death would have compromised the Princess.
The shock is severe, for the poor woman loves her
husband with all her heart.   But she is courageous :
she has made up her mind.   She will divorce him.
She is quite resolved upon it. . . .   Ah ! that is
where M. Octave Feuillet lies in wait for you.   No,
she will not divorce him.   And everything will be
arranged.   She loves :   she forgives.   Love has
infinite treasures of clemency.   And then Roger, at
bottom, is not so black as he seems.   He is weak
rather than wicked.   He was between two women,
and that is a situation from which it is difficult to
extricate oneself advantageously.   Look at all
Racine's lovers, Pyrrhus, Bajazet, Hippolytus, equally
entangled between two loves which they have
inspired :   their position is very delicate, sometimes
even a little ridiculous, and they have their critical

moments. M. d'Épinoy is less innocent than Hippolytus and less excusable than Pyrrhus, but in the end he no longer loves the Princesse de Chagres and loves Juliette who forgives. This is not a conversion, for, as a very amiable old man confided to me the other day, people in love are always the same. But, even if it were a conversion, I would not blame M. Octave Feuillet for it. The author of " M. de Camors " delights to show those faults of the heart, which he excels in describing, culminating in expiation or repentance. Even if one detected a little too much of poetical artifice and moral arrangement, I would not complain of that. On the contrary, it is very agreeable to me that these profane adventures should end, like the stories of the legendary saints, with the definite triumph of the good.

The idea of the final redemption of all creatures is certainly not the idea of a meanly mediocre philosophy. And M. Octave Feuillet's happy endings and moral conclusions are irreproachable from the symbolical point of view. " Le Divorce de Juliette " is but an elegant sketch, but we find in it the hand of a master. I do not speak to-day of " Charybde et Scylla," which is printed at the end of the book: that " proverb " contains in four scenes a witty satire on our public schools for girls and the higher teaching given in them to young ladies. The question is interesting ; we will come to it some day.

What I have in my heart to say now, what I want to declare very emphatically, is my admiration for the finished art with which M. Octave Feuillet composes his novels. They have perfect form: they are statues of Praxiteles. The idea spreads itself through them like life through a harmonious body. They have proportion, they have restraint, and that is worthy of all praise.

Others have wanted to do better, and have constructed monsters. They have fallen into barbarism. They have said: "We must be human." But what is more human, I pray you, than proportion and harmony ? To be truly human is to compose, to connect, to deduce ideas ; it is to have the spirit of sequence. To be truly human is to deliver thoughts under forms which are only symbols ; it is to penetrate into souls and to seize upon the spirit of things.

That is why M. Octave Feuillet is more human in his elegant symmetry and in his passionate idealism than all the naturalists who display indefinitely before us all the works of organic life without conceiving its significance. The ideal is the whole man. " Le Divorce de Juliette " has furnished me with an opportunity of rendering homage to M. Octave Feuillet's accomplished talent.

What charms me profoundly in the master's work is that fine equilibrium, that wise plan, that happy ordering in which I find again the French genius against which so many and such monstrous assaults are committed on all sides.

I feel as it were a grateful piety towards those ordered and luminous talents whose works bear in them that supreme virtue : proportion.

This morning, as I found myself on the hill of Sainte-Geneviève, in the centre of the old land of studies, I entered into the church of Saint-Étienne-du-Mont, driven by the desire of seeing elegant sculpture and charming stained glass, drawn by that irresistible inclination which unceasingly leads meditative minds to the things that speak to them of the

past, and, if a more intelligible reason must be
given, guided by the desire of reading again the
epitaph of Jean Racine, whose life I have the honour
of writing at the present moment. That epitaph,
composed in Latin by Boileau, was thrown down
along with the church of Port-Royal-des-Champs
where it had been placed. It still bears traces of
the violence it has undergone ; the stone is broken
into twenty pieces and the poet's name is a good deal
mutilated. A violence that seems stupid to us
to-day ! Let us realise that our violences, if we
have the misfortune to commit them, will equally
inspire pity two centuries hence. That epitaph is
admirable in its simplicity, and one cannot read its
last phrase without emotion. Boileau, after having
recorded all his friend's titles to the esteem and
admiration of men, concludes with Christian philosophy by these touching words : " O thou, whoever
thou art whom piety leads into this holy house,
recognise by what thou seest the little that life is, and
give to the memory of so great a man prayers rather
than praises. *Tanti viri memoriam precibus potius
quam elogiis prosequere.*" As I left that old house of
stone where the names of Pascal and Racine are
inscribed under the wings of Jean Goujon's pretty
angels, as I came back to the world of the living,
beneath the rain and storm, I applied my thoughts
to the things of the present time, the ideas of the
day, the new books, the " Divorce de Juliette," a
copy of which the publisher had just sent me. And
my thought going on from the book to its author, I
pictured to myself that exemplary life, so well
hidden away, so well shielded, which only the
exquisite books that were its fruits revealed. I
fancied to myself M. Octave Feuillet peaceful and

happy on his little rock of Saint-Lô, in the shadow
of the old church with the tracery of black stone,
in those steep streets where one hears the coopers
putting hoops on the casks in which next harvest's
cider will be made, where heavy-laden bees who
leave behind them the smell of buckwheat are flying
in the sunlight. I also see him going down the
dusty road that leads to the stream in which the
willows dip, and dreaming there of some of those
audacious, perverse, charming, and sometimes chas-
tened characters which are the favourites of his
imagination.

He lives there, securely hidden, the obscure
author of celebrated books. He makes of his family
life a work as conscientious and refined as his novels.
He would like never to leave the banks of the Vire,
where in the days of mourning there sang that good
Basselin whom the English put to death because his
songs made France loved. He would like never to
leave the two spires of Sainte-Croix, nor his little
black, crippled, hunchbacked, crooked-built town,
a town, none the less, surrounded by tender grass
and pure water, over-arched by soft skies, and, like all
the Norman towns, ugly in a pretty way. He only
comes to Paris with great regret and for the sake of
his children's education. But a delicate and faithful
hand has piously transported to the new dwelling
all the family relics, all the mementos of youth ;
not a bond is burst, not a thread broken : the dear
past is still there in its entirety. Shall I follow the
poet-novelist to his retreat at Versailles, where he
rested by performing the labour of labours of his
life ? It was there he was struck, less than a year
ago, by a cruel sorrow which two lives will support
to the end. The day on which M. Octave Feuillet

lost his son, it was made clear to him how universally he is loved. Testimonies of sympathy and respect flowed from all sides into his house. I hope he will not read what in the sincerity of my heart I am writing here. One should not reopen wounds except to bandage them, and my words, though profoundly felt, have not, alas! the virtue of a balm or an electuary.

These were the thoughts that I revolved in my mind as I left Saint-Étienne-du-Mont for the Place du Panthéon, beaten by the wind and rain; and, calling to mind the fine Latin inscription that I had just read, I applied to the author of " Julia de Trécœur " what Boileau said of the memory of his illustrious friend. However worthy of eulogy, however happy, however fruitful a human life be, it is subject to such ordeals and struck by such cruel blows that we must pity what we are most anxious to admire: *Memoriam precibus potius quam elogiis prosequere.*

JOAN OF ARC AND POETRY
VALERAND DE LA VARANNE—M.
ERNEST PRAROND *

NE can say of M. Ernest Prarond, poet and scholar of Abbeville, that he loves his town and loves letters with his whole heart. He has devoted long years to describing and telling the story of his Abbeville and all the antiquities of Ponthieu. To feel the former ages living again in oneself is mightily sweet. I am sure that M. Ernest Prarond has felt it to the full. He possesses that ardent patience, that ever-eager curiosity, that ingenious love of the past, which are always rewarded by admirable visions. Two years ago, as I was passing through Abbeville, I stood and dreamed beneath the ruined vaults of the elegant and fragile collegiate church and in the shade of the square black donjon of the Town Hall. These walls, said I to myself, antique witnesses of the struggles and the longings of men, these vocal stones, whose homely meaning I, a heedless passer-by, scarcely divine, how many touching secrets have they not confided to the poet-historian

* Ernest Prarond : " La Voie Sacrée "—" Valerandi Varanii : De Gestis Joannæ Virginis Francæ Egregiæ Bellatricis." A poem of 1516, republished, analysed, and annotated by E. Prarond.

of the five towns and three hundred villages of
Ponthieu ! Happy are they for whom tombstones
have only words of life, and who find eternal symbols
beneath the moss that covers half-broken images !
Happy are the rare archæologists in whom the letter
has not killed the spirit !

It was yesterday, it seems to me, that I saw
M. Ernest Prarond for the first time ; yesterday, in
truth, in 1871, just after the war and the Commune,
in that little house in the Rue du Four-Saint-Ger-
main where Charles Asselineau finished life with the
politeness of a Parisian bourgeois and the grace of
a man of letters. Since then life has not afforded
me many meetings with the Abbeville poet. Yet
M. Prarond's face has remained in my memory, and
I like to call it to my mind. It is that of a robust
man, very simple and very refined, and in the grand
style : a large open face in which shines an angry
eye. I find that eye again in the generous verses of
the poet, verses that are sometimes angry. M.
Prarond had, when he began, about 1848, a gay and
somewhat mocking manner ; what M. Philippe de
Chennevières calls " the free good-humour of the
old story-tellers of the North of France." He has
since formed for himself a new style, learned, complicated, tormented, and certainly original. The
good public cannot rub itself against these bushes
without being pricked a little by them ; but, under
rinds of strange forms, not a few savoury fruit tickle
the palate of the connoisseur.

It was yesterday, I said, that I met M. Ernest
Prarond, in the little study where the good Asselineau, surrounded by Nanteuil's engravings, used
to dally with the romantic editions that spoke
to him of his youth. During the Commune he

had done his work at the Mazarin Library with heroic exactness. When the soldiers of the Commune rolled barrels of petroleum into the gallery filled with literary treasures, they found before them an old gentleman, very polite and very obstinate, who induced them by force of reasoning to take away their incendiary engines. The library was saved, but Asselineau died in the following year of pain and amazement. I still recall that man of honour, mortally stricken in his patriotism and in his habits, but polite, smiling, doing the honours of his modest table like a sage, and thinking, I imagine, of taking for himself the epitaph that Boufflers had put upon his tomb : " My friends, think that I am sleeping."

On that day, I tested, not without infinite pleasure, M. Ernest Prarond's unexpected turn of mind. With what subtilty his intelligence pierced into things, and how he could make even patriotism original ! His conversation had the broken brilliancy of lightning. Since then—for eighteen years have slipped past like a day—M. Prarond, having retired beneath some old roof in Abbeville, has peacefully pursued his erudite and poetic enchantments, and made innumerable shades appear in his magic mirror. He is of the race of Faust, and would see Helen. But the devil has no power over him.

Like a pious son of Abbeville, he has devoted himself of late years to the elucidation of an old Latin poem which another son of Abbeville, Valerand de la Varanne, Doctor of Theology of the Faculty of Paris, published in 1516, " De Gestis Joannæ virginis, francæ egregiæ bellatricis." This poem, composed on the deeds of Joan of Arc by a

cleric who might in his youth have seen old men
that were contemporaries of the Maid, deserved to
be drawn out of oblivion; and to give us a readable,
correct, and, above all, an attractive edition of it, is
an angelic work. That is what has been done, in
Abbeville, by M. Prarond, a scholiast of a singular
species. The glosses, under his pen, turn into verses,
and it is in sonnets and in odes that he elucidates
his author. He has seized the timely moments and,
detaching these embellishments from the margins of
the old text, he has made a separate collection of them,
which he calls " la Voie Sacrée," not wishing, from a
conscientious scruple, to place the heroine's name
on the poems she has inspired. This respect, joined
to the diligence of the worship, has been rewarded.

" La Voie Sacrée " is perhaps the most genuine
poem Joan of Arc has inspired. Doubtless M.
Ernest Prarond's inspiration preserved something
oblique, sinuous, fugitive, which destines all his
works to the soft twilight of esoteric productions:
there is nothing here that can become popular.
But what a charm there is for adepts in discovering
in it, here and there, profound meanings and rare
truths! When one has lived, as I have done, for
several years with the Maid and her companions,
one cannot read the fourteen poems of " la Voie
Sacrée " without saying to the author: " Well,
brother, so you have also seen that fairy tree to
which Joan used to go with the girls of the district
on Well Sunday, when, as the ploughmen would
say, it was as beautiful as a lily. You were at
Poitiers then when Joan appeared there in her
victorious innocence; in Orleans when it was
delivered at the exultation at Patay, at Reims, at
Compiègne. Alas! then you have heard the sea

beating against the foot of that tower of Crotoy, in which Joan was the prisoner of the English ?

" Yes, you have seen in those hateful days that Bay of Somme, so soft and grey and aglitter with birds, where the foam of the sea embroidered a fringe for the kingdom of lilies, and you have heard the voice of the saint mingling with the voice of the Ocean. Yes, you have seen Joan of Arc's banner, and you have described it with the simplicity of a truthful witness. I, like you, have seen it, why have I not been able to tell about it ? At least I will repeat your words, which bear the full impress of the spirit of the old times " :

" LA BANNIÈRE

" TOURS—ORLEANS

" Jeanne, en avril, commande au peintre sa bannière :
Je veux un tissu blanc, peint de telle manière
Que dans un champ de lys Messire notre Dieu,
Sur le trône du monde, y paraisse au milieu
D'anges agenouillés. Je veux qu'on puisse lire
Sur les côtés : Jésus, Marie. Il faut élire
Une étoffe légère et qui, se déployant,
Déroule bien ces noms, les fleurs, Dieu tout-voyant,
Et les anges. Frangez l'orle avec de la soie,
Afin de faire honneur à l'ordre qui m'envoie,
Et vous-même ainsi, peintre, ouvrez aux bons combats.

Mai fleurit. La Bastille est formidable. Au bas
Un gentilhomme dit, sous l'assiégé qui raille :
' Jeanne, votre étendard a touché la muraille.'
Jeanne s'écrie alors : ' Tout est vôtre : y entrez ! '
Et le flot des Français passe aux murs éventrés." *

---

* " Joan in April orders her banner from the painter : I want a light fabric painted in such a manner that on a field of lilies God, our Lord, on the throne of the world, may appear on it surrounded by kneeling angels. I want people to be able to read on the sides :

That is the strange and graceful fashion in which
M. Ernest Prarond comments upon Valerand de la
Varanne's old poem. But, as I have said, he has
published his poetical gloss separately. The Latin
text, accompanied by notes and followed by an
analysis, was printed however, and here it is,
published to-day. Let us thank M. Prarond for it.
That Doctor of Theology of the Faculty of Paris,
who celebrated in three thousand hexameters her
whom he called *Darcia progenies* and *barricea lux*,
was a great Latinist, but he was a good Frenchman.

He celebrated in his poems the victory of Fornovo
and the taking of Genoa. It was whilst reading the
trial of Joan of Arc that the idea came to him of
composing an epic poem on the Maid's deeds. He
says in one of the dedicatory epistles that accompany
his poem : " If any one wishes to know this history
more thoroughly, let him ask at the Abbey of Saint-
Victor for the book that was lent to me for some
days." And we know that that book was a copy of
the two trials. That is the true source of this
marvellous history. Accordingly, the good Valerand
usually forms a correct enough idea of his heroine.
He is not too extravagant, and except that he always
wants to display his knowledge and his genius, he is
a very honest man. We must forgive him his in-
vocation to Apollo, to the Muses, and to Pan, and

Jesus, Mary. You must choose a light stuff which, as it unfurls,
will well display those names, the all-seeing God, and the angels.
Fringe the orlet with silk to do honour to the order that sends me,
and thus yourself, painter, open up good combats.

" May blossoms. The fortress is formidable. At its foot a nobleman who is beneath the besieged, who are scoffing, says : ' Joan, your
standard has touched the wall.' Joan then exclaims : ' All is yours :
enter in to it ! ' And the flood of Frenchmen crosses the strewn
walls."

allow him to put the names of Phœbus and Nereus
in the mouths of the angels of Paradise. We must
not, above all, be surprised if he continually compares Joan with Camilla and with Penthesilea.
Christine de Pisan and Gerson had done it before
him. The wits of the fifteenth century were much
more enamoured of Greece and Rome than we
imagine. Have you not seen at Pierrefonds the
chimneypiece of the nine female warriors which
Viollet-le-Duc has restored on the model of the
monuments of the epoch. Penthesilea, with her
hand on her shield, figures in it with heroic elegance.
In 1429, a French cleric was living at Rome and was
there composing a chronicle. On the news of the
deliverance of Orleans, he set down in writing the
Maid's exploits, and concluded that the high deeds
of the young girl would appear all the more admirable when they were placed in comparison with
those of the sacred or profane heroines, Deborah,
Judith, Esther, Penthesilea. " Our Maid," he says,
" surpasses them all."

It is none the less true that Valerand wants
simplicity, that he imitates Ovid and Statius too
much, and, lastly, that he is perfectly ridiculous when
he makes Joan of Arc say that she has not come from
the Scythian rocks, that she has dwelt neither in
Ortygia nor in the fields of Phasis.

> " Scythicis non eruta veni
> Rupibus   .   .   .   .   .
>   .   .   . Nec Ortygiam colui, nec Phasidis agros."

On the other hand, he gives an account of the
Poitiers examination, which has unhappily not been
preserved for us, and we may suppose that what he
relates about it is not entirely imaginary. He

paraphrases a letter which Charles VII might have
written to Pope Calixtus III in order to obtain the
rescript which served as a basis for the suit of
rehabilitation, and it is probable that he has not
invented this letter, all trace of which has been lost.
Finally, Valerand may be regarded as an historian,
for he introduces fresh uncertainties.

His is a moderate mind. To judge of him from
the precepts which he supposes to be dictated to
Charles VII by the spirit of Charlemagne, he is a
partisan of the moderate, I was going to say con-
stitutional, monarchy. Would you like a summary
of these precepts ?

" Be pious, honour justice. Assure the liberty of
the judges ; choose them incorruptible ; establish
legislative bodies. Strike at the wicked, for indulgence encourages crime. Chastise the proud.
Do not listen to informers, and fear flattery. Know
how to triumph over thy anger and say to thyself :
I have conquered, as soon as thou hast been able to
conquer. Be chaste, content thyself with the queen.
Have pity on the poor. Ask everything from the
laws alone. Love peace and only make just wars.
Protect the people against the violent. Fix equit-
able laws and be the first to observe them. Restrain
luxury : it is not the purple that strengthens a
kingdom. If war compels thee to raise new taxes,
economise carefully in other matters. The royal
power has fixed limits. Silence enmities which give
birth to divisions in the kingdom. Be merciful to
the conquered ; the levity and harshness of the
French soldier have often aroused the hatred of the
foreigner. Do not desire overmuch to be feared ;
Cæsar and Nero were dreaded : they perished. Do
not depend upon youth, believe the old men. Thus

shalt thou equal thy ancestors and deserve heaven."

It is not doubtful that Valerand lends his own political sentiments to the Emperor Charlemagne. And it must be admitted that our Doctor of Theology has formed a fine idea of a sovereign. Louis XI, assuredly, furnished more than one feature of it. He was a king according to Valerand's heart, both by his love for the weak, and also, a matter of less moment, by the purity of his private morals ; for, conformably with the precept of chastity which is rather out of place in Charlemagne's mouth, Louis XI contented himself with the queen his wife, " even when she was not such," says Commines, " that he could take great pleasure in her."

M. Prarond compares the " Mystère du Siège d'Orléans " with the " De Gestis Joannæ virginis," and very ingeniously opposes " to the hexameters of the too heavily armed legionary the short simply-rhymed lines of the citizen archer." And how he prefers the archer ! How one feels that he would give all Varanius for these eight little lines alone :

" Le Roi.

" Or câ, Jehanne, ma doulce fille,
Vollez vous doncques estre armée ?
Vous sentez vous assez agille
Que vous n'en soyez pas grevée ?
Porter harnoiz sur vostre doux (*dos*),
Vous en serez bien toust lassée.
Belle fille, qu'en dictes vous ?

" La Pucelle.

" Au nom Dieu, le porteroy bien." *

" The King.

* " Come, Joan, my gentle girl, do you wish then to be armed ? Do you feel yourself agile enough not to be encumbered by it ? You

And indeed, nothing could ring more true. If there are poems relative to the Maid that interest and move us, they are those of the fifteenth century because they are pieces of evidence, and in them one hears an inimitable accent. I will mention, in the forefront, the verses of Christine de Pisan. They are the only ones that were written during the heroine's lifetime. They were finished on July 31, 1429, at the moment when Charles VII, master of Château-Thierry, could in three days' march lead his army before Paris. Christine was then old ; she had lived for eleven years cloistered in an Abbey of the Ile-de-France. This lady had her head full of the learned subtleties which formed the whole knowledge of her time ; she was a bit of a pedant, but good, serious and full of compassion. The miseries of France afflicted her. When she heard of the deliverance of Orleans and the Maid's mission, she felt for the first time for eleven years an uplifting of joy :

"Or, à prime me prens à rire." *

It was then that, in the depth of her retreat, the excellent woman wrote some verses which are believed to be the last that ever left her hand. They show the effects of the author's old age and the miseries of the time. They are heavy and awkward. But one discovers in them a grave joy, a pious gladness, a profound feeling of the public good, which renders them worthy of respect and dear to us.

will be wearied out by wearing harness on your back. Fair girl, what do you say ?

"THE MAID.

"In the name of God, I will wear it."

    * "Now, at prime, I am filled with laughter."

"Chose est bien digne de mémoire,"

says the cloistered poetess,

> " Que Dieu par une vierge tendre
> Ait adès voulu—chose est voire (*vraie*),
> Sur France si grant grace estendre.
> Tu Jehanne de bonne heure née
> (*Toi, Jeanne, née en une bonne heure*),
> Benoist (*beni*) soit cil (*celui*) qui te créa.
> Pucelle de Dieu ordonnée (*envoyée*)
> En qui le Saint-Esprit réa (*fit rayonner*)
> Sa grande grace ; et qui ot et a (*et qui ens et as*)
> Toute largesse de hault don.
> M'onc requeste ne te véa (*refusa*)
> Que te rendra assez guardon.
> (*Et il te donnera assez grande recompense*)." *

What above all rejoices the good Christine is that
the salvation comes through a woman.   She is quite
happy at this, without being the least in the world
surprised at it, for she had always set the honour of
her sex very high, and all through her life had
shown herself obstinate for the privileges that the
spirit of chivalry granted to ladies.   For her, as for
many souls of her time, a virtuous lady, a pure
young girl, could become, by the will of God,
superior to evil, stronger than archers and the walls
of towns.   Examples of such a vocation are not
lacking.   Nurtured in sacred and profane letters, she
knew the strong women of the Bible, the sibyls of
Rome and Cumæ, the Amazons and the female
warriors.   She puts Joan, the shepherd girl, above

---

* " It is a thing worthy of remembrance that by means of a
tender virgin God has always willed—the thing is truè—to extend
so great grace on France. Thou, Joan, born in a good hour, blessed
be He who created thee. Maid sent by God, in whom the Holy Spirit
showed his great grace ; and who hast and had all wealth from above.
Never a request did He refuse thee, and He will give thee a great
enough reward."

all these heroines who foretell her coming and prepare for her. She expects from her the deliverance of the kingdom, the resurrection of that great people, more wretched than a dog. (*Tout ce grand people chenin par femme est sours.*) But a Christian as well as a Frenchwoman, she does not limit Joan's mission to the defeat of the English. She foretells that the victorious Maid will lead the King of France to the conquest of the tomb of Jesus Christ and will only die on the soil sanctified by the death of a God.

> " Des Sarrazins fera essart
> En conquérant la sainte terre ;
> Le menra Charles, que Dieu gard' ;
> Ains qu'il muire fera tel erre.
> Cils et cil qui la doit conquerre :
> Là doit elle finer sa vie
> Et l'un et l'autre gloire acquerre,
> Là sera la chose assovye." *

It was wishing for too much ; it was expecting too much from the poor and holy girl. One can anticipate thenceforward, in that fair hour of glory and hope, the coming days of bitterness and deception. Joan was condemned always to conquer. For her, the least defeat was an irreparable fall. Conquered, she could only find refuge in martyrdom.

The people of France, it is consoling to say it, did not forget their saint after the passion she suffered at Rouen, under the English regent. The old poets of the fifteenth century also furnish us with this precious evidence of the piety of Frenchmen towards the memory of their friend.

The " Mystère du Siège d'Orléans," of which we

---

* The Saracens she shall bring to nought by the conquest of the Holy Land. Charles, whom God preserve, she shall thither lead before any rumour spread of her emprise. And whosoe'er be destined to defeat her, there it is she shall end her life. And there shall both of them achieve glory and the whole matter conclude.

were speaking just now, was performed in that town
from the year 1435 onwards, on the anniversary of
the deliverance of the city. This mystery play, in
which God the Father, the Virgin, and the Saints
mingle with the men-at-arms, is composed of twenty
thousand five hundred and twenty-nine verses, says
M. Marius Sépet, whose word I accept. Those
verses are the work of several worthy people who
manufactured them as best they could, with a good
deal of artlessness. The piece ends with the return
of Joan to Orléans, after the battle of Patay, the
rapidest, most joyous, and gladdest of our victories.

I am told that the able manager of the Odéon
theatre, M. Porel, is asking a fresh Joan of Arc from
the poets. I have no advice to give either to the
poets or to M. Porel. But it seems to me that the
best manner of setting this admirable Joan on the
stage would be to construct, not a drama or a
tragedy, but a simple mystery play, composed of
detached scenes which would be taken from the
chronicles and translated into thoroughly popular
language, if possible in very simple and artless verse.
It would be necessary not to have recourse to any
dramatic artifice, and to make the scenes follow on
without joining them one to another, almost as
Shakespeare does in his " Histories." In this task
at once simple and minute, one ought especially to
fear the eloquence of words, for it would injure that
of facts. In its general tone, one would be inspired
by the old and venerable piece of which I have just
spoken. Verse was willingly prosaic in the fifteenth
century. It could not be so to-day. Perhaps it
would be more suitable to replace it with prose each
time that the human personages speak. Only Saint
Michael, Saint Catherine, Saint Margaret, all the

saints, all the angels, would speak in verse and sing
the choruses. They would be visible and present,
and would reveal the mystical sense of the action.
The chorus of angels who sang M. Gounod's music
around Joan of Arc's stake in M. Jules Barbier's
play, created a very fine effect in 1873. This time
I should like Michael, Catherine, and Margaret to
be wholly in the taste of the fifteenth century, and
the two latter saints to be ladies and to represent the
soul of old France. It would be necessary for the
whole flower of Christian poetry to proceed out of
their mouths, and for their songs to be of a religious
character, and to be accompanied on the organ. As
for making Joan herself speak according to the laws
of a versification which dates from Ronsard, that
would shock all those who are scrupulous lovers of
history. Many of the sayings of that admirable girl
have happily been preserved. They could not be
put into verse without disfiguring them, and that
would be a great pity, for they are pearls and jewels
of the purest French tongue. It would only be
necessary to modernise them : the theatre does not
permit archaisms in speech. We are shocked at
hearing obsolete words on youthful lips. To bring
such a work to a successful issue, the collaboration of
a poet and a scholar would not be inadvisable.
Finally, the piece of which I am dreaming is a
chronicle in dialogue, accompanied by music ; for
the ideal must be joined to the real. It is a truly
national and popular work. I do not want it to be,
properly speaking, a work of art. I want something
much more and much better. I want it to be a
work of faith which speaks to souls. I ask that, to
do it well, the authors should for the moment make
themselves men of the fifteenth century, and that,

in the words of Alfred de Vigny's Chatterton, they should consent to " narrow their outlook."

But we were speaking of the old poets. Nine years after Joan's death, the Provost of Lausanne Cathedral, Martin le Franc by name, devoted to the heroine's glorification an episode in his poem " Le Champion des Dames." It is to be noted that Martin le Franc was attached to the Duke of Burgundy to whom he dedicated his book. In that episode, Joan is attacked by a personage whose name indicates his character : he is called Narrow-Understanding. She is victoriously defended by Free-Will. It was she, says the latter,

> " Ce fut elle qui recouvra
> L'honneur des Français tellement
> Que par raison elle en aura
> Renom perpétuellement." *

All these verses are like chestnuts : they have a good flavour but the rind is thick and rough. Here are some of the easiest : they are taken from the " Vigiles du roi Charles VII," brought to a conclusion by Martial d'Auvergne in 1484 :

> " En ceste saison de douleur
> Vint au roy une bergerelle
> Du villasge de Vaucouller
> Qu'on nommait Jehanne la Pucelle.
> C'estoit une povre bergière,
> Qui gardoit les brebis es champs,
> D'une douce et humble manière,
> En l'aage de dix-huit ans.
> Devant le roy on la mena,
> Ung ou deux de sa cognoissance,
> Et alors elle s'enclina
> En luy faisant la reverence.

---

* " It was she who recovered the honour of Frenchmen in such a way that by it she will rightly have perpetual renown."

M

> Le roy par jeu si alla dire :
> ' Ha ! ma mye, ce ne sui-je pas ? '
> A quoi elle respondit : ' Sire,
> C'estes vous, ne je ne faulx pas.
> Au nom de Dieu, si disoit-elle,
> Gentil roy, je vous meneray
> Couronner à Rains, qui que veille
> Et siège d'Orléans leveray '." *

Now it only remains for us to recall Villon's ballad to complete our anthology of the old singers of the good Joan, among whom one regrets not finding that Duke of Orléans whom she loved so much and for whom she did so much good without ever having known him. Why, since he made ballads, did he make none for Joan ?

From the sixteenth century onwards, language and feeling have changed. No poet finds the correct tone in which to sing the Maid. I will quote, for example, an epigram by Malherbe :

> " L'ennemy, tous droits violant,
> Belle amazone en vous bruslant
> Témoigna son âme perfide ;
> Mais le destin n'eut point de tort :
> Celle qui vivoit comme Alcide,
> Devoit mourir comme il est mort." †

---

* " In that season of sorrow there came to the king a shepherd girl of the village of Vaucouller who was called Joan the Maid. She was a poor shepherdess who kept the sheep in the fields in a gentle and humble manner, and her age was eighteen years. One or two who knew her led her before the king ; and then she bowed, doing him reverence. The king began to say in sport, ' Ha ! my dear, it is not I.' To which she answered : ' Sire, it is you unless I am mistaken. In the name of God,' said she to him, ' gentle king, I shall lead you to be crowned at Reims whatever happens, and I shall raise the siege of Orleans '."

† " The enemy, violating all laws by burning you, fair Amazon, showed his perfidious soul ; but destiny made no mistake : She who lived like Alcides should die as he died."

That, certainly, is a ridiculous compliment. I was forgetting four lines attributed to Mademoiselle de Gournay, Montaigne's adopted daughter. Quicherat admired them. The Duc de Broglie does not believe " that the memory of the virgin of Orléans has inspired any that are more touching." I am very far from sharing this opinion. In order that you may be able to judge, I will quote them, although they are fairly well known :

" —Peux-tu bien accorder, vierge du ciel chérie,
La douceur de tes yeux et ce glaive irrité ?
—La douceur de mes yeux caresse ma patrie
Et ce glaive en fureur lui rend sa liberté ! " *

The quatrain is well turned : that is all I can say for it. Nothing in that clumsy antithesis recalls to me the fair visionary of the fields, as Louis Veuillot admirably says, " that lily so slender, so strong, so frank and so fresh, and so well perfumed." It is, moreover, doubtful whether the epigram, in that form, is by Mademoiselle de Gournay. Another version, which is certainly by that lady, is detestable :

" —Pourquoy portes-tu, je te prie,
L'œil doux et le bras foudroyant ?
—Cet œil mignarde ma patrie,
Ce bras chasse l'Anglois fuyant." †

No, that is not poetry. And how could one poetise that divine Joan, already in herself bearing the mark of poetry and steeped in it ?

* " Virgin beloved of heaven, can'st thou reconcile the sweetness of thine eyes and that angry sword ?—The sweetness of my eyes caresses my country, and this sword, in its rage, gives it back its liberty."

† " Why hast thou, I prithee, a gentle eye and a crushing arm ? —This eye fondles my country, this arm is chasing the flying English."

Joan is made of nothing but poetry. She stepped out of the popular poetry of Christianity, the litanies of the Virgin and the Golden Legend, the marvellous stories of those brides of Jesus Christ who put on the white robe of virginity and the red robe of martyrdom. She emerged from the pleasing sermons in which the sons of Saint Francis exalted poverty, candour, and innocence ; she came forth from the eternal fairyland of the woods and the fountains, from those artless tales of our ancestors, from those narratives, as obscure and as fresh as the nature that inspires them, in which girls of the fields receive supernatural gifts ; she was born of the songs of the land of oaks in which Vivien, Merlin, Arthur and his knights live a mysterious life ; she was the breath of that great thought which made a rose of fire bloom above the doors of the churches ; she was the fulfilment of the prophecies by which the poor people of the realm of France foretold a better future ; she was the offspring of the ecstasy and tears of a whole people who, like Mary of Avignon in days of misery, beheld arms in the sky, and thereafter trusted only in her weakness.

She is moulded out of poetry, like the lily out of dew ; she is the living poetry of that gentle France which she loved with a miraculous love.